Errata

Digital Progress and Trends Report 2023

On p. xvii, the last sentence of the first bulleted item should read as follows: However, only one out of four individuals in **low-income** countries used the internet in 2022.

Digital Progress and Trends Report 2023

Digital Progress and Trends Report 2023

ISBN (paper): 978-1-4648-2049-6
ISBN (electronic): 978-1-4648-2050-2
DOI: 10.1596/978-1-4648-2049-6

Cover and interior design: Bill Pragluski / Critical Stages, LLC.

Library of Congress Control Number: 2023924019

Contents

PART 1: PROGRESS

Boxes

Exhibit

Figures

Foreword

Development has entered a new era in which digitalization is profoundly transforming our economies and societies. Significant advances in digital technologies have driven dramatic changes, from the way we communicate and access information to how we conduct business and interact with the environment. Digitalization has opened new avenues for innovation, efficiency, and inclusion, bringing tangible benefits and new possibilities to individuals, organizations, and nations.

Embracing digitalization is no longer a choice but a necessity, as it holds the foundation and potential to shape a more inclusive, resilient, and sustainable world for generations to come. When fast internet becomes available, the probability that an individual is employed increases by up to 13.2 percent, total employment per firm increases by up to 22 percent, and firm exports nearly quadruple. Across Africa, 3G coverage has been linked to a reduction in extreme poverty of 10 percent in Senegal and of 4.3 percent in Nigeria. Analytics and data-driven decision-making can boost the sales of small and medium enterprises and help them to establish a competitive advantage. Digital technologies can reduce greenhouse gas emissions by up to 20 percent by 2050 in the three highest-emitting sectors: energy, materials, and mobility.

However, the progress and distributional impact of digitalization have been highly uneven within and across countries. The inherent characteristics of digital data and digital technologies also generate new risks. In 2022, one-third of the global population remains offline. More than half of firms in Burkina Faso, Ethiopia, Ghana, and Senegal reportedly lack internet connection. Network effects and economies of scale and scope tend to concentrate information, profits, and power. Digital technologies have accelerated automation and displaced workers, while increasing gig work can bring risks to workers, including lack of social protection. Social media platforms and algorithms have contributed to the spread of misinformation and extremism, making society even more divisive. Digital data and technologies also create new privacy and security vulnerabilities. The explosive growth of data and massive digitalization is resulting in significant increases in electricity consumption and greenhouse gas emissions.

As a result, the World Bank is launching the *Digital Progress and Trends Report,* which tracks the global progress of digitalization, summarizes emerging technology and market trends, and highlights policy shifts and debates. The report puts a focus on low- and middle-income countries. It seeks to open dialogue and motivate action among relevant audiences to help to sustain political commitment to closing the digital divide. The report also brings global attention to successful experience as well as to areas where efforts will need to be redoubled.

Unprecedented growth in data and analytical capabilities, including cloud and artificial intelligence (AI), is propelling digitalization to a new era. This inaugural edition highlights two emerging trends: the emergence of the digital public infrastructure (DPI) concept and advances in AI technologies and their implications. DPI—the combination of digital platforms for identity, payments, and data sharing—has become foundational for accessing public and private sector services by individuals and firms. The latest breakthroughs in AI technologies have sparked widespread excitement as well as unease. It is critical for the global community, including low- and middle-income countries, to work together to carve out a new development path to prepare for the AI disruption.

Axel van Trotsenburg
Senior Managing Director
The World Bank

Acknowledgments

Digital Progress and Trends Report 2023 was prepared by a World Bank team led by Yan Liu, under the guidance of Christine Zhenwei Qiang, director for the Digital Development Global Practice. The core team comprised Rami Amin, Hans Christian Boy, Jieun Choi, Saloni Khurana, Yan Liu, Jonathan Marskell, Michael Minges, Anshuman Sinha, and Henry Stemmler, all from the Digital Development Global Practice. Key inputs were received from Rong Chen, Julia Clark, Georgina Marin, and Minita Varghese from the Digital Development Global Practice; Xavier Cirera, Ana Goicoechea, Silvia Muzi, Sara Oliveira, and Nithya Srinivasan from the Finance, Competitiveness, and Innovation Global Practice; and Cem Dener and Kimberly Johns from the Governance Global Practice.

The team is grateful to the many reviewers who provided thoughtful insights and guidance at various stages of the report's preparation. External peer reviewers include Vivien Foster (principal research fellow, Imperial College London; former chief economist for the infrastructure vice-presidency, World Bank), William Lehr (research associate, Massachusetts Institute of Technology), and Anna M. Polomska-Risler (Strategic Partnerships at the United Nations/International Telecommunication Union Broadband Commission). Internal peer reviewers include Mary Hallward-Driemeier, Timothy Kelly, Aart Kraay, Gaurav Nayyar, and Davide Strusani. Additional written comments were received from Adele Moukheibir Barzelay, Carolina Sánchez-Páramo, and David Satola.

The team particularly appreciates the guidance and support of Guangzhe Chen, Pablo Fajnzylber, Sebastian-A Molineus, and Stephane Straub.

Special thanks are due to Andrea Barone, Jerome Bezzina, Julia Clark, Vyjayanti Desai, Doyle Gallegos, Nicole Klingen, Jonathan Marskell, Maria Isabel Neto, Michel Rogy, Sandra Sargent, Rajendra Singh, Randeep Sudan, Casey Torgusson, and Mahesh Uttamchandani for their helpful comments and suggestions.

The team thanks the following organizations for participating in the Digital Industry Leader Survey and providing valuable inputs: Alphabet, Atos Africa, Bureau Veritas, Business Finland, Meta, Microsoft, Mouvement des Entreprises de France International (MEDEF International), MTN Group Limited, Orange, Secure Identity Alliance, Sofrecom, and Visa.

The report was funded by the World Bank and the Digital Development Partnership Trust Fund, which offers a platform for digital innovation and development financing, bringing public and private sector partners together to advance digital solutions and drive digital transformation in low- and middle-income countries.

The communication and dissemination efforts were led by Kelly Alderson and Breen Byrnes. Elizabeth Forsyth and Matthew Robert Zoller edited the report. Caroline Polk coordinated and oversaw its production. Bill Pragluski, Critical Stages, LLC, designed the report's cover and interior. Datapage supplied typesetting services. Dalia Ali provided the team with resource management and administrative support.

Finally, the team apologizes to any individuals or organizations inadvertently omitted from this list. It is grateful for the help received from all who contributed to this report, including those whose names may not appear here.

Executive Summary

The new series *Digital Progress and Trends Report* adopts a holistic framework of digitalization, with selective topics examined in depth in each edition. The framework, which is described in figure ES.1, includes both the production and the adoption sides of digital technologies and their interactions.[1] Box ES.1 explains how the series supports global efforts to study the progress, gaps, benefits, and risks of digitalization. The benefits and risks are also interconnected and reflect the trade-offs and complexity of digitalization: innovation and growth can be accompanied by high concentration and reduced market contestability. Efficiency gains and lower costs for large businesses may mean higher inequality and polarization. Digitalization can create jobs and improve inclusion, but it also results in power asymmetry and makes it easier for governments and companies to monitor and control individuals. Digital innovation creates new possibilities for climate change mitigation and adaptation but expands the carbon footprint of the information and communication technology (ICT) sector. Cybersecurity, privacy, and misinformation are also major risks that can undermine trust in the digital space and circumvent the gains from digitalization. Countries need to maximize the benefits while minimizing the risks of digitalization.

FIGURE ES.1 Report framework

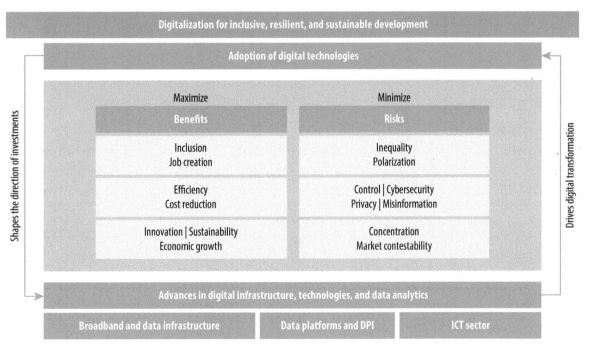

Source: Based on World Bank 2016.
Note: DPI = digital public infrastructure; ICT = information and communication technology.

BOX ES.1 About this report

The report adds to global efforts to study the progress, gaps, benefits, and risks of digitalization in two ways.

1. By compiling, curating, and analyzing data from diverse sources to present a comprehensive picture of digitalization in low- and middle-income countries, including in-depth analyses on understudied topics

Digitalization is cross-cutting and encompasses different dimensions. Data on digitalization are scattered in many sources with varying visibility and accessibility. The differences in the definition, measurement, and update frequency of indicators further hamper over-time and cross-country comparisons.

The rich data compiled and curated by the report team greatly expand the scope of synthesis, shed light on both the production and adoption sides of digitalization, and present a multifaceted picture of the digital landscape in the world, with a focus on low- and middle-income countries.

In its inaugural issue, the report uses a range of data sources, including the World Bank's Findex data, Identification for Development data, and household and business survey data, among others, to examine the adoption of digital technologies by individuals and businesses. It explores the dynamics of digital markets based on venture capital investment data and app performance data. It also uses data compiled from various sources to analyze trends in investments in broadband and data infrastructure, electricity consumption, and greenhouse gas emissions from digital infrastructure. Further, the report team has curated a new information and communication technology (ICT) sector data set to provide more accurate and comprehensive information on value added and employment in the ICT sector.[a]

2. By developing insights on policy opportunities, challenges, and debates and reflecting the views of stakeholders and World Bank operational experiences

The report highlights key policy opportunities, challenges, and debates related to digitalization through regulatory data analysis, literature review, and stakeholder consultations. It reflects inputs from a variety of stakeholders, including leading players in the private sector, partner organizations, policy makers, and academia. It also reflects and incorporates insights and learning from the World Bank's country engagements and operations in more than 100 countries, where appropriate.

Report structure

As an annual series, the *Digital Progress and Trends Report* aims to maintain consistency and comparability in its structure and tracking of progress as well as flexibility to adjust methodologies in light of new trends and available data. Each edition will have two parts. Part 1 will include two to three chapters on digitalization progress. These chapters will be quantitative in nature, enabled by primary and secondary data sets collected and compiled by the World Bank and partner organizations. Part 2 will feature one to two chapters on trends with strategic and real-time relevance. The topics covered in both parts will vary in each edition to capture timely developments, data, and debates. A data appendix will focus on a set of core indicators, which may be expanded as new, comparable data become available.

a. The report includes a data appendix describing the databases used and showing the latest value of core indicators for all countries, regions, and country income groups.

Main findings

While digital adoption is accelerating, the digital divide continues to widen, exacerbating the poverty and productivity divide.

Internet use is speeding up in middle-income countries, but low-income countries are falling further behind.

- The world gained 1.5 billion new internet users during 2018–22. The number of internet users reached 5.3 billion in 2022, representing two-thirds of the global population. The COVID-19 pandemic catalyzed the already accelerating growth in internet users in middle-income countries. However, only one out of four individuals in middle-income countries used the internet in 2022.

- The stark divide in fixed broadband penetration between richer and poorer countries has widened as the pandemic boosted penetration in high-income and middle-income countries but less so in low-income countries. Fixed broadband subscriptions per 100 persons were above 30 in high-income and upper-middle-income countries, but only 4.4 in lower-middle-income countries and 0.5 in low-income countries in 2022.

Larger gaps are forming in internet speed and data use, and the poor quality of internet services is hampering firms' digital transformation in some low- and middle-income countries.

- Internet speed has risen much faster in high-income countries than in middle-income ones since 2019 and has even fallen slightly in low-income countries. In 2023, median fixed and mobile broadband speeds are 10 and 5 times faster, respectively, in high-income countries than in low-income countries.

- The pandemic led to a surge in data traffic, driven by video streaming, which accounted for two-thirds of global internet traffic in 2022. The surge occurred primarily in high-income and upper-middle-income countries, widening the gap with lower-middle-income and low-income countries.

- In 2022, median mobile broadband traffic per capita was more than 20 times higher in high-income countries than in low-income countries, and median fixed broadband traffic per capita was more than 1,700 times higher.

The pandemic and consequent mobility control measures induced substantial and persistent changes in people's behavior.

- The use of business, education, finance, medical, health, and shopping apps got a significant boost from mobility restrictions during the pandemic. The increase was driven mainly by a surge in new users.

- Lockdown stringency during the pandemic was a strong predictor of higher downloads, greater use of business, education, games, and health apps, and lower use of travel apps. The effects on total time spent can persist even one year after the initial mobility restrictions.

Firms with greater digital readiness before the pandemic and those that invested in digital solutions during the pandemic showed greater resilience.

- While the pandemic drove firms of all sizes online, large firms led investments in digital solutions. From April 2020 to December 2022, the percentage of firms investing in digital solutions doubled from 10 percent to 20 percent for micro firms (0–4 employees) but tripled from 20 percent to 60 percent for large firms (more than 100 employees).

- Firms' prepandemic digital readiness[2] and management practices[3] predicted a higher probability of investing in and using digital solutions during the pandemic. Firms with greater digital readiness before the pandemic and those that invested in digital solutions during the pandemic also showed greater resilience in sales.

The digital sector is driving innovation, economic growth, and job creation, generating positive spillovers on the broader economy.

The digital sector continues to be an engine of innovation and growth. However, lower-income countries have yet to exploit the productivity spillovers from information technology (IT) services.

- Global patent publications in computer technology soared 27-fold between 1980 and 2021. Patent publications in other ICT fields also surged more than 10-fold, compared to just 2-fold in other fields of technology.

- The IT services segment was the most vibrant and fastest-growing segment of the global economy over the past two decades. The compound annual growth rate of global value added and employment for IT services reached 8 percent and 6.7 percent, respectively, during 2000–22, far outstripping the 5.1 percent and 1.2 percent growth of the global economy.

- IT services were increasingly used as intermediate inputs in other sectors. From 2000 to 2020, IT services contributed to a much larger share of total intermediate inputs across all sectors. The input intensity of IT services almost doubled in high-income and upper-middle-income countries during 2000–20 but did not grow at all in lower-middle-income countries.

- Most countries experienced robust job creation in IT services. Global employment in IT services quadrupled from 8 million in 2000 to 32 million in 2022. China, Israel, Malaysia, Nigeria, the Philippines, Viet Nam, and several Central and Eastern Europe countries (Hungary, Poland, and Romania) had the fastest employment growth thanks to the burgeoning local IT services industry and roaring exports.

- Women made up 29 percent of total employment in the male-dominated IT services industry in 2020, up from 23 percent in 2010. Albania, Bangladesh, Brunei Darussalam, Cyprus, the Arab Republic of Egypt, Iceland, the Islamic Republic of Iran, the Kyrgyz Republic, Tanzania, and Uganda achieved significant progress in bringing more women into the IT services workforce.

Diversification of the global value chain and surging demand in IT and IT-enabled services are creating new opportunities for countries to pursue export-led growth.

- Intensifying geopolitical tensions between China and the United States, the pandemic, and the war in Ukraine have galvanized multinational corporations to accelerate diversification of their global value chain, creating opportunities for other countries close to major markets and suppliers. India and countries in the Association of South East Asian Nations have been among the biggest beneficiaries.

- The IT services segment was the most dynamic category of international trade for the past decade, creating an export-led growth pathway for countries to expand and diversify their economies. During 2010–22, IT services grew by 12 percent annually, surpassing all other service categories. By 2022, it was the third largest category of service exports, right after transport and travel.

At the same time, homegrown digital firms are springing up in low- and middle-income countries, filling important market gaps, driving innovation, and often generating more spillovers than foreign firms.

- Many low- and middle-income countries have received an influx of venture capital funding since 2020. Most venture capital deals in low- and middle-income countries are in e-commerce, fintech, health, education, and entertainment.

- India minted 50 new digital unicorns[4] during 2020–22, up from just 4 unicorns during 2017–19. Digital unicorns also popped up in Argentina, Brazil, Chile, Colombia, Egypt, Indonesia, Malaysia, Mexico, Nigeria, the Philippines, Senegal, South Africa, Türkiye, and Viet Nam.

- The app market is becoming more local and less global, and this trend has accelerated since the pandemic. Countries with a large domestic market, unique language, strong cultural identity, and prolific IT talents have enabled and incentivized local firms to cater to their home markets.

- From 2015 to 2022, domestic apps made up an increasing share of the 100 most downloaded apps in 54 of 63 economies. Argentina, Brazil, Chile, India, Indonesia, the Russian Federation, Saudi Arabia, South Africa, Türkiye, Ukraine, and the United Arab Emirates experienced the largest increase in the share of domestic apps between 2015 and 2022.

- Nonetheless, the growth potential of digital firms in low- and middle-income countries remains to be seen. While localization has been key to their success in home markets, their products and business models may be less relevant or transferrable to foreign markets. For US apps, foreign users made up four out of five users in 2022. The share of foreign users of most apps developed by low- and middle-income countries is less than 20 percent.

Unprecedented growth in data and analytical capabilities is propelling digitalization to a new era, with profound implications for low- and middle-income countries.

Low- and middle-income countries need to expand and upgrade their broadband infrastructure to handle the explosive growth in data and enable broader digitalization.

- The volume of data created, stored, transferred, and used globally has been growing exponentially from 2 zettabytes[5] in 2010 to an expected 120 zettabytes in 2023; it is forecast to exceed 180 zettabytes by 2025 (Hack 2021).

- Investment priorities in the telecommunication sector are shifting to higher-speed access infrastructure such as fiber optic cable to the premises, next-generation mobile network connectivity, and wireless technologies. GSMA forecasts that mobile operators alone will invest more than US$600 billion between 2022 and 2025, of which 85 percent will be for 5G.

- Governments can catalyze private investment and improve the efficiency of telecommunication investment by phasing out legacy 2G and 3G networks, reducing spectrum costs, and promoting infrastructure sharing.

- To reduce spectrum costs, governments can allow operators to use unallocated spectrum for free or low cost, make spectrum technology and service neutral,[6] and allow operators to reuse their current spectrum for 5G. Governments that have not yet allocated frequency for 5G should do so, particularly the new mmWave band, which can offer high-speed indoor coverage.

- Aggregation of mobile and unlicensed Wi-Fi spectrum will also help to increase network throughput. Regulators need to enhance institutional capacity to secure and release enough spectrum, including globally harmonized pioneer bands, while avoiding the risk of spectrum fragmentation that prevents 5G from delivering on the performance desired.

- Infrastructure sharing of wireless base station towers and cable ducts lowers costs and reduces greenhouse gas emissions. Regulatory frameworks that encourage network sharing can substantially reduce the costs for 5G.

Data infrastructure—internet exchange points (IXPs), data centers, and cloud computing—has become vital to the digital economy.

- Investment is also needed in middle-mile infrastructure[7] to transmit, store, and exchange data, especially IXPs, connected data centers,[8] and cloud computing.

- As of 2022, low- and middle-income countries accounted for less than half of total public IXPs and one-quarter of connected data centers, respectively.

- To lower costs and improve quality, IXPs need to attract major content and cloud service companies to become members. Among lower-middle-income and low-income countries in 2022, the retail price for 1 gigabyte per month in countries that have IXPs with leading content providers was less than one-fifth of that in countries that do not have an IXP. Mobile data consumption was nearly three times higher.

- Governments in low- and middle-income countries should liberalize the IXP environment and ensure that internet service providers (ISPs) with significant market power do not discourage the use of IXPs (Qassrawi 2022).

- To encourage private investment in data centers, governments need to create a favorable investment climate and introduce targeted financial and other instruments, such as state aid, venture capital funding, public-private co-financing mechanisms, or tax incentives. These instruments can vary depending on a data center's location, size, energy efficiency, and environmental footprint.

- Aggregating demand at the regional level and bringing together stakeholders to achieve economies of scale might also be a potential solution for lower-income countries to attract private sector investment.
- Regional harmonization of regulations for data security, protection, and sovereignty could help encourage major cloud providers to establish a presence in low- and middle-income countries. Governments could also promote cloud services through the adoption of cloud technologies for their own use.

The emergence of digital public infrastructure (DPI) concept reflects a paradigm shift from using siloed vertical approaches for digitalization to building cross-cutting horizontal enablers.

- "DPI" is a new term referring to the basic capabilities that are building blocks for developing digital services at a societal scale. DPI is the intermediate layer between physical infrastructure (for example, broadband and data centers) and sectoral applications (for example, social protection and e-commerce). The most common types of DPI are platforms and systems for digital identification, digital payments, and data sharing.
- DPI rose in prominence during the COVID-19 pandemic. The countries with elements of DPI in place reached three times more beneficiaries with emergency cash transfers. Countries with good DPI also were able to keep government services, commerce, hospitals, schools, and other operations functioning through online channels.
- Globally, 850 million people still lack any form of official identification. Five billion people live in countries without digital identification that can be used for secure online access to public and private sector services.
- Only 57 percent of adults in low- and middle-income countries made or received some sort of digital payment in 2021, and only 37 percent made a merchant payment.

AI development has arrived at a new stage, attaining a level of sophistication previously unimaginable.

- The ability of large language models to interpret natural language prompts correctly and generate completely original text, audio, image, and video content that is indistinguishable from human-made content has propelled them to the forefront of AI research and commercialization (Brown et al. 2020).
- New generative AI start-ups have been entering the market at a swift pace, with content generation and generative AI infrastructure gaining the most traction from investors. In the first half of 2023, the space saw US$14.1 billion in equity funding (including US$10 billion to OpenAI), more than five-fold compared to full-year 2022.

AI has huge potential to accelerate productivity growth and bring vast benefits to the global economy and society, but it also presents new risks and challenges, especially for low- and middle-income countries.

- AI holds huge potential to help low- and middle-income countries to tackle issues in crucial areas, notably in agriculture, health care, education, energy, financial inclusion, climate resilience, and insurability.
- In Mexico, companies like Clínicas de Azúcar are using AI to analyze data and improve health outcomes for thousands of at-risk diabetic patients (Sonneborn and Graf 2020). In Africa, companies like Azuri Technologies are using AI to optimize power consumption by learning home energy needs and adjusting power output accordingly (automatically dimming lights, slowing fans, or managing how quickly devices are charged).
- However, AI could potentially widen the gap between rich and poor countries. Digital technologies including AI tend to give rise to natural monopolies, creating a small set of superstar firms that are headquartered in a few "superstar countries" and reaping all of the rents associated with the development of AI. Rich countries also have stronger incentives and better complementary skills and institutions to adopt AI than poor countries.
- AI could deteriorate the terms of trade and devalue the comparative advantage of low- and middle-income countries, eventually reversing the convergence in standards of living between rich and poor countries.

The AI era calls for a new playbook for policy making and closer coordination across stakeholders and regulatory and jurisdictional spheres.

- There is a lot of uncertainty about the direction, pace, scale, and effect of changes brought by AI. It is critical for the global community, including low- and middle-income countries, to shape the direction of AI innovations jointly, to coordinate the pace and scale of their applications, to forecast, monitor, and assess the impacts, and to prepare to ameliorate the adverse effects.

- While some common foundational principles guide AI regulation, distinct variations exist in the specific approaches and priorities adopted by different countries. The European Union has opted for a structured, risk-based legislative framework, with the AI Act proposing exhaustive regulations governing AI applications across diverse sectors. The United States has adopted a more diverse, flexible approach to AI regulation, characterized by a combination of soft law, self-regulation, responsible use, and legislation at various levels within different domains.

- Multistakeholder efforts, such as the Rome Call on AI Ethics and the United Nations Educational, Scientific, and Cultural Organization's Recommendation on the Ethics of AI, have also sought to maximize the synergy of foundational research, technological advancements, standardized norms, and balanced regulations in fostering responsible deployment of AI.

- Regulatory strategies must navigate the complexities and potential biases inherent in AI, addressing the juxtaposition of economic growth, efficiency, transparency, privacy, national security, and societal impacts. Regulatory fragmentation may hinder AI innovation and development, create enforcement gaps and trade barriers, lead to regulatory arbitrage, and diminish the effectiveness of such regulations.

Rapid advances in AI also highlight the urgency for low- and middle-income countries to build digital infrastructure, develop digital skills, and carve out new development paths to prepare for the disruption.

- A range of countries, including Egypt, Ghana, Kenya, Mauritius, Rwanda, South Africa, and others, have initiated efforts to develop AI policies and strategies, with a heavy focus on building digital infrastructure, developing AI skills, and adopting AI solutions. Such efforts echo the views of industry leaders, who emphasize the urgency for low- and middle-income countries to invest in digital infrastructure and prepare the workforce for the disruptions that AI may bring.

- Policy makers in low- and middle-income countries can intentionally steer the direction of AI adoption toward labor augmentation; leverage AI to improve the efficiency and effectiveness of taxation, redistribution, and social protection; rethink their sectoral strategies; and explore services-led growth pathways.

Notes

1. "Digital technologies" often refers to electronic tools, systems, devices, and resources that generate, store, or process data. "Digitalization" is the use of digital technologies and data as well as the interconnection that results in new activities or changes to existing activities (OECD 2019).

2. Digital readiness is measured as the number of pre-COVID-19 digital practices applied out of three indicators: online sales or payment, online social media, and use of enterprise resource planning software and systems.

3. Management practices are measured as the number of structured management practices applied out of three indicators for firms: targets, advertisements, and promotion of employees.

4. Unicorns are privately held start-up companies with a value of more than US$1 billion.

5. One zettabyte is 2^{70} bytes. It is equal to 1 trillion gigabytes.

6. Technology-neutral licenses enable spectrum to be used efficiently by mobile operators rather than being tied to declining technologies and services. The most important development is the ability to refarm—repurpose—bands so that they are used simultaneously for several technologies, including 4G and 5G. This repurposing allows for the introduction of newer technologies in line with increasing demand for mobile broadband, while at the same time supporting legacy users.

7. The mile framework is useful for understanding the telecommunication value chain, which stretches from the point where the internet enters a country (the first mile), passes through that country (the middle mile), and eventually reaches the end user (the last mile), including certain hidden elements in between (the invisible mile). Refer to World Bank (2016).

8. Connected data centers house the computing and networking equipment of tenants and include interconnection facilities. Connected data centers serve a variety of tenants, including companies from a range of industries, governments, ISPs, content and cloud providers, as well as IXPs.

References

Brown, Tom B., Benjamin Mann, Nick Ryder, Melanie Subbiah, Jared Kaplan, Prafulla Dhariwal, Arvind Neelakantan, Pranav Shyam, Girish Sastry, Amanda Askell, et al. 2020. "Language Models Are Few-Shot Learners." arXiv preprint arXiv:2005.14165.

Hack, Ulrike. 2021. "What's the Real Story behind the Explosive Growth of Data?" *Redgate* (blog), September 8, 2021. https://www.red-gate.com/blog/database-development/whats-the-real-story-behind-the-explosive-growth-of-data.

OECD (Organisation for Economic Co-operation and Development). 2019. "Going Digital: Shaping Policies, Improving Lives." OECD, Paris. https://www.oecd.org/digital/going-digital-synthesis-summary.pdf.

Qassrawi, Zaher. 2022. "Internet Exchange Points—Beyond Configuration Issues." *RIPE Labs*, March 24, 2022. https://labs.ripe.net/author/zaher-qassrawi/internet-exchange-points-beyond-configuration-issues/.

Sonneborn, William, and Lana Graf. 2020. "How AI Can Help Developing Countries Rebuild after the Pandemic." *Digital Development* (blog), September 16, 2020. https://blogs.worldbank.org/digital-development/how-ai-can-help-developing-countries-rebuild-after-pandemic.

World Bank. 2016. *World Development Report 2016: Digital Dividends*. Washington, DC: World Bank. https://elibrary.worldbank.org/doi/abs/10.1596/978-1-4648-0671-1.

Abbreviations

AI	artificial intelligence
API	application programming interface
ASEAN	Association of South East Asian Nations
BPO-ITES	business process outsourcing and IT-enabled services
BPS	Business Pulse Survey
CAGR	compound annual growth rate
DPI	digital public infrastructure
EADC	East Africa Data Center
EBIA	Emerging Brazilian Artificial Intelligence Strategy
FAT	Firm Level Adoption of Technology
FDI	foreign direct investment
GDP	gross domestic product
GNI	gross national income
GTMI	GovTech Maturity Index
G2P	government-to-person
HIC	high-income countries
ICT	information and communication technology
ICTD	ICT Sector Data Set
ID	identification document
ID4D	Identification for Development
IoT	Internet of Things
ISP	internet service provider
IT	information technology
IXP	internet exchange point
KIXP	Kenyan Internet Exchange Point
LIC	low-income countries
LLM	large language module
LMIC	lower-middle-income countries
OECD	Organisation for Economic Co-operation and Development
OTT	over the top
PPP	purchasing power parity
PV	photovoltaic
QoQ	quarter over quarter
R&D	research and development
SDG	Sustainable Development Goal
tCO_2e	tons of carbon dioxide equivalent

TESPOK	Technology Service Providers of Kenya
TiVA	Trade in Value-Added
TWh	terawatt-hour
UMIC	upper-middle-income countries
UN	United Nations
VA	value added
VC	venture capital
VPN	virtual private network

PART 1
Progress

Digital Adoption: Accelerating Postpandemic, yet a Widening Divide | 1

Yan Liu, Rami Amin, and Henry Stemmler

KEY MESSAGES

- The world gained 1.5 billion new internet users from 2018 to 2022, with accelerated growth in middle-income countries amplified by the COVID-19 pandemic. However, low-income countries are falling behind, with only one in four people using the internet in 2022.

- Affordability continues to be a main barrier to internet use. Median fixed broadband prices in low-income countries accounted for one-third of monthly gross national income per capita in 2022. Even the cheapest smartphone accounts for more than 14 percent of annual income for persons living on less than US$2 a day.

- Larger gaps are forming in internet speeds and data use. In 2023, median fixed and mobile broadband speeds in high-income countries are 10 and 5 times faster, respectively, than speeds in low-income countries. Median mobile broadband traffic per capita in high-income countries was more than 20 times higher than traffic in low-income countries, and median fixed broadband traffic per capita was more than 1,700 times higher in 2022.

- The COVID-19 pandemic and consequent mobility control measures induced some durable changes in people's habits. Time spent on business, education, finance, medical, health, and shopping apps increased significantly during and after the COVID-19 pandemic.

- Firms' digital readiness and management practices before the pandemic predicted a higher probability of investment in and use of digital technology during the pandemic. Firms with greater digital readiness before the pandemic and firms that invested in digital solutions during the pandemic also showed greater resilience in sales.

Introduction

Digital technologies and internet connectivity are transforming lives, creating opportunities, and advancing economic development around the world. For households and individuals, digital technology has significantly improved access to timely information and lowered transaction costs, boosting educational outcomes, labor force participation, income, consumption, and welfare (Aker 2010; Bahia et al. 2020; Derksen, Michaud-Leclerc, and Souza 2022; Hjort and Poulsen 2019; Jensen 2007; Rodriguez-Segura 2022; Viollaz and Winkler 2022). For businesses, digital technology can improve decision-making, increase efficiency, facilitate innovation, and expand markets (Bar-Gill, Brynjolfsson, and Hak 2023; Bloom, Sadun, and Van Reenen 2012).

Despite the potential of digital technologies to create enormous socioeconomic benefits, their uneven deployment, adoption, and use have created so-called "digital divides" across individuals, businesses, and countries. For instance, in Africa, mobile internet covers 84 percent of the population, but only 22 percent make use of it (Begazo, Blimpo, and Dutz 2023). This underutilization is driven by significant barriers, including high costs of devices and services, limited digital skills, quality of service, and relevance, including the perception of relevance, among other factors such as cultural attitudes and concerns about digital trust and safeguards. Among enterprises in low- and middle-income countries, high costs, lack of digital skills, and weak digital infrastructure are preventing the productive use of digital technologies (Atiyas and Dutz 2021; Cirera, Comin, and Cruz 2022). Vast digital divides also exist across countries. More than 90 percent of people in high-income countries used the internet in 2022, compared with 25 percent in low-income countries.

This chapter highlights trends in digital adoption and identifies remaining barriers to adoption, placing particular focus on low- and middle-income countries, where the lingering presence of well-known obstacles to adoption are the most profound. The chapter also analyzes how the COVID-19 pandemic has affected the patterns of internet use and examines how firms have adopted and invested in digital technologies. It provides high-level policy insights on how to promote digital adoption, close usage gaps, and mitigate emerging divides in the quality of adoption.

The share of Internet users in middle-income countries is moving closer to that in high-income countries, while the share in low-income countries continues to lag

The world gained 1.5 billion new internet users between 2018 and 2022, as the COVID-19 pandemic amplified and accelerated growth in low- and middle-income countries. The number of internet users reached 5.3 billion in 2022, representing two-thirds of the global population. In 2020, the first year of the COVID-19 pandemic, the share of global population using the internet increased by 6 percent (500 million people), the highest jump in history, as mobility restrictions drove many activities online (refer to figure 1.1, panel a). While growth slowed in 2021 and 2022, it remained faster than most years during the past two decades, as vast populations in both low-income and lower-middle-income countries began using the internet (refer to figure 1.1, panel b).

Middle-income countries, especially India, drove the surge in internet users. In 2018, only one in five Indians used the internet. However, between 2018 and 2022, India recorded a staggering 170 percent growth in internet users. Contributions to the surge included the rise in internet literacy among women, cheaper mobile data prices, pandemic restrictions, and government initiatives like the Unified Payments Interface and the Digital India Initiative.[1] Consequently, as of 2022, more than half of Indians were active internet users. Mongolia experienced even faster growth, as more than one-third of its population became internet users during 2019–21. In addition, since 2018, the Arab Republic of Egypt, Ghana, the Lao People's Democratic Republic, and Thailand also brought a quarter of their population online.

COVID-19 has significantly narrowed the gap between middle-income and high-income countries in the share of internet users, although low-income countries continue to lag. In 2022, 92 percent of the population in high-income countries used the internet, up from 87 percent in 2018. At the same time, the share of internet users grew much faster in middle-income countries, narrowing the gap with high-income countries. By 2022, the share of internet users in upper-middle-income countries reached 79 percent, while the share in lower-middle-income countries reached 56 percent, reflecting an increase of 16 percent and 25 percent, respectively, since 2018

FIGURE 1.1 Internet users as a share of population, global and by country income group, 1990–2022

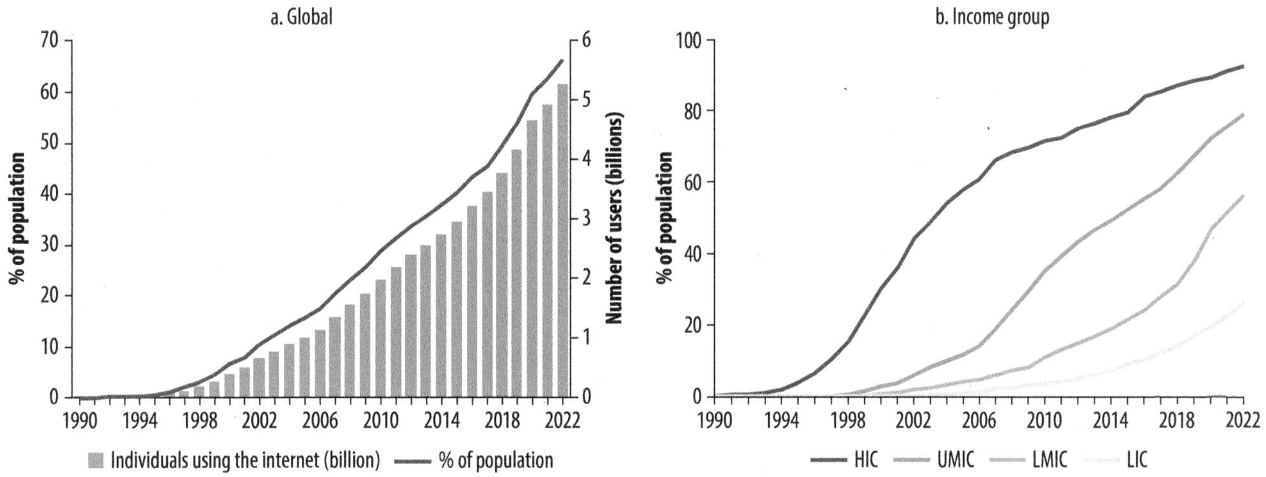

Sources: World Development Indicators and International Telecommunication Union data (https://www.itu.int/en/ITU-D/Statistics/Pages/stat/default.aspx).
Note: HIC = high-income countries; LIC = low-income countries; LMIC = lower-middle-income countries; UMIC = upper-middle-income countries.

(refer to figure 1.1, panel b). Low-income countries also experienced accelerated growth of internet users, especially between 2021 and 2022, but the gap with high-income countries remains substantial. As of 2022, only one in four individuals in low-income countries used the internet (refer to figure 1.1, panel b). As such, 2.7 billion people remain unconnected globally, mostly in low- and middle-income countries.

Both high-income and middle-income countries have made significant progress since 2019 to narrow the gaps between urban and rural areas, age groups, and genders. However, in low-income countries, these gaps have widened, as most new internet users are young males in urban areas. Internet use is much more prevalent among individuals residing in urban areas than among those residing in rural areas. The urban-rural gap stands out as the widest of the three gaps (urban-rural, youth-adult, and male-female) across low- and middle-income countries, indicating broader economic disparities between urban and rural areas (refer to figure 1.2). The urban-rural gap is particularly pronounced in lower-middle-income countries, with three-quarters of urban residents using the internet in 2022, compared with only two in five rural residents. Regardless of income group, youth between the ages of 15 and 24 are more likely to use the internet than the older population, although the gap is greatest in upper-middle-income countries. The gender gap has largely been closed in high-income countries but persists in lower-middle-income and low-income countries, where the share of men using the internet surpasses that of women by as much as 15 percentage points.

The stark divide in fixed broadband penetration between rich and poor countries widened as the pandemic boosted penetration in high-income and middle-income countries, but not in low-income countries. Fixed broadband connections provide high-speed internet to a fixed location like a residence or a business. In 2022, fixed broadband penetration reached 38 percent of the population in high-income countries. [2] Upper-middle-income countries were close behind, with fixed broadband penetration standing at 31 percent in 2022. However, fixed broadband penetration was merely 4 percent in lower-middle-income countries and almost zero in low-income countries as of 2022 (refer to figure 1.3, panel a) due to a lack of infrastructure and high prices. The nearly nonexistent

FIGURE 1.2 Location, age, and gender digital divides, by country income group, 2019 and 2022

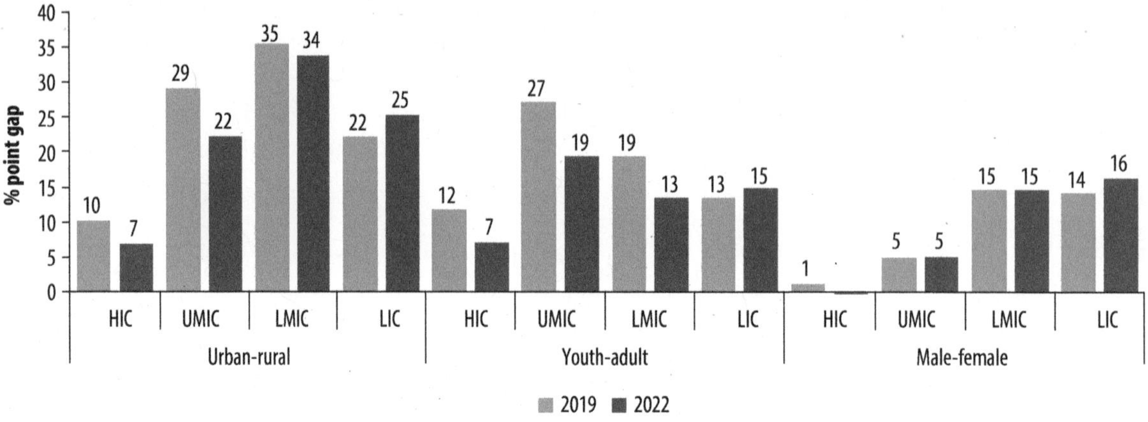

Source: Original calculations for this publication using International Telecommunication Union data.
Note: HIC = high-income countries; LIC = low-income countries; LMIC = lower-middle-income countries; UMIC = upper-middle-income countries.

penetration of fixed broadband in lower-middle-income and low-income countries also implies very limited computer use by households and businesses, as desktop computers often use fixed broadband based on its capacity to offer faster speed and lower latency than mobile broadband.

Mobile broadband penetration is much higher than fixed broadband penetration and continues to rise steadily across income groups, although growth in low income countries has been lackluster. As mobile devices such as smartphones, tablets, and smartwatches become more powerful and versatile, mobile broadband has replaced fixed broadband as the main gateway to internet use. People are no longer tied to their home or office for online engagement. They can access information and all sorts of online applications while on the go. There were 4.4 billion unique mobile internet users in 2022, representing about three-quarters of the global population ages 15 and above. Furthermore, active mobile broadband subscriptions surpassed fixed broadband subscriptions globally in 2008, and mobile subscriptions grew 15-fold between 2008 and 2022, reaching 6.9 billion in 2022. During the same time, fixed broadband subscriptions only doubled, reaching 1.4 billion at the end of 2022. Mobile broadband penetration has been growing at similar speeds in high-income and middle-income countries, while low-income countries have failed to keep pace (refer to figure 1.3, panel b). As a result, the gaps in mobile broadband penetration between low-income countries and countries at other income levels have widened since 2015.

Fixed broadband remains unaffordable for most people in low-income countries, while mobile broadband's affordability continues to rise. Lack of fixed broadband remains an important barrier to universal connectivity, as most people in low-income countries still cannot afford it. In the past few years, median prices for mobile broadband have dropped across income groups, while median prices for fixed broadband have stagnated. Furthermore, the median price for the cheapest fixed broadband plan has been stable in high-income and middle-income countries since 2020, but has trended upward in low-income countries. In 2022 the median price for a fixed broadband plan was 50 percent higher in low-income countries than in countries at other income levels (refer to figure 1.4, panel a), accounting for nearly one-third of monthly gross national income per capita (ITU 2023). Conversely, the median price for a mobile broadband plan dropped across income groups in 2022, resuming a downward trend that was interrupted by the COVID-19 pandemic

FIGURE 1.3 Fixed and mobile broadband penetration, by country income group, 2015–22

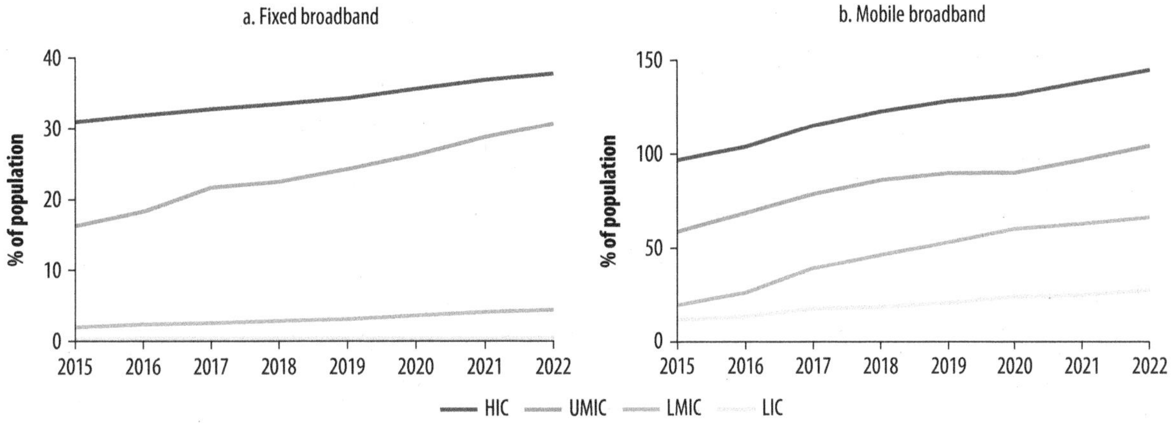

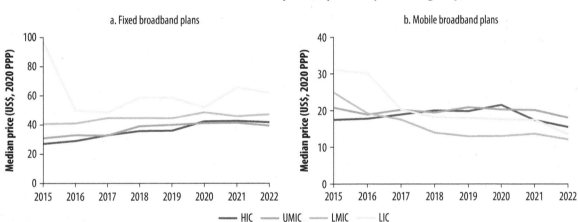

Source: International Telecommunication Union data.
Note: HIC = high-income countries; LIC = low-income countries; LMIC = lower-middle-income countries; UMIC = upper-middle-income countries.

FIGURE 1.4 Price of fixed and mobile broadband plans, by country income group, 2015–22

Source: Original calculations for this publication using International Telecommunication Union data.
Note: The retail price of a fixed broadband basket includes 1 gigabyte and 5 gigabytes of data for 2015–17 and 2018–22, respectively. The retail price of a mobile broadband basket includes postpaid computer-based data (1 gigabyte) for 2015–17, data-only mobile broadband (1.5 gigabytes) for 2018–20, and data-only mobile broadband (2 gigabytes) for 2021–22. HIC = high-income countries; LIC = low-income countries; LMIC = lower-middle-income countries; PPP = purchasing power parity; UMIC = upper-middle-income countries.

(refer to figure 1.4, panel b). The number of countries meeting the Broadband Commission's mobile broadband affordability target increased from 96 in 2021 to 103 in 2022.[3]

Mobile phones are the primary way in which people connect to the internet in low- and middle-income countries. Smartphone penetration is similarly converging between high-income and middle-income countries, while low-income countries remain far behind. Based on International Telecommunication Union data, in 2022, more than 95 percent of individuals in high-income countries owned a mobile phone (including smartphones, feature phones, and basic phones). The share of mobile phone owners was 76 percent in upper-middle-income countries, 66 percent in lower-middle-income countries, and only 49 percent in low-income countries. Smartphones have long replaced basic and feature phones for most mobile phone users. The rise of touchscreens, sophisticated mobile apps, built-in Global Positioning System, camera advancements, and other features have made smartphones the single most used digital device compared to personal computers, tablets, and wearables. As such, the number of smartphone connections exceeded the total population in high-income countries in 2022 (refer to figure 1.5, panel a).[4] Upper-middle-income countries are rapidly catching up with high-income countries, with smartphone connections approaching 100 percent. Smartphone connections also grew rapidly in lower-middle-income countries, although the pace has slowed since 2020. Progress in low-income countries has been too slow to narrow the gap with other income groups.

Similar to fixed broadband, lack of affordability is a main barrier contributing to the divide in smartphone penetration across countries. Even the cheapest smartphones are too expensive for the lowest-income groups, with prices accounting for 14 percent or more of annual income for persons living on less than US$2 per day. Lower-cost feature phones provide a more accessible option for lower-income individuals, although such phones lack the more advanced capabilities and features of smartphones, manifesting a key digital divide with regard to type of device. While only 8 percent of mobile connections use basic or feature phones in high-income countries, the figure jumps to 46 percent in Sub-Saharan Africa countries (refer to figure 1.5, panel b).

Even greater digital divides are present in the rate of computer ownership, which varies considerably between high-income and low-income countries and between urban and rural households. More than 80 percent of households in Australia, Belgium, Estonia, Israel, Japan, and Poland owned a computer during 2017–21. These countries had almost no urban-rural gap in computer ownership. In contrast, fewer than 20 percent of households in the Kyrgyz Republic, Malawi, Mali, Mozambique, Myanmar, and Nigeria owned a computer (refer to figure 1.6, panel a). Computer ownership is higher in other lower-income countries, although it is heavily skewed toward urban households, as in Angola, Bhutan, or Niger. In Latin America and the Caribbean, more than half of urban households, on average, possessed a computer or tablet, while only 38 percent of rural households possessed such devices. In rural Colombia, Haiti, and Nicaragua, these devices were present in only about 15 percent of households (refer to figure 1.6, panel b).

FIGURE 1.5 Smartphone penetration, by income group, region, and type of connection, 2015–22

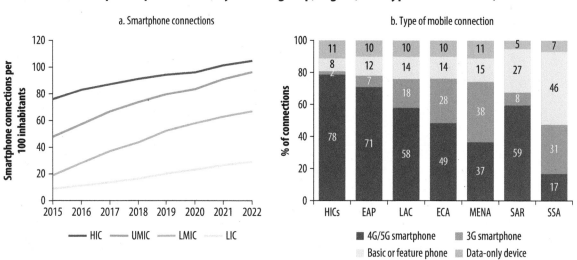

Sources: Original calculations for this publication using GSMA and World Development Indicators data; GSMA 2022, fig. 1.6.
Note: EAP = East Asia and Pacific; ECA = Europe and Central Asia; HIC = high-income countries; LAC = Latin America and the Caribbean; LIC = low-income countries; LMIC = lower-middle-income countries; MENA = Middle East and North Africa; SAR = South Asia; SSA = Sub-Saharan Africa; UMIC = upper-middle-income countries.

FIGURE 1.6 Rural and urban households with a computer or tablet, by country income group, various years

a. % of households with a computer

b. % of households with a computer or tablet

● HIC   ● UMIC   ● LMIC   ● LIC

Sources: Original calculations for this publication using International Telecommunication Union data for 2017–22 (panel a) and on World Bank High-Frequency Survey data for 2021 for Latin America and the Caribbean (panel b).
Note: HIC = high-income countries; LIC = low-income countries; LMIC = lower-middle-income countries; UMIC = upper-middle-income countries.

Larger gaps are forming in internet speeds and data use

Internet speeds have risen sharply since the start of the pandemic, resulting in improved service quality and enhanced user experience with more data-intensive applications. However, speeds rose much faster in high-income countries than in middle-income countries and even fell slightly in low-income countries. International bandwidth, which mirrors the overall capacity of a network, has been increasing across all income groups, but the pace has been much faster in high-income countries than in middle-income countries (refer to figure 1.7). Bandwidth continues to be very low in low-income countries. Similarly, download speeds leaped in high-income countries between 2019 and 2023, widening the gap in quality of service and end user experience compared to lower-income countries (refer to figure 1.8).

Divides in device ownership, connection quality, and affordability have contributed to the significant gaps in data traffic per capita, with low-income countries representing a small fraction of both fixed and mobile broadband data traffic. The pandemic has driven a surge in internet traffic since 2019, especially among high-income and upper-middle-income countries. Fixed broadband traffic per capita grew most rapidly in high-income countries from 2019 to 2020, but decelerated afterward. Mobile broadband traffic per capita continued to soar during 2019 to 2022. Both types of traffic per capita more than doubled in

FIGURE 1.7 Use of bandwidth per user, by country income group, 2015–22

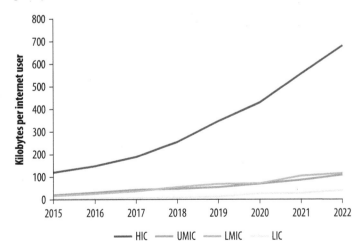

― HIC   ― UMIC   ― LMIC   ― LIC

Source: Original calculations for this publication using International Telecommunication Union data.
Note: Median across countries in the same income group. HIC = high-income countries; LIC = low-income countries; LMIC = lower-middle-income countries; UMIC = upper-middle-income countries.

FIGURE 1.8 **Median speed of fixed and mobile downloads, by country income group, 2019 and 2023**

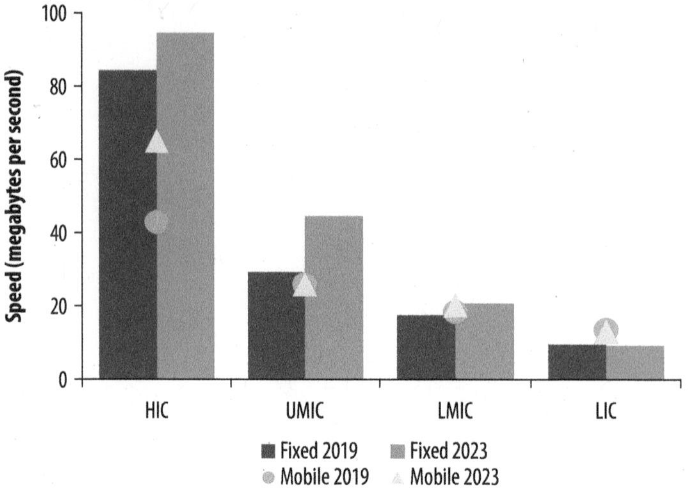

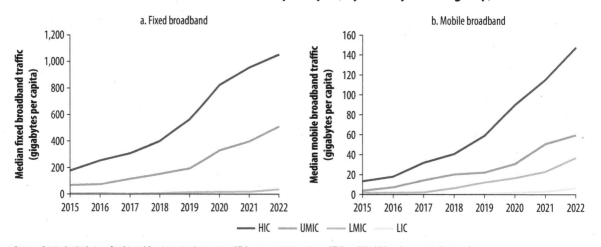

Source: Original calculations for this publication using Ookla data.
Note: Median across countries in the same income group. HIC = high-income countries; LIC = low-income countries; LMIC = lower-middle-income countries; UMIC = upper-middle-income countries.

FIGURE 1.9 **Fixed and mobile broadband traffic per capita, by country income group, 2015–22**

Sources: Original calculations for this publication using International Telecommunication Union (ITU) and World Development Indicators data.
Note: Figure depicts median traffic per capita by income group, using ITU available data between 2015 and 2022. Mobile broadband traffic includes internet traffic both within and outside the country. HIC = high-income countries; LIC = low-income countries; LMIC = lower-middle-income countries; UMIC = upper-middle-income countries.

upper-middle-income countries between 2019 and 2021 (refer to figure 1.9). Between 2019 and 2022, the median traffic per capita of fixed and mobile broadband grew by almost nine and seven times, respectively, in low-income countries. However, this traffic started from extremely low levels, effectively widening the gap in data traffic between high-income and upper-middle-income countries versus lower-middle-income and low-income countries. Median mobile broadband traffic per capita was more than 20 times higher in high-income countries than in low-income countries, and median fixed broadband traffic per capita was more than 1,700 times higher in 2022.

COVID-19 boosted the use of business, education, finance, medical, health, and shopping apps

The pandemic significantly boosted the use of business, education, finance, medical, health, and shopping apps. In March 2020, more than 100 governments enforced full or partial lockdowns to contain the virus.[5] Remote work, online schooling, telemedicine, and online shopping enabled daily activities to continue during a period of enforced lockdown and social distancing. While people used computers primarily for remote work and online schooling in higher-income countries, patterns of smartphone use also reveal that downloads (proxying the number of new users) of business, education, finance, medical, health, and shopping apps all grew significantly in the first half of 2020; total time spent using these apps also was higher than before the pandemic (refer to figure 1.10a).

Among all categories of apps, business apps have grown the most in scale and length of use. Business apps consist largely of video conferencing and business communication apps (like Zoom), professional networking and hiring platforms (like LinkedIn), business procurement apps, products and services selling apps (like Amazon seller), and corporate digital solutions apps (remote desktop, cloud, file management). Downloads of business apps peaked at more than 300 million in May 2020, 75 percent higher than the level in January 2019, and total time spent more than doubled (refer to figure 1.10, panel b). Most of the increase in downloads of and total time spent using business apps was driven by video conferencing apps. China, India, the United States, Indonesia, Brazil, and Mexico supplied most of the new downloads, while Bulgaria, Romania, Uruguay, Nigeria, the Philippines, and Peru had the highest growth rates in downloads.

The pandemic induced a durable acceleration in digital payments and online shopping in many countries. Finance and shopping apps are the other two categories of apps with persistently high downloads. Countries in Sub-Saharan Africa (Burkina Faso, Ghana, Malawi, Nigeria) and the Middle East and North Africa (Kuwait, Saudi Arabia, the United Arab Emirates) recorded the highest growth in finance app downloads, while several European Union countries (Bulgaria, Finland, Hungary, Ireland), India, and Senegal recorded the highest growth in shopping app downloads

FIGURE 1.10 **Impact of COVID-19 on patterns of smartphone use, by type of app, 2019–22**

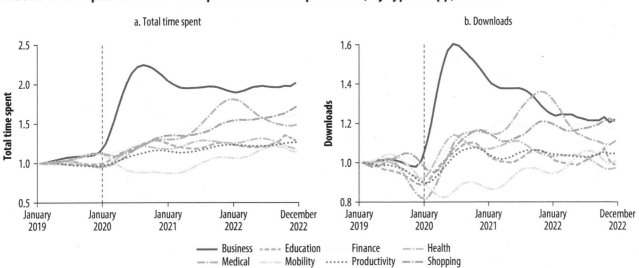

Source: Original calculations for this publication using Apptopia data for all active apps in Google Play and Apple Store globally.
Note: Values for time spent in January 2019 are normalized to 1, and values are smoothed over six months.

(refer to figure 1.11). Countries where the use of digital payments and online shopping were already prevalent before the pandemic had much lower growth in downloads.

Countries that adopted more stringent lockdowns witnessed higher downloads and greater use of business, education, games, and health apps and much lower downloads and use of travel apps. Lockdown stringency was a strong predictor of monthly downloads and total time spent for several types of apps. On a scale of 0–100, a 1 unit increase in a country's lockdown stringency predicted a 0.6 percent increase in business app downloads, a 0.2 percent increase in game app downloads, and a 0.5 percent drop in travel app downloads in the same month (refer to figure 1.12, panel a). A 1 unit increase in lockdown stringency also boosted total time spent on business apps by 0.3 percent, education apps by 0.1 percent, and game apps by 0.07 percent and reduced the total time spent on travel

FIGURE 1.11   Growth in app downloads, by country and type of app, 2019–22

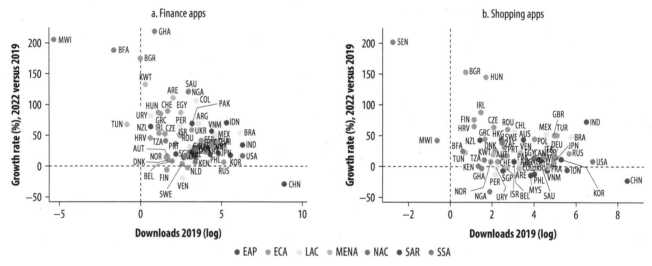

Source: Original calculations for this publication using Apptopia data for the top 500 most downloaded apps in Google Play and Apple Store in each country.
Note: EAP = East Asia and Pacific; ECA = Europe and Central Asia; LAC = Latin America and Caribbean; MENA = Middle East and North Africa; NAC = North America; SAR = South Asia; SSA = Sub-Saharan Africa. For a list of country and economy codes, refer to https://www.iso.org/obp/ui/#search.

FIGURE 1.12   Effect of lockdown stringency on downloads and total time spent on apps, by category of app, 2020–22

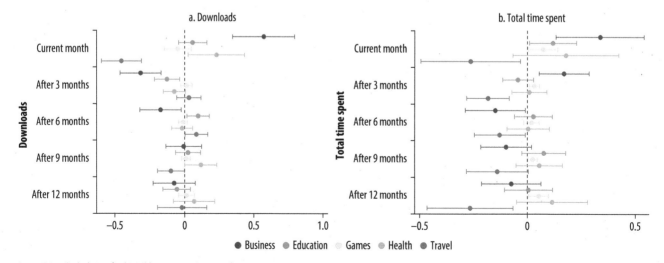

Source: Original calculations for this publication using Apptopia data.
Note: The figure displays the coefficients and 95% confidence interval of a 1 unit increase in a country's lockdown stringency (on a scale from 0 to 100) on the total downloads and total time spent on a certain category of app in the current month and after 3, 6, 9, and 12 months. Control variables include the number of new COVID-19 cases per million population, country fixed effects, and month-year fixed effects.

apps by 0.26 percent (refer to figure 1.12, panel b). While the effects of lockdowns on app downloads (a proxy for new users) were immediate and limited largely to the same month, the effects on total time spent persisted. For instance, for 3 months after the initial lockdown, total time spent on business apps remained much higher in countries that imposed harsher lockdowns. Further, the negative effect on the use of travel apps persisted for 12 months after the initial lockdown. The effects on downloads and use of the top 500 apps were even larger and more persistent.

Digital uptake by businesses varies significantly across countries and types of technology

This section compares firms' digital uptake in 14 countries from four regions based on the World Bank's Firm Level Adoption of Technology (FAT) survey conducted during 2019–22. Each country was only surveyed in one wave, so the data do not allow an analysis of trends. An appendix at the end of the report provides more details about the FAT survey. For all cross-country comparisons presented in this section, the value is the predicted value after controlling for firm age, firm size, and sector.

While companies in high-income countries continue to integrate the latest digital technologies— like generative artificial intelligence (AI) platforms—into their products, services, and business functions, many companies in low- and middle-income countries, particularly small and medium enterprises, were without a computer or internet connection in 2022. The World Bank's FAT survey revealed significant disparities in firms' access to basic technology enablers across countries. After controlling for firm age, size, and sector, almost all firms in Brazil, Chile, Georgia, India, the Republic of Korea, Poland, and Viet Nam had a computer for business purposes and internet connection. In contrast, only half of firms in Bangladesh, Burkina Faso, and Ethiopia had computers, illustrating the wide divide between businesses and the use of internet technology across countries (refer to figure 1.13).

In some low- and middle-income countries, firms with access to a computer and the internet face limits in pursuing broader digital transformation due to outdated connection methods and poor quality of internet services. Dial-up internet, long phased out in most countries, requires users to link their phone line to a computer. In Burkina Faso, this outdated method of connecting to the internet is still the fastest type of connection for more than 70 percent of firms. In addition to low internet speeds, firms in some low- and middle-income countries also suffer frequent disruptions in internet service. In Bangladesh, internet service is predicted to crash seven times per month on average. Such frequent

FIGURE 1.13 **Share of firms with a computer or internet connection across countries, 2019–22**

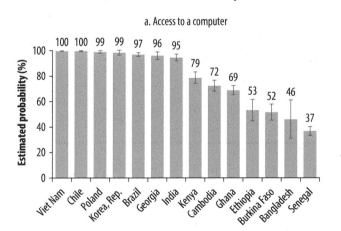

a. Access to a computer

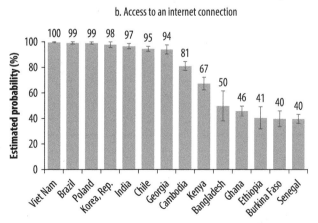

b. Access to an internet connection

Source: Original calculations for this publication using World Bank Firm Level Adoption of Technology survey data.
Note: The panels illustrate the estimated probability, with 95% confidence intervals, after controlling for country, sector, firm size, and firm age.

disruptions make it difficult to maintain business continuity and compete with other firms in the global digital economy. Many competing firms in higher-income economies not only experience fewer disruptions but also enjoy the assurance of redundancy, designed to reduce disruptions not only in internet connection but also in the energy systems that power use of the internet and digital devices.

In most high-income markets, it is essential for businesses to use a website or social media account to boost visibility, reach potential customers, gain market insights, and grow their brand. However, website and social media use remains low among firms in some poorer countries relative to similar firms in richer countries. After controlling for firm age, size, and sector, survey results predicted that more than half of firms in Brazil, Chile, Ghana, Kenya, and Poland have a website. Further, results indicated that four in five firms in India use social media accounts for business purposes. In contrast, only around 13 percent of firms in Burkina Faso, Ethiopia, and Senegal have a website; these three countries are also the least likely of the countries surveyed to use social media for business purposes (refer to figure 1.14). One (of many) reason that these countries have such low figures is that digital platforms are not as useful or as effective in reaching customers in their markets because their customers may lack access to digital technologies and means of internet connectivity at this time.

Use of advanced technology services like cloud computing is even more rare in most of the low- and middle-income countries surveyed. Businesses can benefit from cloud computing in multiple

FIGURE 1.14 **Use of website, social media, and cloud computing for business purposes in select countries, 2019–22**

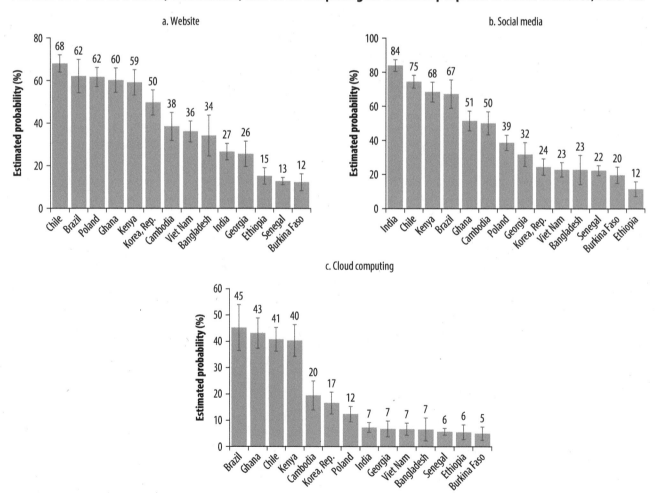

Source: Original calculations for this publication using World Bank Firm Level Adoption of Technology survey data.
Note: Figures illustrate 95 percent confidence intervals.

ways, ranging from cost savings, scalability and flexibility, enhanced collaboration and productivity, increased reliability and data security, and better decision-making through advanced analytics and insights. Cloud adoption is already mainstream in high-income countries. About 80 percent of US businesses surveyed by the PricewaterhouseCoopers cloud business survey reported using cloud services in most or all parts of their businesses in 2021. [6] Among the countries surveyed in the FAT survey, Brazil, Chile, Ghana, and Kenya reported the highest cloud adoption, at around 40 percent of firms. In most other countries surveyed, cloud adoption remains rare. Fewer than 10 percent of firms in Bangladesh, Burkina Faso, Ethiopia, Georgia, India, Senegal, and Viet Nam used cloud computing services during 2019–22 (refer to figure 1.14).

Firms in low- and middle-income countries continue to have huge untapped potential in the use of digital technology for payments and sales. While firms in these poorer economies lag on the extensive margin (whether technology is used or not), the gap is even larger on the intensive margin (how frequent technology is used). Only one in five firms in Bangladesh, Burkina Faso, Ethiopia, Ghana, and Senegal use online banking for payments. Further, almost none of the firms in these countries use online banking as the most common method for payments (refer to figure 1.15). Use of an online

FIGURE 1.15 Use of technologies applied to payment methods in select countries, 2019–22

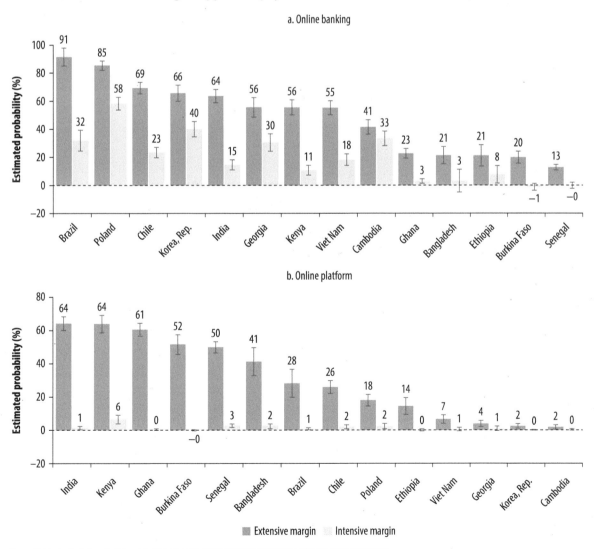

Source: Original calculations for this publication using World Bank Firm Level Adoption of Technology survey data.
Note: Figures illustrate 95 percent confidence intervals.

platform for payments is less common than online banking across economies. Use of digital platforms, company websites, and electronic orders to manage sales is also limited in the countries surveyed, especially on the intensive margin (refer to figure 1.16). This digital divide in adoption has enormous implications for firms in low- and middle-income countries, as their ability to connect with customers efficiently and effectively in an increasingly competitive digital economy relies on narrowing the divide through greater digital uptake.

FIGURE 1.16 Use of technologies applied to sales methods in select countries, 2019–22

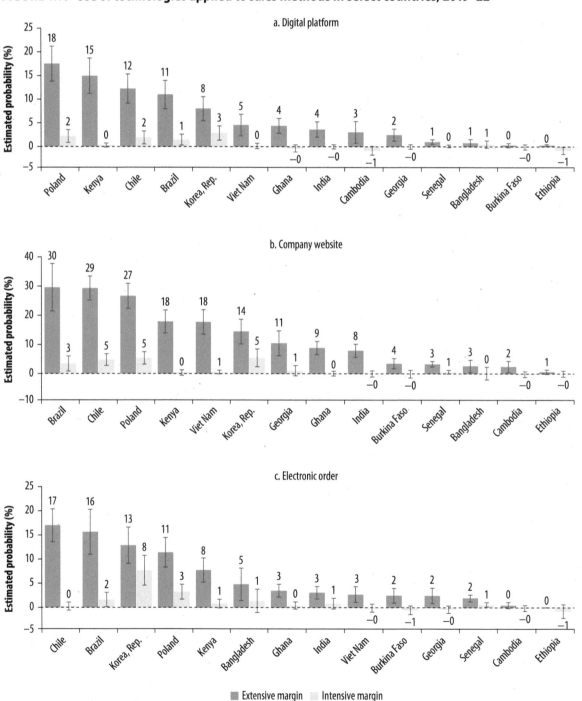

Source: Original calculations for this publication using World Bank Firm Level Adoption of Technology survey data.
Note: Figures illustrate 95 percent confidence intervals.

Firms with greater digital readiness before the pandemic and those that invested in digital solutions during the pandemic were more resilient

This section uses the World Bank's Business Pulse Survey (BPS) to track firms' digital uptake since the outbreak of COVID-19. The BPS was conducted in several waves from April 2020 to December 2022 to assess the impact of the pandemic on businesses in dozens of countries around the world. These surveys also captured information on how much firms invested in and used digital solutions before and during the pandemic. The appendix provides more details about BPS data.

The share of firms investing in digital solutions increased significantly over the course of the pandemic. While COVID-19 drove firms of all sizes online, the pandemic widened the gap between small and large firms investing in digital solutions. Based on the BPS conducted in dozens of countries across six regions, about 16 percent of firms invested in digital technologies during the early phase of the pandemic from April to August 2020. This share increased to 26 percent during the second phase of the pandemic from September 2020 to June 2021 and increased to 33 percent during the final phase of the pandemic from July 2021 to December 2022. This increase in investment in digital technologies transpired for firms of all sizes, but most dramatically for large firms, contributing to a widening of digital divides despite widespread investment globally. Over the course of the pandemic from April 2020 to December 2022, the percentage of micro firms investing in digital solutions doubled from 10 percent to 20 percent, but the percentage of large firms tripled from 20 percent to 60 percent (refer to figure 1.17).

The use of digital solutions was highest during the middle phase of the pandemic (September 2020 to June 2021), declining slightly after mid-2021. Still, use remained much higher in 2022 than in early 2020. This finding holds true for firms across all sizes and in all sectors, after controlling for time, firm size, sector, and region fixed effects (refer to figure 1.18). Normalcy started to return in late 2021, as people obtained protection from infection and received vaccines and earlier strains were replaced by the less virulent Omicron variants. As a result, in-person interaction began to increase. Thus, the final phase of the pandemic is associated with the likelihood that the firms surveyed would use digital solutions less often than in the second phase. Still, the probability of using digital solutions at the end of 2022 remained much higher than in early 2020.

Firms' digital readiness and management practices before the pandemic predicted a higher probability of investment in and use of digital solutions during the pandemic. Digital readiness was measured as the number of pre-COVID-19 digital practices applied out of three indicators: online sales or payment, online social media, and use of enterprise resource planning software and systems. Management practices were measured as the number of structured management practices applied out of three indicators among firms: targets, advertisements, and promotion of employees. The numbers were then used to generate firm capability scores. A score of 0 indicated no digital preparedness or poor management practices before

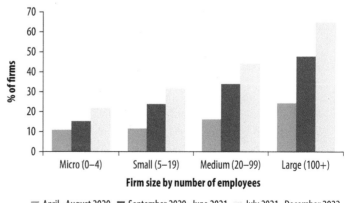

FIGURE 1.17 Share of firms investing in digital solutions during COVID-19, by firm size, 2020–22

Source: Original calculations for this publication using World Bank Business Pulse Survey data.
Note: Firm owner is not counted as an employee.

FIGURE 1.18 Predicted probability of using digital solutions over time, by size of firm and sector, 2020–22

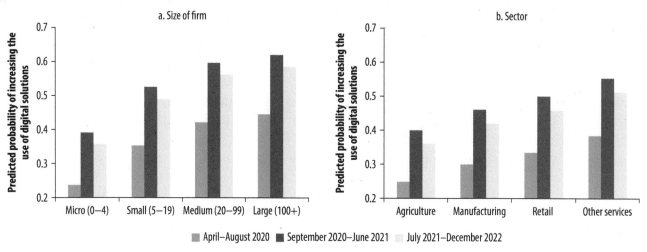

Source: Calculation based on World Bank Business Pulse Survey data.

FIGURE 1.19 Association between firms' capabilities and digital investment and use, 2020–22

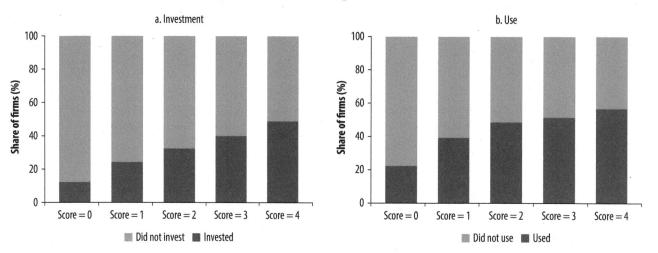

Source: Calculation based on World Bank Business Pulse Survey data.

the pandemic, while a score of 4 indicated the highest digital readiness and best management practices. BPS results revealed that the firms with higher scores were more likely to invest in and use digital technologies (refer to figure 1.19).

Firms with greater digital readiness before the pandemic and those that invested in digital solutions during the pandemic also recorded greater resilience in sales. Firms with higher digital readiness before the pandemic had a higher share of sales during the pandemic due to their use of digital platforms (refer to figure 1.20). Firms that invested in digital solutions during the pandemic also experienced a much smaller decline in sales relative to firms that did not invest across all levels of prepandemic digital readiness.

FIGURE 1.20 Association between firms' resilience in sales and digital investment and use, 2020–22

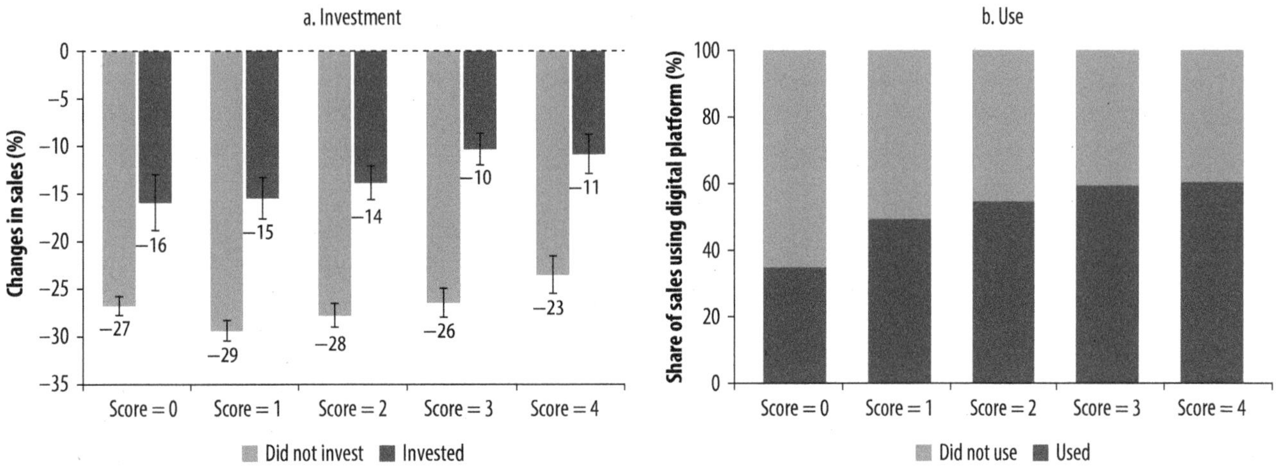

a. Investment

b. Use

Did not invest ▪ Invested

Did not use ▪ Used

Source: Calculation based on World Bank Business Pulse Survey data.
Note: A higher score indicates higher digital readiness and better management practices prepandemic.

Digital adoption and diffusion must be facilitated to narrow the digital divide

To boost economic growth, the diffusion and adoption of digital technologies are arguably just as critical as their invention. The contribution of new technology to economic growth can only be realized when and if the new technology is widely diffused and used. Technology's diffusion relies on a series of decisions by people and organizations based on comparing uncertain technological benefits with uncertain adoption costs. Well-informed and skilled individuals along with pioneering companies, often located in high-income economies, have frequently extolled the positive impact of digital technology and reaped hefty rewards due to their technological understanding. However, much of the world is still at the start of the digital adoption journey.

Governments can play a key role in speeding up the adoption of technology. Identifying what type of market failure justifies government support, determining the size of the market failure, and articulating why and under what conditions government support could lead to higher adoption and not waste public resources are critical initial steps for public policy. Governments can catalyze private investment in digital infrastructure to connect the unconnected. These catalysts include removing restrictions on foreign participation and ownership in internet service providers and spectrum-based operators, promoting infrastructure sharing, ensuring competition, and monitoring the quality of internet services (ITU 2020).

Addressing the affordability of devices is one tangible means of closing the use gap of individuals living within the range of a broadband signal but not using the services. Government can promote affordable entry-level devices in several ways. Import duty reductions and tax exemptions can lower the cost of devices but have fiscal implications. Financing schemes should be based on a risk-sharing model that subsidizes devices between parties with an interest in bringing more individuals online, including manufacturers, retailers, consumers, app partners, and governments. Successful pilot subsidy programs exist, but providing subsidies at scale remains a challenge.

While much has been achieved over the last decade to narrow the divide in internet access, more work is needed to minimize the divide in smartphone and computer ownership, fixed broadband penetration, internet speeds, data traffic, digital skills, and productive use—particularly in the face of emerging and disruptive digital technologies—as much as possible. It is critical for policy makers and development stakeholders to monitor developments in the latest digital technologies like generative AI, which has been adopted rapidly in 2023. Broader generative AI applications have enormous potential to simplify digital tasks at all levels of complexity, including coding and data analysis, and offer new opportunities for facilitated learning of both digital and other skills. At the same time, if global adoption and use rates mirror the general digital divides between higher-income and lower-income economies (as discussed in this chapter), it will only further exacerbate the asymmetrical distribution of benefits yielded by these new technologies. Chapter 5 discusses the latest AI developments, the associated benefits and risks, trends in AI governance, and the implications for low- and middle-income countries.

Notes

Xavier Cirera, Ana Goicoechea, Silvia Muzi, Sara Oliveira, and Nithya Srinivasan provided key inputs to this chapter.

1. "Rural Net Users See Steep 45% Rise in 3 Years," *Times of India,* May 6, 2022 (https://timesofindia .indiatimes.com/business/india-business/rural-net-users-see-steep-45-rise-in-3-years/articleshow /91357551.cms) and "Over 50% Indians Are Active Internet Users Now; Base to Reach 900 Million by 2020: Report." *The Hindu,* May 4, 2023 (https://www.thehindu.com/news/national/over-50 -indians-are-active-internet-users-now-base-to-reach-900-million-by-2025-report).
2. As one fixed broadband subscription in a household or business often has multiple users, fixed broadband subscriptions per 100 inhabitants (fixed broadband penetration) tend to be much lower than mobile broadband subscriptions.
3. The target is met when the retail price of 2 gigabytes of data-only mobile broadband is below 2 percent of monthly gross national income per capita.
4. Total smartphone connections can exceed a country's population for several reasons. Some people have multiple SIM cards or smartphones for different purposes. Dual-SIM smartphones allow users to use two SIM cards simultaneously. Tourists and visitors may purchase local SIM cards or use roaming services, which contribute to the overall number of smartphone connections.
5. "Coronavirus: The World in Lockdown in Maps and Charts," *BBC News,* April 7, 2020 (https://www.bbc.com/news/world-52103747).
6. "The PwC's Cloud Business Survey" (https://www.pwc.com/us/en/tech-effect/cloud/cloud-business -survey.html).

References

Aker, Jenny C. 2010. "Information from Markets Near and Far: Mobile Phones and Agricultural Markets in Niger." *American Economic Journal: Applied Economics* 2 (3): 46–59.

Atiyas, İzak, and Mark A. Dutz. 2021. *Digital Technology Uses among Informal Micro-Sized Firms.* Washington, DC: World Bank.

Bahia, Kalvin, Pau Castells, Genaro Cruz, Xavier Pedros, Tobias Pfutze, Carlos Rodriguez Castelan, and Hernan Jorge Winkler. 2020. "The Welfare Effects of Mobile Broadband Internet: Evidence from Nigeria." Policy Research Working Paper 9230, World Bank, Washington, DC.

Bar-Gill, Sajit, Erik Brynjolfsson, and Nir Hak. 2023. "Helping Small Businesses Become More Data-Driven: A Field Experiment on eBay." NBER Working Paper w31089, National Bureau of Economic Research, Cambridge, MA.

Begazo, Tania, Moussa P. Blimpo, and Mark A. Dutz. 2023. *Digital Technologies: Enabling Technological Transformation for Jobs.* Washington, DC: World Bank.

Bloom, Nicholas, Raffaella Sadun, and John Van Reenen. 2012. "Americans Do IT Better: US Multinationals and the Productivity Miracle." *American Economic Review* 102 (1): 167–201.

Cirera, Xavier, Diego Comin, and Marcio Cruz. 2022. *Bridging the Technological Divide: Technology Adoption by Firms in Developing Countries.* Washington, DC: World Bank. https://elibrary .worldbank.org/doi/full/10.1596/978-1-4648-1826-4_ch7.

Derksen, Laura, Catherine Michaud-Leclerc, and Pedro C. L. Souza. 2022. "Restricted Access: How the Internet Can Be Used to Promote Reading and Learning." *Journal of Development Economics* 155 (March): 102810.

GSMA. 2022. *The State of Mobile Internet Connectivity Report 2022.* London: GSMA. https://www .gsma.com/r/wp-content/uploads/2022/12/The-State-of-Mobile-Internet-Connectivity-Report-2022. pdf?utm_source=website&utm_medium=download-button&utm_campaign=somic22.

Hjort, Jonas, and Jonas Poulsen. 2019. "The Arrival of Fast Internet and Employment in Africa." *American Economic Review* 109 (3): 1032–79.

ITU (International Telecommunication Union). 2020. *Connecting Humanity: Assessing Investment Needs of Connecting Humanity to the Internet by 2030.* Geneva: ITU.

ITU (International Telecommunication Union). 2023. "The Affordability of ICT Services 2022." ITU, Geneva.

Jensen, Robert. 2007. "The Digital Provide: Information (Technology), Market Performance, and Welfare in the South Indian Fisheries Sector." *Quarterly Journal of Economics* 122 (3): 879–924. doi:10.1162/qjec.122.3.879.

Rodriguez-Segura, Daniel. 2022. "EdTech in Developing Countries: A Review of the Evidence." *World Bank Research Observer* 37 (2): 171–203.

Viollaz, Mariana, and Hernan Winkler. 2022. "Does the Internet Reduce Gender Gaps? The Case of Jordan." *Journal of Development Studies* 58 (3): 436–53.

The Digital Sector: A Driver of Innovation, Growth, and Job Creation | 2

Yan Liu and Henry Stemmler

KEY MESSAGES

- Value added growth of information technology (IT) services averaged 8 percent annually between 2000 and 2022, growing nearly twice as fast as the global economy. Employment in IT services grew by 7 percent annually during the same period, far outstripping the meager 1 percent growth in total employment.

- IT services are also being used increasingly as intermediate inputs in other sectors. The input intensity of IT services almost doubled in high-income and upper-middle-income countries during 2000–20, but it did not grow at all in lower-middle-income countries.

- Globally, IT services exports grew at 12 percent annually during 2010–22, eclipsing all other types of services exports. Low entry barriers and soaring demand led to remarkable growth in IT services exports in many low- and middle-income countries.

- Digital start-ups from low- and middle-income countries have received an influx of venture capital (VC) funding since 2020, with most VC deals being in e-commerce, fintech, health, education, and entertainment.

- The app market has become more local and less global. From 2015 to 2022, 54 out of 63 countries where data are available witnessed an increase in the share of domestic apps in the list of top 100 most downloaded apps. Low- and middle-income countries with vast domestic markets, unique language, and strong cultural identity are especially well positioned to develop homegrown giants, and firms from smaller economies can still prosper in niche markets.

Introduction

The information and communication technology (ICT) sector combines manufacturing and services industries whose products fulfill or enable the function of information processing and communication primarily by electronic means, including transmission and display (UN 2008). Due to variations in industry and product classifications across countries or sources and the increasingly blurred lines between industries, this chapter adopts a slightly modified definition of the ICT sector (refer to figure 2.1). It presents a granular breakdown of ICT manufacturing and ICT services, whenever possible, to allow for more accurate and detailed analysis.

Today, digital platforms comprise some of the largest ICT companies by market capitalization. Digital platforms have also transformed businesses in other sectors and blurred traditional industry lines. A digital platform is an economic agent with a business model that permits interactions and

FIGURE 2.1 Key segments in the digital sector

Sector	Segment	Firm examples
ICT manufacturing	Electronic components	Intel, Nvidia, Qualcomm, TSMC
	Computers and peripheral equipment	Apple, Dell, Lenovo
	Communications equipment	Apple, Ericsson, Huawei, Samsung
	Consumer electronics	Apple, Samsung, Sony
ICT services	Publishing, broadcasting, audiovisual	BBC, Blizzard, Netflix
	Telecommunication	AT&T, Verizon, Vodafone
	Data centers and cloud computing	Alphabet, AWS, Microsoft
	AI and big data analytics	DeepMind, OpenAI
	IT consulting services	Accenture, IBM
	IT outsourcing	Infosys, Wipro
	Operating software	Meta, Microsoft, Apple
	Application software (including information platforms, search engines, social media, and others)	Citrix, Meta, Microsoft, Oracle, SAP, Tencent Zoom
BPO-ITES	Call centers, accounting, human resources, marketing, and others	Concentrix, Teleperformance
Other digital platforms	Digital financial services	Alipay, PayPal, Venmo
	E-commerce	Alibaba, Amazon, Flipkart
	Employment and sharing platforms	Airbnb, TaskRabbit, Uber, Upwork
	Other digital platforms	Coursera, Redfin, Teladoc

(The ICT sector comprises ICT manufacturing and ICT services; the digital sector comprises the ICT sector, BPO-ITES, and Other digital platforms. IT services spans Data centers and cloud computing through Application software.)

Source: World Bank.
Note: AI = artificial intelligence; BPO-ITES = business process outsourcing and IT-enabled services; ICT = information and communication technology; IT = information technology.

exchanges of information, goods, or services between multiple types of users—which can include producers, consumers, or a community—through digital means. While some digital platforms like Google and Meta belong to the ICT sector, others such as Amazon and Uber are often mapped to other sectors. Digital platforms have spread to many different industries, including real estate (Redfin), health (Teladoc), education (Coursera), and so forth. Traditional businesses have increasingly embraced the platform-based model as well. For instance, Walmart has become an e-commerce giant, while banks have launched their own apps and digital wallets. Digital platforms have widened firms' boundaries and businesses to bring increasingly diverse and unrelated business lines together to create digital ecosystems, further complicating the industry classification of such firms.

Business process outsourcing and information technology (IT)-enabled services (BPO-ITES) refers to contracting business activities and functions to third-party providers. Business processes are often IT based or delivered electronically over the internet or through telecommunication networks. Common outsourced business processes include call center or customer services, accounting and bookkeeping, human resources, data entry, editing and typesetting, design, marketing, and so forth. BPO-ITES has created abundant job opportunities and improved inclusion by providing new sources of income for youth, women, the disabled, and people from remote areas.

The ICT sector, BPO-ITES, and digital platforms (hereafter referred to as "the digital sector") both address and exacerbate several market failures. The digital sector can enhance innovation and boost efficiency by overcoming information barriers, augmenting production factors, transforming products, and reducing searching, matching, and transaction costs (Beuermann, McKelvey, and Vakis 2012; Paunov and Rollo 2016; World Bank 2016). The Internet and data are borderless by nature, nonrival, and sometimes nonexcludable, exhibiting characteristics of global public goods (Buchholz and Sandler 2021). At the same time, network externalities, economies of scale and scope, and "winner-takes-most" characteristics tend to result in high market concentration and power imbalance. Thus, the characteristics of the digital sector necessitate government intervention to alleviate market failures.

First, this chapter examines how the digital sector contributes to economic growth and job creation. Next, it shows different pathways for countries to create value in the digital sector and identifies outperforming economies in each pathway. The chapter seeks to answer the following questions: (1) How much does the digital sector contribute to growth and job creation? (2) What are the opportunities and pathways for countries to create value in the digital sector? (3) What factors have contributed to the success of certain low- and middle-income countries in different pathways?

The digital sector drives growth, creates jobs, and generates huge positive spillovers

ICT was the most innovative field of technology during the past few decades and a key enabler of innovation in other sectors. Fields related to ICT technology have been among the most rapidly growing fields in patent publications (refer to figure 2.2); their share of total patent publications grew from less than 10 percent in 1980 to 26 percent in 2021. From personal computers, the internet, digital platforms, 4G/5G, smartphones, and cloud services to artificial intelligence (AI), the most significant technological breakthroughs during the past few decades were dominated by the ICT sector. The world's seven biggest spenders on research and development in 2020 were all ICT companies: Alphabet, Amazon, Apple, Huawei, Meta, Microsoft, and Samsung. Generative AI tools such as ChatGPT and Stable Diffusion dazzled the public in late 2022. As a general-purpose technology (GPT), ICT enables and accelerates innovation in other sectors. For example, AlphaFold2—a software that uses AI to predict the shape of proteins—has opened new paths for the discovery and design of drugs.

The IT services segment has been the fastest-growing segment in the global economy over the past two decades, growing twice as fast as the rest of the economy. Based on the ICT sector data set compiled by this report team (refer to the appendix for more information), the total value added of the ICT sector exceeded US$6.1 trillion in 2022, representing around 6 percent of global gross domestic

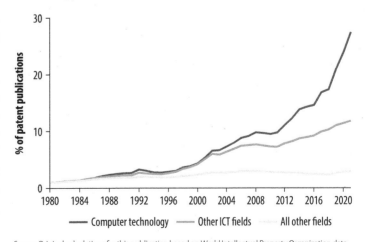

FIGURE 2.2 **Global annual patent publications, by field of technology, 1980–2020**

Source: Original calculations for this publication based on World Intellectual Property Organization data.
Note: Computer technology is a subset of ICT. Value in 1980 is normalized to 1; ICT = information and communication technology.

product (GDP) (refer to figure 2.3).[1] Within the ICT sector, value added is increasingly captured in IT services rather than in hardware manufacturing or telecommunication. The value added growth rate of IT services is nearly twice the growth rate of the global economy, surpassing all other sectors in the past two decades, based on information in the Trade in Value-Added (TiVA) data set.

Similar to other GPTs, such as electricity, digital technology's growing importance is not reflected in national accounts. Some people are puzzled by the conflict between the ubiquitous presence of digital technologies and their modest share in global GDP. As a new general-purpose technology matures and becomes widely adopted, the price of technology often drops more than the expansion of output, resulting in a stable or contracting share of the technology-producing sector in GDP. Part of the explanation also reflects a measurement problem. The variety and quality of digital goods and services have soared over the past few decades, but they are not captured accurately in price indexes. The welfare gains from a few popular digital services—many of which are free to users—amount to an estimated 6 percent of GDP. These digital services also disproportionately benefit lower-income groups (Brynjolfsson, Li, and Raymond 2023).

Value added in ICT manufacturing and ICT services is highly concentrated in high-income economies, and the concentration increased further during the past decade. China and the United States account for more than half of global value added in the two industries. Furthermore, the top six economies account for 80 percent of global value added in ICT manufacturing and 70 percent in ICT services. These shares have increased further since 2010, as economies of scale and scope, network effects, and winner-takes-most characteristics of the ICT sector have cemented and escalated dominance by the world's leading economies.

Several Central and Eastern European countries achieved impressive growth in both ICT manufacturing and ICT services production in the past few years. Bosnia and Herzegovina, Bulgaria, Iceland, Lithuania, Malta, North Macedonia, Slovenia, and Türkiye achieved double-digit growth in ICT manufacturing value added during 2015–22 (refer to figure 2.4, panel a). Bulgaria, Croatia, Cyprus, Czechia, Estonia, Latvia, Lithuania, Malta, and Romania achieved double-digit growth in ICT services (refer to figure 2.4, panel b). Other countries such as Chile, Costa Rica, Senegal, and Viet Nam also experienced brisk growth in ICT manufacturing, while China, Ghana, Ireland,

FIGURE 2.3 **Value added of ICT manufacturing and ICT services, by subsector, 2000–22**

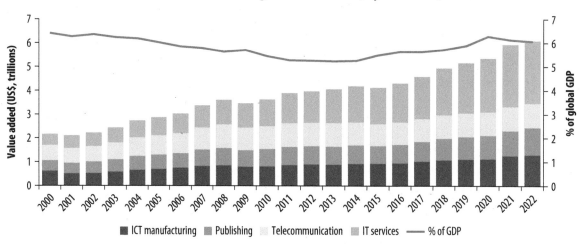

Source: Original calculations for this publication based on the World Bank ICT sector data set compiled for this report.
Note: GDP = gross domestic product; ICT = information and communication technology; IT = information technology.

Kenya, Saudi Arabia, and Singapore excelled in ICT services. Most of these countries achieved such growth by integrating into the global ICT value chain.

ICT goods and services are also increasingly used as intermediate inputs in other sectors. Based on the TiVA database, the share of ICT goods inputs increased modestly from 2000 to 2020 in all sectors (refer to figure 2.5a). The intensity of telecommunication inputs remained stable (refer to figure 2.5b). The share of IT services inputs rose dramatically across sectors, especially in modern services (refer to figure 2.5c), highlighting the substantial spillovers that IT services generate in the broader economy.

FIGURE 2.4 **Value added growth in ICT manufacturing and services, select countries, 2015–22**

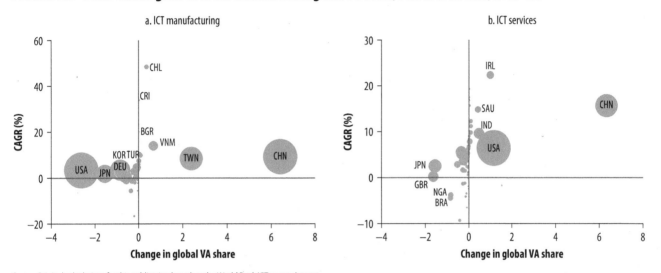

Source: Original calculations for this publication based on the World Bank ICT sector data set.
Note: ICT = information and communication technology; CAGR = compound annual growth rate; VA = value added. For a list of country and economy codes, go to https://www.iso.org/obp/ui/#search. Only major economies and the fastest growing economies are labeled. Bubble size represents the economy's share of the global ICT value added.

FIGURE 2.5 **Intensity of ICT inputs, by sector, 2000 and 2020**

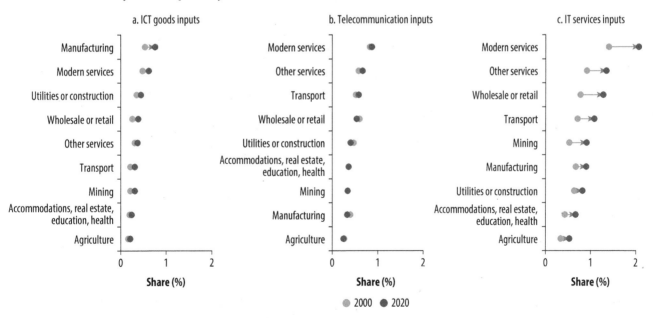

Source: Original calculations for this publication using Organisation for Economic Co-operation and Development Trade in Value-Added (2022) data.
Note: Modern services include publishing and broadcasting, telecommunications, IT services, finance and insurance, and professional and scientific services. Input share is calculated as the percentage of ICT manufacturing, telecommunication, and IT services in all intermediate inputs. ICT = information and communication technology; IT = information technology.

There is a growing digital divide in production. Gaps in the use of IT services have widened both within and across country income groups. In 2000, the finance industry's IT services intensity was below 1 percent in most middle-income countries and between 1 percent and 2 percent in high-income countries (refer to figure 2.6). Between 2000 and 2020, IT services intensity in the finance sector barely increased in low- and middle-income countries, while it doubled in most high-income countries. The dispersion within income groups also widened. Similar trends can be observed in professional services. These findings strongly suggest that productivity gains from the use of IT services have not been fully exploited in low- and middle-income countries.

The ICT sector directly employs a small but growing share of workers, driven largely by the IT services subsector. Global employment in the ICT sector reached 68 million in 2022, up from about 37 million in 2000. The ICT sector's contribution to the share of global employment grew modestly from 1.3 percent in 2000 to 2 percent in 2022, with most new jobs added in IT services (refer to figure 2.7). The compound annual growth rate (CAGR) of employment in IT services averaged nearly 7 percent during 2000–22, significantly eclipsing the 1 percent growth of total employment.

FIGURE 2.6 **Intensity of IT services inputs in select industries, by country income group, 2000 and 2020**

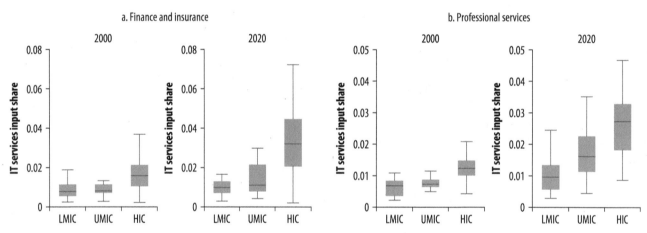

Source: Original calculations for this publication using Organisation for Economic Co-operation and Development Trade in Value-Added (2022) data.
Note: Whiskers represent 95% confidence intervals. HIC = high-income countries; IT = information technology; LMIC = lower-middle-income countries; UMIC = upper-middle-income countries.

FIGURE 2.7 **ICT sector as a share of employment, by subsector, 2000–22**

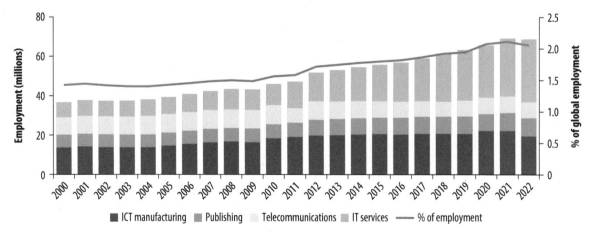

Source: Original calculations for this publication based on the World Bank ICT sector data set.
Note: ICT = information and communication technology; IT = information technology.

ICT manufacturing jobs withered in Brazil, France, Japan, the United Kingdom, and the United States, while they mushroomed in China and Viet Nam during the past two decades. As the world's factory floor, China's ICT manufacturing sector employed around 13 million people in 2021, accounting for nearly 60 percent of global employment in ICT manufacturing. Viet Nam's ICT manufacturing employment approached 1 million in 2021 and grew at an astonishing 21 percent annually during the past two decades. ICT manufacturing employment also grew in China; India; Malaysia; Mexico; and Taiwan, China.

Rapid technological advances and explosive demand have made the IT services industry one of the most desirable employers in the 21st century. The sector has created some of the most well-paid jobs, minted a vast new middle class, and increased social mobility. The increasing dependence on digital technologies has spurred tremendous demand for app developers, software engineers, data analysts, cloud architects, and many other professions that did not even exist 20 years ago. The IT services industry houses some of the world's most valuable companies by market capitalization and provides jobs with opportunities for professional success. In the United States, IT services occupations were among the most well-paid occupations in 2022. In China since 2020, the IT services industry has replaced financial services as the highest-paying industry. The IT services industry employs many more people and offers more social mobility than traditional lucrative industries like medicine, law, and finance. There are also more routes of entry into the IT industry as well as lower costs to attain the required qualifications and skills.

China created by far the most jobs in IT services during the past two decades, followed by India. China's IT services employment approached 10 million by the end of 2022, a 30-fold increase from 0.3 million in 2000 (refer to figure 2.8, panel a). Underpinning this jobs spurt is the remarkable growth of China's homegrown technology firms, enabled by a massive domestic market, vast pool

FIGURE 2.8 Size and growth of IT services and gender ratio in IT services, 2000–22

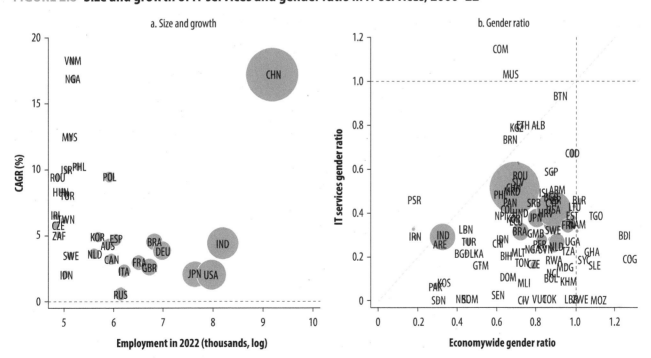

Source: Original calculations for this publication based on the World Bank ICT sector data set.
Note: The gender ratio is the ratio of women to men. CAGR = compound annual growth rate; IT = information technology. For a list of country and economy codes, refer to https://www.iso .org/obp/ui/#search.

of talent, enormous investments, and policy support. India maintained second place, behind China, during the past two decades. In India, more than 3 million people worked in IT services in 2022, up from 1.4 million in 2000. Direct employment in India's ICT and BPO-ITES sector is estimated to have been around 5.1 million in 2022.[2]

Israel, Malaysia, Nigeria, the Philippines, Viet Nam, and several Central and Eastern European countries (Hungary, Poland, Romania) saw the fastest growth in employment thanks to the burgeoning local IT services industry and roaring IT exports. Viet Nam has emerged as a major software hub in Southeast Asia. The country's IT services job sector grew at a breakneck annual rate of 20 percent during the past two decades, thanks to its young and growing population, low labor costs, and strong science, technology, engineering, and math education. Similarly, Nigeria's tech industry has been on the rise, with start-ups and tech hubs popping up across the country. Hungary, Malaysia, the Philippines, Poland, and Romania have become increasingly attractive destinations for IT services outsourcing. Companies are drawn by their skilled workforce, competitive labor costs, and favorable business environment.

The gender gap in the IT services industry is narrowing, with low- and middle-income countries leading the progress. Back in 2010, women only accounted for 23 percent of global employment in the IT services industry, 6 percentage points below the level in 2020. Many low- and middle-income countries led the progress, as educated women joined the tech industry in droves to pursue their career ambitions. The Kyrgyz Republic had the largest increase in female participation in IT services, with the ratio of women to men jumping from 0.04 in 2010 to 0.79 in 2020 (refer to figure 2.8, panel b). Albania, Bangladesh, Brunei Darussalam, Cyprus, the Arab Republic of Egypt, Iceland, the Islamic Republic of Iran, Tanzania, and Uganda also achieved remarkable progress in bringing more women into the IT services workforce.

Pathways to create value in the digital sector

Countries have two main pathways to develop their digital sector: export oriented and domestic market oriented. While each pathway has its own set of prerequisites, they complement and reinforce each other. Not all countries need a large domestic digital sector; however, many low- and middle-income countries could benefit from developing their local digital sector. Both ICT manufacturing and ICT services present huge potential for export-led growth. At the same time, a vibrant local digital sector can better serve domestic demand, generate more positive spillovers in the economy than foreign firms, and ultimately stimulate innovation and growth (Keller 2002; Sampson 2023). For low- and middle-income countries, the export-oriented pathway is often the first step in creating value within the digital sector. Global value chains have enabled them to focus on specific tasks in the digital sector without having to build the entire industry from scratch. Through export activities, countries accumulate capital, skills, and knowledge that prove to be invaluable in the domestic market. As the local digital sector develops, it paves the way for the emergence of domestic entrepreneurs. These entrepreneurs establish firms specializing in local ICT manufacturing, ICT services, and local digital platforms. Subsequently, these homegrown digital firms expand and internationalize, fueling exports in return.

In the short term, countries need to assess their comparative advantage in different segments of the digital sector and to formulate strategies accordingly. The digital sector is vast, complex, and rapidly evolving, and almost no single country can produce a product without any foreign inputs. Countries' endowments, stage of development, and industry structure play a key role in determining their comparative advantage in different segments of the digital sector. Leveraging current strengths through tailored pathways is a more pragmatic approach for many low- and middle-income countries in the short term.

However, comparative advantage is not destiny. In the longer term, low- and middle-income countries can identify the most promising global opportunities for creating value and formulate strategies to overcome existing constraints through innovative approaches. Constantly evolving technologies in the digital sector present opportunities for countries to circumvent existing constraints and move up the value chain. For example, smaller and less developed economies have been hindered by the lack of availability of large data sets to train AI models. However, with synthetic data, the lack of data may be less of a constraint. Similarly, cloud computing can help countries to overcome some of their constraints in computing power. Policy makers and the private sector can work together to identify promising opportunities in the digital sector and leverage innovative approaches to move into more complex tasks that promote technological spillovers. Reshaping their comparative advantage toward more sophisticated tasks can lead to long-term economic growth and prosperity.

Policies and institutions also need to keep adapting to a country's level of maturity and market dynamics in the digital sector. As countries move up the digital value chain and their domestic digital sector matures, innovation and market contestability become more important. It is ineffective and inefficient for policy makers to sustain labor-intensive ICT manufacturing when wages are high. Similarly, premature efforts to leapfrog into cutting-edge segments without adequate digital infrastructure, skills, and innovation ecosystems are likely to flop. Governments need to adapt their policies and regulations constantly based on the country's position in the digital value chain.

This section analyzes the latest global trends, highlights well-performing countries in each pathway, and identifies factors contributing to their success. Data on ICT goods and services exports are used to examine the export-oriented pathway. Venture capital and private equity investment data are used to examine the emergence of domestic digital start-ups in low- and middle-income countries. Finally, app performance data are used to shed light on the performance of digital start-ups in low- and middle-income countries and to highlight the intersection of the two pathways—that is, how local digital firms in low- and middle-income countries can go global.

Promoting ICT goods and ICT and BPO-ITES exports

Global ICT goods exports grew faster than total merchandise exports during the past decade. Global ICT goods exports expanded from US$1.7 trillion in 2010 to US$2.9 trillion in 2021, driven mainly by communications equipment and semiconductors (refer to figure 2.9). Their share in total merchandise exports also edged up from 11 percent to 13 percent during the past decade.

China's dominance in ICT goods exports has weakened slightly since 2013, as its demographic dividend has been running out. China; Germany; Hong Kong SAR, China; the Republic of Korea; Malaysia; Singapore; Taiwan, China; Thailand; the United States; and Viet Nam were the top 10 exporters of ICT goods in 2021. Together they accounted for 82 percent of global ICT goods exports. China became the largest ICT goods exporter in the early 2000s, and its export share peaked at 31 percent in 2013 (refer to figure 2.10), the same time as its working-age population peaked. Consequently, the concentration of ICT goods exports also peaked around 2013. As China's demographic dividend runs out and labor costs creep up, its dominance in labor-intensive assembly tasks has slipped.

Czechia, Hungary, India, Mexico, Poland, Thailand, and Viet Nam have become new hotspots for ICT manufacturing. From 2015 to 2021, Viet Nam gained a significant share of global exports in all four categories of ICT goods and became one of the top five ICT goods exporters (refer to figure 2.11). Thailand increased its export share of computers and communication equipment. The picture for Mexico is mixed, as its share of computer exports increased, while its share of

FIGURE 2.9 **Global exports of ICT goods, by category, 2000–21**

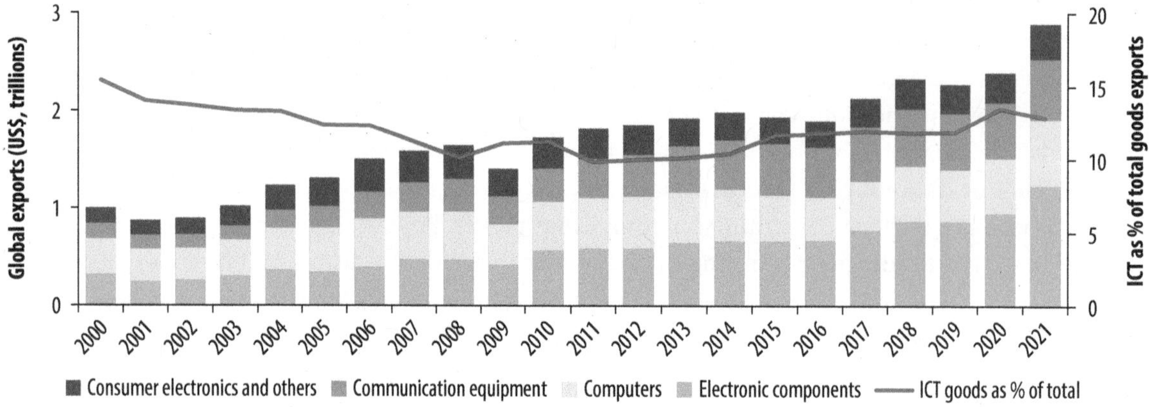

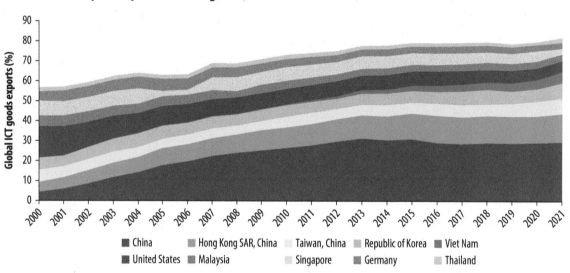

Source: Original calculations for this publication based on United Nations Conference on Trade and Development ICT goods trade data, ICT services trade data (https://unctadstat.unctad.org/EN/BulkDownload.html), and World Integrated Trade Solution data (https://wits.worldbank.org/).
Note: Mirror data are used to fill in missing values in ICT goods exports. ICT = information and communication technology.

FIGURE 2.10 **Top 10 exporters of ICT goods, 2000–21**

Source: Original calculations for this publication based on United Nations Conference on Trade and Development ICT goods trade data, ICT services trade data (https://unctadstat.unctad.org/EN/BulkDownload.html), and World Integrated Trade Solution data (https://wits.worldbank.org/).
Note: Mirror data are used to fill in missing values in ICT goods exports. ICT = information and communication technology. For a list of country and economy codes, refer to https://www.iso.org/obp/ui/#search.

communication equipment and consumer electronics dropped. Smartphone production in India ramped up from a very low base and continues to grow. Czechia, Hungary, and Poland all showed increases in ICT goods exports and have become regional ICT manufacturing hubs for Europe.

Attracting foreign direct investment (FDI) has been instrumental in jump-starting and accelerating ICT goods exports in most low- and middle-income countries. ICT goods manufacturing is dominated largely by multinational corporations. The long and highly complex global value chains for ICT goods create high entry barriers for domestic firms in low- and middle-income countries. Most of the major ICT goods exporters in these countries relied on FDI to build up an incipient ICT manufacturing industry focused on labor-intensive production and assembly. The entrance of Intel in Costa Rica, Malaysia, and the Philippines catalyzed FDI from other multinational corporations

FIGURE 2.11 Economies with the largest changes in share of exports of global ICT goods, 2015–21

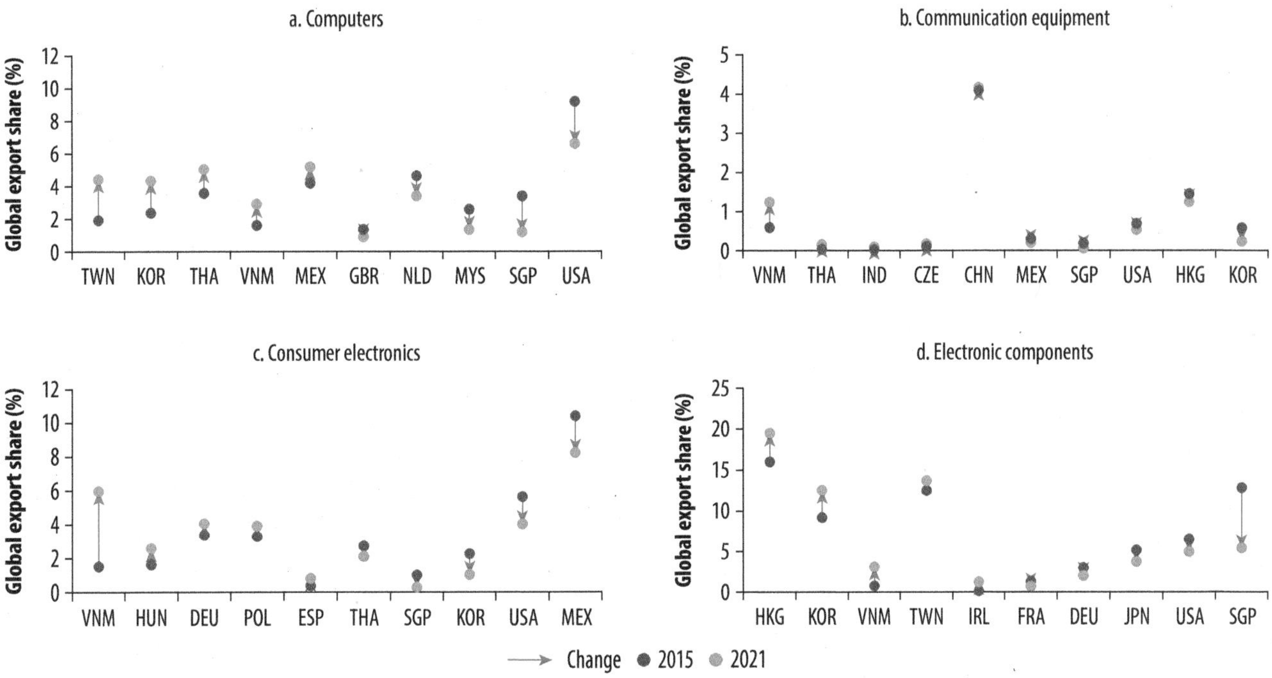

Source: Original calculations for this publication based on United Nations Conference on Trade and Development data on ICT goods trade (https://unctadstat.unctad.org/EN/BulkDownload.html).
Note: Each panel shows the five economies with the largest increase and the five economies with the largest decrease. ICT = information and communication technology. For a list of country and economy codes, refer to https://www.iso.org/obp/ui/#search.

and transformed the industry structure and export basket of these economies (Awan et al. 2017; Freund and Moran 2017; Qiang, Liu, and Steenbergen 2021). China's rise as a behemoth in ICT manufacturing is linked inextricably to FDI. Samsung has turned Viet Nam into a leading ICT goods exporter. Mexico, Thailand, and, more recently, many Central and Eastern European countries similarly owe their success in ICT manufacturing to FDI. These economies often lured multinational corporations with proactive investment promotion, generous tax incentives, infrastructure building, cheap labor, and a conducive business environment. Over time, multinational corporations in these economies have shifted their operations into higher value added activities and developed local suppliers, some of which have become multinational corporations themselves.

Intensifying geopolitical tensions between China and the United States, the pandemic, and the war in Ukraine have galvanized multinational corporations to accelerate diversification of their global value chains, creating opportunities for low- and middle-income countries near major markets and suppliers. The trade war between China and the United States reached an inflection point in July 2018. Since then, geopolitical tensions between the two countries have worsened, with ICT sector conflict at the forefront of the superpower competition. On top of this conflict, the COVID-19 pandemic and the Russian Federation's invasion of Ukraine further laid bare the vulnerabilities of placing too much dependence on a single country. Furthermore, China's unpredictable and heavy-handed policies during recent years have alarmed global investors. As a result, more and more ICT giants are eyeing alternative locations and weakening their reliance on China. Members of the Association of South East Asian Nations, Eastern Europe, India, and Mexico have been primary choices. Apple plans to start making its MacBook computers in Viet Nam and is expanding production in India (Roy, Kubota, and Wen 2023). Sony Group has transferred production of cameras sold in the European, Japanese, and US markets to Thailand from China (Furukawa 2023).

FIGURE 2.12 Global export of ICT services, by category, 2005–22, and top 10 exporters of ICT services, 2010–22

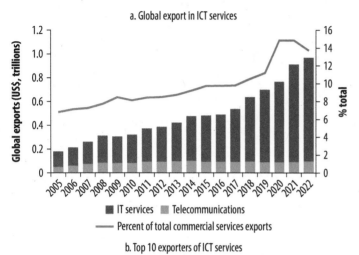

a. Global export in ICT services

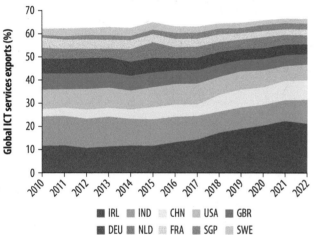

b. Top 10 exporters of ICT services

Source: Original calculations for this publication based on International Monetary Fund balance of payments data.
Note: IT services include computer services and information services. ICT = information and communication technology; IT = information technology. For a list of country and economy codes, refer to https://www.iso.org/obp/ui/#search.

The Intel plant in Costa Rica was reactivated in 2020 with an announced investment of US$350 million that ultimately grew to US$1 billion (Murillo 2022).

ICT services exports have grown much more rapidly than ICT goods during the past two decades, with growth accelerating during and after the pandemic. Global ICT services exports nearly quadrupled between 2005 and 2019, owing primarily to IT services (refer to figure 2.12, panel a). The share of ICT services in total services exports also rose steadily from 7 percent to 11 percent during the same period. ICT services exports grew 19 percent in 2021, the fastest pace since 2008. IT services, the core element of ICT services exports, were up by 43 percent in 2022 compared to 2019. The share of ICT services in total services exports jumped to an unprecedented 15 percent in 2021 and declined to 14 percent in 2022 as travel rebounded.

China's rise as a major ICT services exporter has eroded India's market share, although the latter's outlook remains strong. India's booming IT industry has long been celebrated as a great success story in the country's economic rise. India's IT industry thrived on its vast engineering talent and a vibrant start-up ecosystem; its ICT services exports raked in US$100 billion in foreign exchange in 2022 and grew by nearly 8 percent annually during 2010–22 (refer to figure 2.12, panel b). However, India's growth was outpaced by China's 19 percent growth rate during the same period. Riding on its domestic market success as a testing ground and stepping stone, Chinese software and IT firms are increasingly foraying into foreign markets and have propelled China's ICT services exports. As the domestic market matures and competition stiffens, Chinese software and internet firms are looking overseas to expand their revenue sources.

The IT services segment has been the most vibrant category of international trade for the past decade and has created a new export-led growth pathway for countries to expand and diversify their economies. During 2010–22, IT services grew by 12 percent annually, surpassing all other service categories. In 2022, IT services became the third largest category of services exports, right after transport and travel (refer to figure 2.13). Countries around the world are embracing the IT services sector as a new driver of growth, economic diversification, and job creation. For high-income economies, exporting IT services extends the global reach and influence of their technology firms. For resource-rich, landlocked, and lower-income countries, IT services exports offer a tantalizing opportunity to diversify their economies and integrate into the global economy. For most other economies, IT services exports create well-paid jobs and improve inclusion.

Several upper-middle-income countries have enjoyed exuberant growth in IT services exports since the pandemic. Among upper-middle-income countries, 6 out of the top 10 performers are from the Europe and Central Asia region, including Albania, Armenia, Georgia, Kazakhstan, Moldova, and Montenegro (refer to figure 2.14). These economies achieved annual growth ranging from 30 percent to 130 percent during 2019–22. Among countries that exported more than US\$1 billion in IT services, Indonesia achieved a whopping 41 percent annual growth, followed by 30 percent in Pakistan, 28 percent in Türkiye, 26 percent in Brazil, 23 percent in Serbia, 21 percent in Bulgaria and Ukraine, and 16 percent in China, Costa Rica, and India.

FIGURE 2.13 Global services exports, by category, 2022

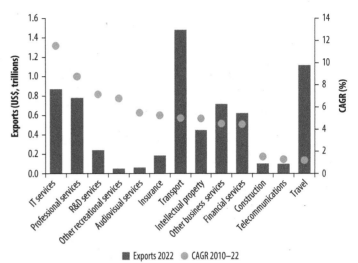

Source: Original calculations for this publication based on International Monetary Fund balance of payments data.
Note: CAGR = compound annual growth rate; IT = information technology; R&D = research and development.

The pandemic turbocharged the nascent computer services sector in several lower-middle-income countries, but many low-income countries failed to partake in the rally. Bangladesh, Egypt, Ghana, India, the Kyrgyz Republic, Pakistan, Tunisia, Ukraine, and Uzbekistan led the growth of IT services exports during 2019–22 (figure 2.14). Among low-income countries, Madagascar and Uganda were the only two countries that reported decent growth, albeit from a low base. Hampered by weak digital infrastructure, a dearth of ICT

FIGURE 2.14 Growth of IT services exports, by country income group, 2019–22

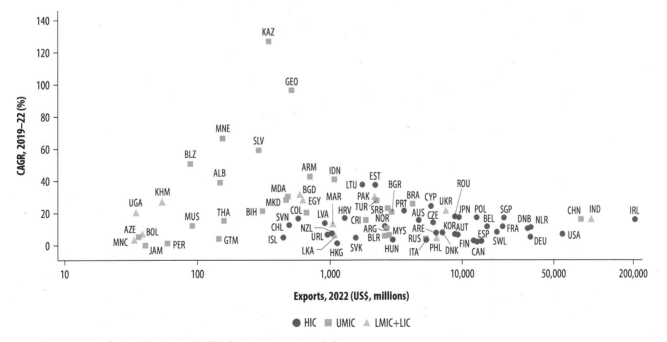

Source: Original calculations for this publication using World Trade Organization services trade data.
Note: HIC = high-income countries; UMIC = upper-middle-income countries; LMIC = lower-middle-income countries; LIC = low-income countries. For a list of country and economy codes, refer to https://www.iso.org/obp/ui/#search.

talents, and a less favorable business environment, many low-income countries failed to realize pandemic-fueled growth and continue to struggle to develop their IT services industry.

More broadly, the pandemic spurred booming BPO-ITES exports around the world and unlocked growth opportunities for low- and middle-income countries to create jobs and combat the brain drain. Digital technologies have driven a paradigm shift in how services are supplied, delivered, and consumed across borders. Worldwide, digitally delivered services grew from below 52 percent of services exports in 2019 to 64 percent in 2020 (UNCTAD 2021). To cut costs and tap into the vast pool of global talent, companies are increasingly outsourcing and offshoring business functions from data entry, customer service, human resource management, finance, and administration to business research, data analytics, legal processes, and other professional services. The global software and BPO services market reached US$2.4 trillion in 2022 and is expected to reach US$3.9 trillion in 2026 at a CAGR of 12 percent.[3] The huge growth potential and wide range of activities involved in BPO-ITES offer opportunities for countries and companies of all sizes. IT and BPO-ITES services also help to retain talent and to combat the brain drain that many low- and middle-income countries are experiencing.

Nurturing domestic digital start-ups

Homegrown digital firms fill important gaps in low- and middle-income countries and can better serve domestic demand and drive innovation. Digital markets in many countries remain too shallow or too small to appeal to global tech giants (Ungerer 2021). Furthermore, most global digital platforms are tailored to high-income markets and may not be suitable for drastically different local settings. Ample opportunities exist for homegrown firms, especially in e-commerce, fintech, entertainment, edtech, and e-health subsectors. Digital start-ups in low- and middle-income countries are leveraging digital technology to facilitate transactions in specific markets or to offer services that are otherwise not available. As a result, these start-ups are filling important gaps in the market and creating new avenues for economic growth. This section uses data on venture capital investment to document trends in low- and middle-income countries' digital start-ups.

VC plays an important role in the highly dynamic and innovative digital sector, as it is a critical source of funding for start-ups and firms with high growth potential. ICT firms and internet-based businesses usually require significant investments in research and development to bring their ideas to fruition. For young start-ups, such investments are hard to come by, as their high growth potential is accompanied by high risk. Venture capitalists not only mobilize the funding that digital start-ups may otherwise struggle to obtain, but also provide valuable guidance to entrepreneurs on strategy, marketing, and business development. In addition, they often have extensive networks to connect start-ups with potential partners, customers, and additional investors.

The pandemic sparked a significant increase in VC funding for digital start-ups in many low- and middle-income countries. With record-low interest rates, start-up investments have soared, resulting in higher valuations across various sectors and regions from 2021 to mid-2022. As the pandemic acted as a catalyst for the digital sector, venture capitalists went on a funding frenzy and plowed money into companies developing digital infrastructure, software, and digital solutions. The birth of digital unicorns hit an unprecedented 470 in 2021, breaking the most recent record of 90 in 2020. Among low- and middle-income countries, Brazil, Chile, China, Egypt, India, Indonesia, Mexico, Nigeria, Pakistan, Türkiye, and Viet Nam have seen an influx of VC funding (refer to map 2.1).

Most of the VC deals in low- and middle-income countries are in e-commerce, health, education, entertainment, and fintech. High-income countries received 70–80 percent of all VC deals in all subsectors except for ICT manufacturing during 2017–22. Low- and middle-income countries are gaining momentum in consumer-facing digital platforms (refer to figure 2.15). In the business and productivity subsector, VC deals more than tripled in Côte d'Ivoire, Morocco, Nigeria, Senegal, Tunisia, and Uganda between 2017–19 and 2020–22, driven by digital financial services. In the education and health subsector, investments have been on an upswing in Bangladesh, Nigeria, Peru, and Türkiye. In the entertainment subsector, Nigeria, the Philippines, Türkiye, and Viet Nam are highflyers. The e-commerce subsector had the highest share of VC deals going to low- and middle-income countries in both periods, and the share rose nearly 6 percentage points. Bangladesh, Ghana, Morocco, Pakistan, Tunisia, and Uganda registered the fastest growth in e-commerce deals.

Although low- and middle-income countries are catching up with high-income countries in the business-to-consumer segment, the gap in the business-to-business segment remains huge. While fintech and e-commerce are among the top three subsectors attracting VC investments in countries

MAP 2.1 **Absolute change in the number of investment deals, 2020–22 versus 2017–19**

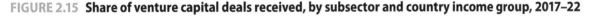

IBRD 47700 | DECEMBER 2023

Change in number of investments

■ 500 to 700　■ 100 to 500　■ 50 to 100　■ 20 to 50　 1 to 20　 0 to 1　 −100 to 0　 No data

Source: Original calculations for this publication using CB Insights (2023) data.

FIGURE 2.15 **Share of venture capital deals received, by subsector and country income group, 2017–22**

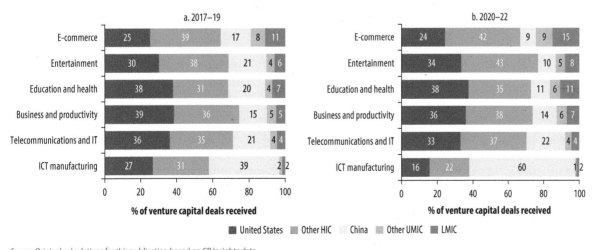

Source: Original calculations for this publication based on CB Insights data.
Note: HIC = high-income countries; ICT = information and communication technology; IT = information technology; LMIC = lower-middle-income countries; UMIC = upper-middle-income countries.

at all income levels, high-income countries attract by far the largest share of investments in the business-to-business segment, such as business management tech, big data and analytics, security tech, software, and software as a service (Zhu et al. 2022).

VC investments, however, have plummeted since late 2022 amid runaway inflation and rising interest rates. As global VC funding continues to cool off in 2023, start-ups in low- and middle-income countries, which are heavily reliant on foreign capital, are feeling the squeeze. Following a bleak 2022, global venture funding decreased by 13 percent quarter over quarter (QoQ) in Q1 2023. Except for the United States, where funding remained stable, all other regions experienced a double-digit drop in funding. Latin America saw the largest QoQ drop, at 54 percent, with only US$0.6 billion raised in the first quarter of 2023. Funding also shriveled 30 percent in Africa and 27 percent in Asia. AI start-ups are the only bright spot, although they are concentrated primarily in high-income countries (CB Insights 2023).

Despite the inevitable pain that comes with market correction and consolidation, significant growth and value creation still lie ahead for digital start-ups in low- and middle-income countries. Most of these countries are only beginning their journey of digital transformation, as fintech and e-commerce are still underused. Excluding China, only 40 percent of adults in low- and middle-income economies made digital merchant payments using a card, phone, or the internet in 2021 (Demirgüç-Kunt et al. 2022). Cash is still used in 90 percent of transactions in Africa. Thus, there is huge potential for growth. McKinsey estimates that revenues for African fintech could grow by up to eight times between 2020 and 2025 (McKinsey and Company 2022). Accelerated digitalization during the pandemic has created a more fertile environment for new technology players to thrive.

From localization to globalization

The previous section examined VC funding in the digital sector and highlighted burgeoning digital start-ups in certain low- and middle-income countries. Expanding on this examination, this section analyzes two overarching questions: Can digital firms from low- and middle-income countries compete with global giants in local, regional, and global markets? How can digital firms from low- and middle-income countries move from localization to globalization? This section uses app intelligence data from Apptopia to shed light on these questions. Box 2.1 illustrates the growing importance of apps and provides an overview of Apptopia data.

The app market is becoming more local and less global, and this trend has accelerated postpandemic. Low- and middle-income countries with a large domestic market, unique language, strong cultural identity, and prolific IT talents have enabled and incentivized local firms to cater to their home markets. From 2015 to 2022, domestic apps made up an increasing share of the 100 most downloaded apps in 54 out of 63 economies (refer to figure 2.16). The use of domestic apps also varies widely across markets. China is the most localized market, and its localization continues to increase over time. Domestic apps also dominate in Japan, Korea, and the United States, although their dominance has recently weakened. Brazil, Denmark, Germany, India, Norway, Russia, Türkiye, and Viet Nam had the next highest share of domestic apps in 2022. Argentina, Brazil, Chile, India, Indonesia, Russia, Saudi Arabia, South Africa, Türkiye, Ukraine, and the United Arab Emirates had the largest increase in the share of domestic apps between 2015 and 2022.

The development of the local IT services industry, pandemic-induced changes in patterns of app use, and policies favoring localization all contributed to the rising popularity of domestic apps in low- and middle-income countries. As previous sections have shown, the IT services industry is growing rapidly in many countries. The industry's rise has naturally inclined domestic digital firms to enter the app market and offer more relevant local content and services. The increased

BOX 2.1 **The importance of apps and an overview of Apptopia app performance data**

Over the past decade, the importance of apps has grown significantly and continues to grow as smartphones become an indispensable part of modern life. Apps allow users to access digital services and content simply by tapping their mobile devices. Individual users can customize apps to suit their preferences and needs. The ease of use and personalization are complemented by device features such as a camera, Global Positioning System, and sensors. Altogether, these features make apps more powerful than mobile websites. Today, many big companies and government agencies offer their own apps to gain competitive advantage, enhance customer experience, collect valuable user data, and improve efficiency.

Data on app performance can offer rich insights into companies' performance, industry trends, and shifts in consumer preferences and behavior, including downloads, active users, session length, total time spent, and average revenue per user.

This report uses Apptopia data collected from Android's Google Play and Apple's App Store. Together, these two systems represented 99 percent of smartphone operating systems in 2022. This chapter uses app-level data for the monthly top 500 most downloaded apps in Google Play and the App Store for each country from January 2015 to December 2022.

The data are available in 65 countries across all World Bank regions. These economies accounted for 90 percent of total mobile internet users in the world by the end of 2022. In addition to the main high-income countries, data are available for many major low- and middle-income countries: Argentina, Bangladesh, Brazil, Bulgaria, Burkina Faso, China, Colombia, the Arab Republic of Egypt, Ghana, India, Indonesia, Jordan, Kenya, Malawi, Malaysia, Mexico, Nigeria, Pakistan, Peru, the Philippines, the Russian Federation, Senegal, Serbia, South Africa, Tanzania, Thailand, Tunisia, Türkiye, Ukraine, Uruguay, República Bolivariana de Venezuela, and Viet Nam. Global aggregate data are also available.

The main variables used in this report include downloads, monthly active users, total time spent, average session length, and average sessions per user.

- Downloads are the number of total downloads for an app during a given period.

- Total time spent measures the total time all users spent on an app during the specified period.

- Average session length measures how long users are actively engaged with the app. Things like switching apps without quitting the app, phone lock, and even swiping down the notification screen will end a session. Background activities are not counted in session length.

- Average number of sessions per user measures the average number of sessions per user per day (or month) and shows how frequently users use an app.

The data come with a few caveats:

- Apptopia estimates performance for many apps. Metrics on less popular apps may be less accurate.

- Publishers self-select app categories. It is also inherently challenging to classify apps accurately, given the versatility of some apps. Google Play and the App Store have different systems of categorization, so the same app can have different categories in the two stores. This report has cleaned and harmonized the two systems into 20 categories.

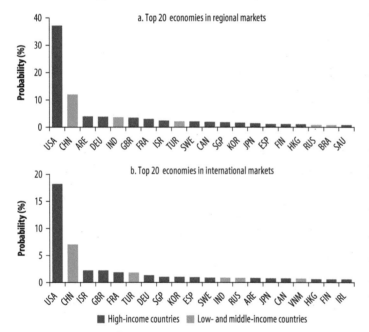

FIGURE 2.16   Share of domestic apps among the 100 most downloaded apps, 2015–22

Source: Original calculations for this publication based on Apptopia data (https://apptopia.com/).
Note: The figure displays only the 45 largest of the total 63 economies and includes only apps that have information on the publisher's country. For a list of country and economy codes, refer to https://www.iso.org/obp/ui/#search.

FIGURE 2.17   Probability of being among the top 50 most downloaded apps in international markets, 2022

Source: Original calculations for this publication based on Apptopia data (https://apptopia.com/).
Note: Regional markets are markets in the same World Bank region as the app publisher's economy. International markets are markets in other World Bank regions. For a list of country and economy codes, refer to https://www.iso.org/obp/ui/#search.

use of health, medical, shopping, fintech, and tools apps after the pandemic has also fueled the rise of domestic apps. These categories are either heavily regulated or require deep knowledge of the local market; thus, homegrown firms have a leg up in developing apps that cater properly to local users. Policies and regulations have also spurred the popularity of domestic apps. For instance, the Indian government has banned more than 200 Chinese apps since 2020, and domestic apps have been quick to fill the void. The interlinkage of these three elements have jointly accelerated the localization of apps.

In addition to being competitive in domestic markets, apps from a few low- and middle-income countries are conquering foreign markets, including high-income markets. US apps continue to rule the world, as they remain most likely to appear in the top 50 most downloaded apps in regional and international markets (refer to figure 2.17). Additionally, apps developed by China are also widely used in regional and international markets, although the gap with the United States remains huge. Despite the dominance of China and the United States, Brazil, India, Russia, Türkiye, and the United Arab Emirates have developed successful apps in regional markets. Furthermore, apps from India, Russia, Türkiye, and Viet Nam have also competed successfully in international markets, especially in the gaming category.

Mobile games developed by low- and middle-income countries have the strongest appeal in foreign markets. Apps from high-income countries have a much larger share of international users across categories. In 2022, four out of five users of apps developed by US publishers were foreign. By contrast, most apps developed by low- and middle-income countries have less than 20 percent of foreign users. While regional and international users only accounted for about 40 percent of all users of apps produced by upper-middle-income countries, users from regional and international markets represented 80 percent of users of game apps (refer to figure 2.18). Apps produced by lower-middle-income countries have a smaller share of users from other countries, but games still stand out as the most internationalized category of apps. Türkiye has become a prominent exporter of mobile gaming. In fact, mobile games developed by Turkish studios accounted for 20 percent of the most downloaded games in the United States (Obedkov 2021). Turkish developers of mobile games have attracted billions of dollars in funding since 2017. Government incentives to export Turkish games abroad also helps. The Turkish government covers the commission fees charged by Apple's App Store and Google's Play Store, making it much easier for Turkish developers of mobile games to go international (Lee 2022).

For digital start-ups in low- and middle-income countries, leveraging home court advantage and offering deeply localized products are often key to gaining traction and getting off the ground. Domestic start-ups often have home court advantage over global giants in terms of time and space. Time refers to the head start and first mover advantage that local companies have before global giants enter or capture market share. Space refers to the deep knowledge that local companies have about their country and its consumers (Moed 2019). Naturally, most start-ups will focus on creating localized products in their home markets. The Vietnamese browser and search engine Cốc Cốc has challenged Google's growth in Viet Nam by factoring in Vietnamese language tones and accents, focusing on locally relevant search results, and embracing a video-first approach, given the affinity of local consumers for video content. Offering fast local delivery, accepting payment in local currency, and providing an online shop in a local language can all be critical in gaining a competitive advantage in e-commerce and enabling the emergence of e-entrepreneurship, even in small national markets such as in the Western Balkans (Ungerer 2021). Government support is also a critical aspect of home court advantage, as such support can facilitate access to finance and address information asymmetry.

Digital start-ups blessed with vast domestic markets have more time to accumulate experience and resources before they go global. Start-ups in smaller markets often face a localization paradox.

FIGURE 2.18 **Geographic distribution of users, by category of app and country income group of the app publisher, 2022**

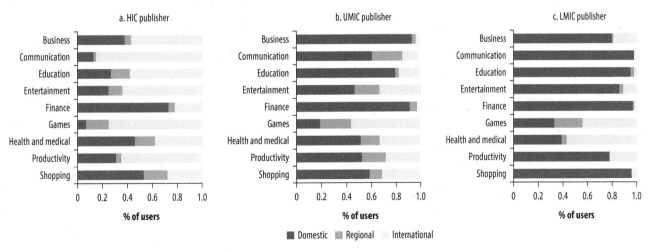

Source: Original calculations for this publication based on Apptopia data (https://apptopia.com/).
Note: Regional markets are markets in the same World Bank region as the app publisher's economy. Global markets are markets in other World Bank regions. HIC = high-income countries; LMIC = lower-middle-income countries; UMIC = upper-middle-income countries.

Start-ups from many smaller countries are forced early on to choose between a bigger market or a more customized product. However, if a start-up initially forgoes a deeply localized product and instead builds a more general product to cater to several markets at once, the firm's product may never get the initial boost of domestic engagement and adoption needed to get off the ground.

When start-ups look to expand abroad, their original products and business models, which are tailored to domestic needs, may not be nearly as relevant or as transferable to other countries. Regional markets are often the first step in start-ups' foreign expansion, but even large regional markets like Latin America, Southeast Asia, and Sub-Saharan Africa, often thought of as consolidated, can be quite distinct and fragmented. For example, M-Pesa achieved remarkable success in East Africa but failed to gain a foothold in South Africa due to product-market mismatch. WeChat was wildly successful in China, with the features offered by Amazon, Apple Pay, Facebook, Grubhub, Messenger, WhatsApp, Uber, and Venmo all living in one app. However, WeChat failed to offer comparable capabilities to foreign users, and its China-centric design further alienated foreign users.[4]

Governments can play a crucial role in supporting their digital start-ups by facilitating access to funding, information, markets, and skills. Access to finance is often the first obstacle that aspiring entrepreneurs must overcome when turning their idea into a viable business. The challenge is particularly pronounced in low- and middle-income countries with underdeveloped start-up investment markets. Governments can attract foreign VC funding, explore innovation grants and loan guarantees, and set up incubators, accelerators, and other support mechanisms that help entrepreneurs to develop and commercialize their ideas. It is equally important to develop the domestic VC market. China, India, Japan, Korea, Saudi Arabia, and the United Arab Emirates all developed a thriving local VC market; consequently, domestic VC investors funded as much as 90 percent of the VC deals in these countries in 2022. To overcome information asymmetry, the government can connect their digital start-ups with potential buyers and investors in their own country and in the global market. Technical assistance, mentoring, training, and other types of capacity building can upskill existing talents in the country. Governments can also streamline visa requirements to attract foreign digital talents.

Market harmonization through trade and investment agreements and international coordination are needed to remove excessive barriers to cross-border online activity. Data localization requirements, onerous and unnecessary technology security standards, differences regarding electronic authentication and signatures, and electronic payment platforms are common barriers that hinder digital firms' access to foreign markets. To reduce trade and investment barriers for digitally deliverable services, policy makers need to ensure holistic market openness through multistakeholder dialogue to ensure interoperability across regulatory regimes, including for cross-border data flows and related privacy and security considerations (OECD 2019). Africa's Continental Free Trade Area and the European Union's Digital Single Markets are useful examples.

As the domestic digital sector grows and matures, intellectual property protection, competition, taxation, and innovation policies become more important. The winner-takes-most characteristics of the digital market and the tendency of incumbents to deploy anticompetitive strategies typically increase as a country's digital market matures. This situation can reduce market contestability, harm consumers and businesses, and slow down innovation. In addition, dominant digital firms may also shift profits overseas to avoid paying their fair share of taxes. To alleviate these concerns, a country must provide stronger intellectual property protection and other policy support to forge a dynamic innovation ecosystem as the country's digital firms approach the technological frontier.

Notes

Hans Christian Boy and Jieun Choi contributed to this chapter.

1. If optical products and publishing, broadcasting, and audiovisual activities are excluded, the ICT sector contributed 5 percent of global GDP in 2022, slightly higher than the 4.5 percent in 2017 estimated by UNCTAD (2019).
2. "Employment Generation," India Ministry of Electronics and Information Technology (https://www .meity.gov.in/content/employment#:~:text=Directpercent20employmentpercent20inpercent20theper cent20IT,topercent20bepercent20overpercent2012.0percent20million).
3. "Software and BPO Services Global Market Report 2022 by Type, Organisation Size, End-Use Industry," *Business Wire,* September 5, 2022 (https://www.businesswire.com/news/home/20220905005136/en /Software-And-BPO-Services-Global-Market-Report-2022-Emergence-of-Startups-as-Major-Clients -of-Software-and-BPO-Service-Providers-Driving-Growth---ResearchAndMarkets.com).
4. "WeChat: A Winner in China but a Loser Abroad" (https://d3.harvard.edu/platform-digit/submission /wechat-a-winner-in-china-but-a-loser-abroad/).

References

Awan, Adnan, Lucky Nurrahmat, Shijir Ochirbat, and Alex Pham. 2017. "Philippines Electronics Components Manufacturing: Steps to Regain Competitiveness." Global Competitiveness Report, Institute for Strategy and Competitiveness, Harvard Business School, Cambridge, MA. https://www .isc.hbs.edu/Documents/resources/courses/moc-course-at-harvard/pdf/student-projects/Philippines _Electronics_2017.pdf.

Beuermann, Diether Wolfgang, Christopher McKelvey, and Renos Vakis. 2012. "Mobile Phones and Economic Development in Rural Peru." *Journal of Development Studies* 48 (11): 1617–28.

Brynjolfsson, Erik, Danielle Li, and Lindsey R. Raymond. 2023. *Generative AI at Work.* Technical Report. Cambridge, MA: National Bureau of Economic Research.

Buchholz, Wolfgang, and Todd Sandler. 2021. "Global Public Goods: A Survey." *Journal of Economic Literature* 59 (2): 488–545.

CB Insights. 2023. "State of Venture 2023 Q1 Report: Global." CB Insights, New York. https://app .cbinsights.com/research/report/venture-trends-q1-2023/.

Demirgüç-Kunt, Asli, Leora Klapper, Dorothe Singer, and Saniya Ansar. 2022. *The Global Findex Database 2021: Financial Inclusion, Digital Payments, and Resilience in the Age of COVID-19.* Washington, DC: World Bank.

Freund, Caroline, and Theodore Moran. 2017. "Multinational Investors as Export Superstars: How Emerging-Market Governments Can Reshape Comparative Advantage." PIIE Working Paper 17-1, Peterson Institute for International Economics, Washington, DC.

Furukawa, Keiichi. 2023. "Sony Separates Production of Cameras for China and Non-China Markets." *Nikkea Asia,* January 29, 2023. https://asia.nikkei.com/Business/Electronics /Sony-separates-production-of-cameras-for-China-and-non-China-markets#:~:text=TOKYO percent20percent2Dpercent2Dpercent20Sonypercent20Grouppercent20has,cameraspercent 20forpercent20thepercent20domesticpercent20market.

Keller, Wolfgang. 2002. "Geographic Localization of International Technology Diffusion." *American Economic Review* 92 (1): 120–42.

Lee, Alexander. 2022. "Turkey Is Now the 'Silicon Valley' of Mobile Gaming: Why Hyper-Casual Games Are Mass-Produced." *Digiday,* February 8, 2022. https://digiday.com/marketing/why-turkey-is -becoming-the-silicon-valley-of-mobile-gaming/.

McKinsey and Company. 2022. "Fintech in Africa: The End of the Beginning." McKinsey and Company, August 30, 2022. https://www.mckinsey.com/industries/financial-services/our-insights/fintech-in -africa-the-end-of-the-beginning.

Moed, Jonathan. 2019. "The Real Reason It's Hard for Start-ups to Scale Internationally." *Forbes,* February 28, 2019. https://www.forbes.com/sites/jonathanmoed/2019/02/28/the-real-reason-its -hard-for-startups-to-scale-internationally/?sh=5365451c5f0b.

Murillo, Álvaro. 2022. "Costa Rica Emerges as the Winner in 'Chip War' between China and the United States." *El País,* October 11, 2022. https://english.elpais.com/economy-and-business/2022-10-11 /costa-rica-emerges-as-the-winner-in-chip-war-between-us-and-china.html.

Obedkov, Evgeny. 2021. "Report: 20% of Most Downloaded Mobile Games in US Developed by Turkish Studios." *Game World Observer,* November 5, 2021. https://gameworldobserver.com/2021/05/11 /report-20-of-most-downloaded-mobile-games-in-us-developed-by-turkish-studios.

OECD (Organisation for Economic Co-operation and Development). 2019. "Going Digital: Shaping Policies, Improving Lives." OECD, Paris. https://www.oecd.org/digital/going-digital-synthesis -summary.pdf.

Paunov, Caroline, and Valentina Rollo. 2016. "Has the Internet Fostered Inclusive Innovation in the Developing World?" *World Development* 78 (C): 587–609.

Qiang, Christine Zhenwei, Yan Liu, and Victor Steenbergen. 2021. *An Investment Perspective on Global Value Chains.* Washington, DC: World Bank.

Roy, Jajesh, Yojo Kubota, and Philip Wen. 2023. "Top Apple Supplier Foxconn Plans Major India Expansion." *Wall Street Journal,* March 4, 2023. https://www.wsj.com/articles/top-apple-supplier -plans-major-india-expansion-f2908b88.

Sampson, Thomas. 2023. "Technology Gaps, Trade, and Income." *American Economic Review* 113 (2): 472–513.

UN (United Nations). 2008. *International Standard Industrial Classification of All Economic Activities (ISIC), Rev. 4.* Statistical Papers Series M No. 4/Rev.4. New York: Department of Economic and Social Affairs Statistics. https://unstats.un.org/unsd/publication/seriesm/seriesm_4rev4e.pdf.

UNCTAD (United Nations Conference on Trade and Development). 2019. *Digital Economy Report 2019: Value Creation and Capture: Implications for Developing Countries.* Geneva: UNCTAD.

UNCTAD (United Nations Conference on Trade and Development). 2021. "Trade Data for 2020 Confirm Growing Importance of Digital Technologies during COVID-19." UNCTAD, Geneva. https://unctad .org/news/trade-data-2020-confirm-growing-importance-digital-technologies-during-covid-19.

Ungerer, Christopher. 2021. "The Emerging Markets E-Commerce Opportunity." *Brookings Commentary,* March 26, 2021. https://www.brookings.edu/blog/future-development/2021/03/26/the-emerging-markets -e-commerce-opportunity/.

World Bank. 2016. *World Development Report 2016: Digital Dividends.* Washington, DC: World Bank. https://elibrary.worldbank.org/doi/abs/10.1596/978-1-4648-0671-1.

Zhu, Tingting Juni, Philip Grinsted, Hangyul Song, and Malathi Velamuri. 2022. *A Spiky Digital Business Landscape: What Can Developing Countries Do?* Washington, DC: World Bank.

Digital Infrastructure: The Continual Need for Upgrading and Greening | 3

Michael Minges

KEY MESSAGES

- The volume of data created has been growing exponentially—from 2 zettabytes[1] in 2010 to an expected 120 zettabytes in 2023—and is forecast to exceed 180 zettabytes by 2025.

- Internet exchange points (IXPs) have evolved from keeping data within the country to bringing data in at low cost from abroad. As of 2022, less than half of global public IXPs were in low- and middle-income countries.

- To reduce costs and improve quality, IXPs need to attract major content and cloud services companies to become members. The retail price for 1 gigabyte of data was nearly six times higher in countries that do not have IXPs than in countries that have IXPs with leading content providers.

- Multitenant, connected data centers provide a venue for all types of companies to exchange data and house IXPs. They are essential for providing an "on-ramp" to cloud computing. Connected data centers grew by 72 percent during 2018–22. In 2022, low- and middle-income countries accounted for only a quarter of the nearly 5,000 connected data centers.

- The information and communication technology (ICT) sector has emerged as the biggest purchaser of renewable energy in the world. Major ICT companies are increasingly using their scale to nurture renewable energy markets, potentially making low- and middle-income countries with clean grids attractive digital hubs for investors. By liberalizing their energy markets, other countries could leverage the expertise and scale of multinational ICT companies to expand the use of renewable energy.

Introduction

Digital infrastructure is a crucial prerequisite for the creation and adoption of various digital technologies. This chapter begins by analyzing the investment trends in broadband infrastructure and provides policy recommendations for low- and middle-income countries. The recommendations aim to catalyze private sector investment and improve investment efficiency. The chapter then emphasizes the growing importance of data infrastructure, including internet exchange points (IXPs), connected data centers, and cloud computing. It highlights how low- and middle-income countries can upgrade their data infrastructure and make them more environmentally friendly, thus contributing to a more inclusive and sustainable digital future.

Telecom network investment moves from coverage toward upgrading

Today, mobile broadband coverage is nearly ubiquitous. By the end of 2022, less than 3 percent of the global population were not covered by a basic mobile signal, while only 5 percent were covered by a mobile broadband signal (that is, 3G, 4G, or 5G) (refer to figure 3.1). Approximately 400 million people are not covered by a mobile broadband signal, with the majority residing mainly in rural and remote areas.

FIGURE 3.1   **Global mobile coverage, 2000–22**

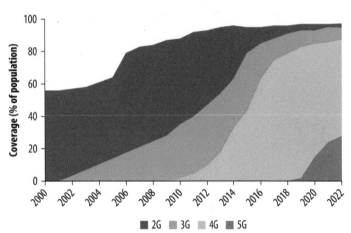

Source: International Telecommunication Union data.

Faster and more widely accessible broadband is accelerating digitalization and spurring unprecedented data growth. Never in human history have data, information, and knowledge been as plentiful and as readily accessible as they are today. Each day, the sheer magnitude of data generated is astounding, with more than 1 billion TikTok videos viewed, 9 billion queries searched on Google (Mohsin 2023), and nearly 350 billion emails sent globally (Kolmar 2023). The volume of data created, stored, transferred, and used globally has been growing exponentially, from 2 zettabytes in 2010 to an expected 120 zettabytes in 2023. This growth is forecast to exceed 180 zettabytes by 2025 (Hack 2021). Similarly, global mobile data traffic per smartphone has soared, from 2.6 gigabytes per month in 2017 to 16 gigabytes per month in 2022, and is projected to reach 42 gigabytes per month by 2027 (refer to figure 3.2, panel a). Data traffic for laptops and tablets is also ballooning. In the coming years, access to 5G and fixed wireless will drive much of the new data traffic (refer to figure 3.2, panel b).

FIGURE 3.2   **Projected growth in data traffic, by device and technology, 2017–27**

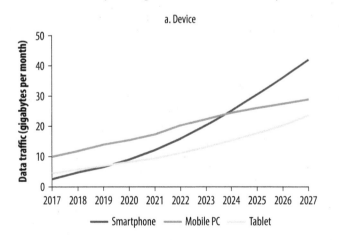

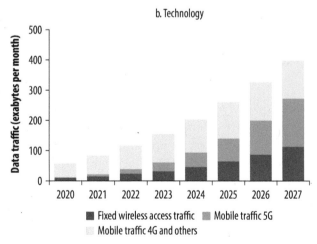

Source: Ericsson 2023.
Note: PC = personal computer.

Rapid advancements in digital technologies catalyzed the data explosion by greatly expanding the range and capacity of the types of data generated, stored, and processed. Faster and more efficient computer chips have caused computing power to grow exponentially, enabling the advent of supercomputers, while cloud computing has allowed on-demand computing power at cost-effective prices. A deluge of data has been produced through the rise of the Internet of Things (IoT)—a network of physical devices, vehicles, home appliances, and other items embedded with electronics, software, sensors, and connectivity. In 2022, more than 13 billion IoT devices were in use. Driven largely by the almost real-time connectivity of 5G technology, these devices are expected to more than double between 2023 and 2028. Meanwhile, the portability, data capacity, and versatility of smartphones have made these devices into ubiquitous data collection tools, capturing text, audio, video, and Global Positioning System data virtually anywhere, anytime. Social media platforms have revolutionized connectivity in the social realm, with individuals sharing copious amounts of data in the form of posts, likes, pictures, music, videos, and more. Businesses have also contributed to the data explosion by collecting all sorts of information on their products, processes, transactions, suppliers, and customers.

While broadband investment in the previous decade focused on expanding internet coverage, the coming decade will concentrate on capacity by upgrading networks to support burgeoning data traffic and by broadening digitalization. The digital divide is now less about coverage and more about use and quality. Thus, high-speed network deployment characterized by fiber optic, 5G, and beyond will play an important role in the coming decade, enabling innovation and digitalization across different sectors of society. As of 2022, the share of the population covered by at least 4G mobile broadband was three times greater in high-income countries than in low-income countries, pointing to an ongoing digital divide in internet coverage. However, data consumption in high-income countries is tens or even *hundreds* of times greater than consumption in low-income countries, revealing a much starker divide in use and quality. The contrast between Curaçao and Sub-Saharan Africa is an illustrative example, as Curaçao leads the world by consuming 131 gigabytes of mobile data per capita per month, while nearly 30 countries, mainly in Sub-Saharan Africa, consume less than 1 gigabyte per capita of mobile data per month. As such, in the years ahead, many low- and middle-income countries will require high-quality broadband infrastructure to ensure that their digital economies are vibrant, inclusive, and sustainable.

After a slight dip in 2020 due to COVID-19, telecommunication investment rebounded in 2021, exceeding prepandemic levels. Even though COVID-19 induced a drop in telecommunication investment in 2020, the network was robust and able to handle the massive increase in digital use spurred by lockdown measures. This outcome was largely due to previous investment as well as to measures taken by many governments to ensure the stability of networks, such as granting operators additional spectrum (GSMA 2021). Investment in telecommunication networks amounted to an estimated US$344 billion around the world in 2021, exceeding prepandemic levels (refer to figure 3.3, panel a). Three regions—East Asia and Pacific, Europe and Central Asia, and North America—accounted for nearly 90 percent of global telecommunication investment, while low- and middle-income regions, including Latin America and the Caribbean, South Asia, and Sub-Saharan Africa, accounted for less than 10 percent of total investment in 2020 (refer to figure 3.3, panel b).

A significant amount of investment is going toward fiber optic and 5G mobile networks. GSMA, a mobile industry association, forecasts that mobile operators alone will invest more than US$600 billion between 2022 and 2025; 85 percent of this investment will be for 5G (GSMA 2022). Furthermore, by 2025, one-third of the world's population will have 5G coverage, while 1.2 billion connections will be on 5G networks.[2] Swedish equipment manufacturer, Ericsson, forecasts

FIGURE 3.3 **Amount and regional distribution of global investment in telecom networks, 2017–21**

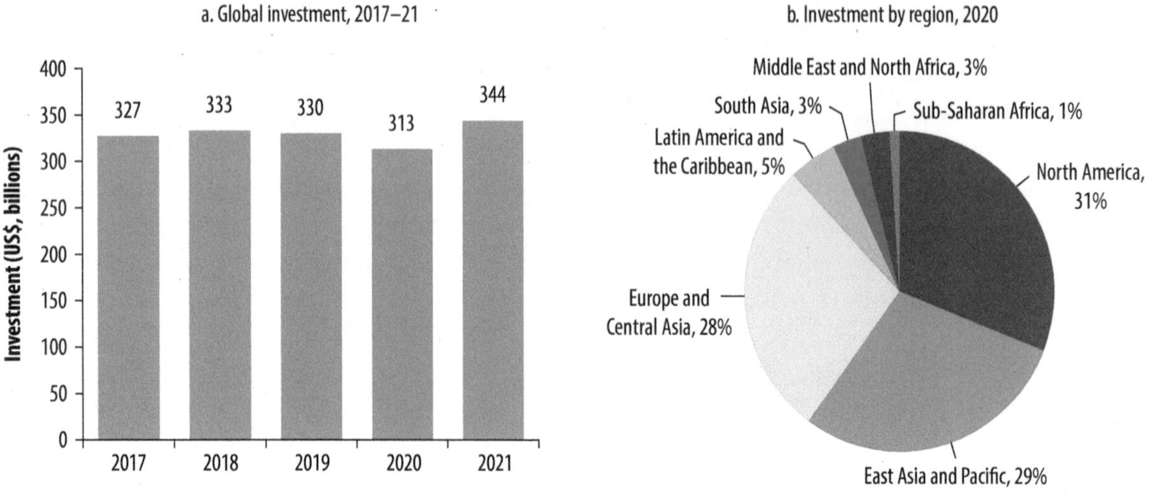

a. Global investment, 2017–21

b. Investment by region, 2020

Sources: Original calculations for this publication using data from the International Telecommunication Union, Eurostat, national regulatory agencies, national statistical offices, and operator reports.
Note: Data are inconsistent regarding the inclusion of spectrum purchases as investment.

that 85 percent of the world will be covered by 5G in 2028, with 5 billion 5G mobile subscriptions (Ericsson 2023). Investment is also needed in national and international fiber optic backbones as well as fiber to the premises, particularly in the aftermath of COVID-19, where working from home, often in hybrid form, has continued for many (McKinsey Global Institute 2020).

Despite concerns about the detrimental impact of over the top (OTT) applications on their revenues (ITU 2020b), major telecommunication operators continue to make significant investments. Revenue streams have diversified from voice to data and financial services, reducing the impact of OTT. At the same time, some of the biggest OTT players are making notable investments in data infrastructure.

Most telecommunication investment comes from the private sector, especially publicly listed multinational companies. Due to network effects and economies of scale, large telecommunication groups dominate the market in many low- and middle-income countries, bringing investment, scale, and expertise. While private unlisted companies and the state also provide investment for telecommunication networks, figures are often unavailable or opaque, making it difficult to gauge their impact. In Latin America and the Caribbean in 2021, 11 private telecommunication groups accounted for more than 90 percent of mobile subscriptions (Parungo 2022). Three of them accounted for around two-thirds of subscriptions and telecommunication investment in the region. In Sub-Saharan Africa, a few multinational telecommunication companies account for around 60 percent of mobile subscriptions and more than three-quarters of telecommunication investment.

Governments can increase the efficiency of telecommunication investment

Governments in low- and middle-income countries can boost private investment by removing monopolies and lifting restrictions on foreign investment in telecom services. Government monopoly of telecom services or poor governance structures often deter the entry of foreign telecom companies. Opening previously restricted markets can boost investments significantly. Ethiopia—with 4G mobile coverage of just 10 percent of the population in 2021—had until recently been the most populous country in the world with a monopoly telecommunication sector. In 2018, a license was awarded for US$850 million to a consortium of companies headquartered in Japan, Kenya, South Africa, and the United Kingdom that is expected to invest US$8.5 billion over the next 10 years.[3] The consortium includes telecommunication group Vodacom as well as its associate Safaricom in Kenya and parent Vodafone. The operating entity, Safaricom Ethiopia, launched commercial operations in October 2022.[4]

In recent years, the mobile market has been consolidating. One of the justifications for consolidation has been to allow operators to acquire the capital investment required to compete. The implications of 5G for investment have prompted renewed calls to allow further consolidation in some markets. Countries need to consider carefully how to balance competition and investment incentives among mobile network operators in light of both new competitive dynamics generated by 5G as well as enhanced opportunities for significant cost savings from increased infrastructure sharing and more flexible approaches to spectrum and licensing.

Governments can phase out legacy wireless networks to make telecom investment more efficient. Shutting down older wireless networks allows their frequencies, particularly those that provide wide coverage, to be reused for higher-performance 4G and 5G networks. Maintaining 2G or 3G networks is also not an efficient use of capital expenditure since their average revenue per user is lower than that of 4G or 5G. Since mobile operators in Japan shut down their 2G networks more than a decade ago, more and more countries have followed. GSMA forecasts that between 2021 and 2025 more than 50 2G and 3G networks will be shut down, freeing up spectrum. Africa is lagging due to the high coverage of 2G and 3G and low adoption of smartphones.

Innovative spectrum management can also promote efficient use of spectrum. During the COVID-19 pandemic, several governments allowed operators to use unallocated spectrum for free or low cost to handle the spike in demand. Consideration should be given to continuing this practice, particularly since it lowers prices for consumers. Governments should make spectrum technology and service neutral and allow operators to reuse their current spectrum for 5G. Those who have not yet allocated frequency for 5G should do so; the new mmWave band is ideal for high speeds and low latency, albeit with lower coverage (Ericsson 2023). Spectrum management should also consider indoor and outdoor coverage. The majority of communication required is still indoor. mmWave can offer high-speed indoor coverage, and other frequencies can offer better capacity for outdoor coverage. Such coverage will lead to better spectral efficiency. Aggregation of mobile and unlicensed Wi-Fi spectrum will also help to increase network throughput.

Regulators need to enhance institutional capacity to secure and release enough spectrum, including globally harmonized pioneer bands, while avoiding the risk of spectrum fragmentation that prevents 5G from delivering the performance desired. Given that spectrum allocation not only will be of interest to traditional telecom operators but also may be relevant for industry verticals operating private networks, regulators will need to be strategic in balancing competing demands for spectrum from new and incumbent users. The design of spectrum assignment methods, pricing, and licensing regimes all have a material impact on the viability of 5G networks and associated investment incentives. Regulators should be mindful of the transparency of spectrum assignments and the affordability of spectrum fees. Since the 5G non-standalone pathway leverages existing 4G infrastructure, taking a technology-neutral approach to spectrum licensing is particularly important, as is allowing licensees to refarm (that is, repurpose) spectrum to the most efficient use; such an approach could achieve significant gains. To address increasing data traffic in 5G, spectrum authorities also need to pay attention to the role of unlicensed technologies such as next-generation Wi-Fi, balancing the use of licensed and unlicensed spectrum in the spectrum management framework.

Infrastructure sharing is another main approach to increasing investment efficiency. Infrastructure sharing of wireless base station towers and cable ducts lowers costs and reduces greenhouse gas emissions. Regulatory frameworks that encourage network sharing can lower substantially the costs of 5G. Examples include enabling passive sharing of fixed infrastructure—such as towers—and allowing a combination of passive and active sharing of backbone infrastructure, which can lead to further savings. Moreover, if single networks are allowed in remote rural areas (where competition is lacking), costs could fall further. Some countries have also developed wholesale 4G or 5G networks with a single facilities-based wholesale operator that offers services to retail providers. However, several countries have reversed course due to a lack of motivation by resellers to market the service, particularly when they also own other mobile networks in the country (Mbugua 2022). Box 3.1 discusses approaches to investing in efforts to connect the unconnected population.

BOX 3.1 **Connecting the unconnected: a US$400 billion investment is needed**

In recent years, telecommunication investment has increasingly aimed at upgrading networks and expanding capacity rather than building out last mile coverage. Nevertheless, millions of people remain unconnected with no network coverage. According to ITU (2020a), an investment of around US$400 billion is needed to connect the unconnected between 2020 and 2030. Investments to equip populations around the world with necessary basic digital skills and development-relevant content are estimated to require US$40 billion over the International Telecommunication Union's 10-year time frame, representing about 10 percent of the total investment required.

Table B3.1.1 highlights the so-called "golden rules" as prerequisites for achieving widespread connectivity.

TABLE B3.1.1 **Golden rules for achieving widespread connectivity**

Area addressed	Golden rules	
	Fixed broadband	**Mobile broadband**
Market approach	General authorization regime	Band migration allowed
Infrastructure sharing	Infrastructure sharing mandated	Co-location or site sharing mandated
Competition	Full competition in cable modem, DSL, fixed wireless broadband	Phone number portability available to consumers and required from mobile operators
	Legal concept of dominance or significant market power	Full competition in international mobile telecommunications (for example, 3G, 4G) services
	Full competition in international gateways	Full competition in international gateways
Foreign participation or ownership	Foreign participation or ownership in internet service providers	No restrictions to foreign participation or ownership in spectrum-based operators
Quality of service	Quality of service monitoring required	Quality of service monitoring required

Source: ITU 2020a.
Note: DSL = digital subscriber line.

Data infrastructure—IXPs, data centers, and cloud computing— is a vital part of the digital economy

While the preceding discussion focused on investment in telecom networks, IXPs, data centers, and cloud computing are also critical pieces of digital infrastructure. In fact, the historical segregation of networks and data centers is gradually disappearing. Open radio access network, disaggregation, and virtualization are already leading to a telecommunication cloud. Some cloud services and large content providers are also making significant investments in fiber optic backbones, particularly undersea cable (O'Shea 2021). As part of the "middle mile"[5] digital infrastructure, IXPs, data centers, and cloud computing providers store and exchange data among different players and provide a location for organizations to house their servers and exchange data with others. This infrastructure not only lowers the cost of data exchange but also enables the digitalization of all kinds of companies and government services, supporting development of the digital economy. Although there are no comprehensive official global statistics on investment in data centers and cloud services, available data suggest that it is growing rapidly.

Capital expenditure in data-hosting infrastructure in the United States, the world's largest data center market, grew by 60 percent between 2018 and 2021.[6] In 2021, it reached US$41 billion, accounting for about 20 percent of capital expenditure in the information and communication technology (ICT) sector. Investment by hyperscale cloud providers was estimated at more than US$200 billion in 2022, a figure that has grown, on average, 20 percent a year since 2016.[7] In addition to capital expenditure, large publicly listed data center companies and private equity have made several recent purchases of privately owned data centers in low- and middle-income countries (the latter with a reported figure of almost US$50 billion in 2022) (Cappella 2022; Moss 2023).

Low- and middle-income countries often struggle to attract private investments in data centers due to immature digital markets, unstable electricity supply, and rigid regulatory frameworks. Investments in data centers and cloud computing are similarly dominated by the private sector. A combination of factors, such as the costs and reliability of energy, availability of digital infrastructure, and favorable regulatory environment, bias private sector investments in cloud infrastructure toward larger, wealthier, and more digitally mature countries.

Development funding for data centers is increasing to fill the financing gaps. In Africa, where an estimated annual investment of between US$4 billion and US$7 billion is needed to bridge the region's data center gap, the US International Development Finance Corporation is providing funding of US$300 million to Africa Data Centers to support the expansion and development of seven existing and greenfield data centers in five African countries.[8]

IXPs started out in the early 1990s to save on the cost of international bandwidth by having locally destined traffic exchanged among internet service providers (ISPs) within the country. According to Packet Clearing House, there were 735 active public IXPs around the world at the end of 2022 (refer to figure 3.4).[9] More than half are in Europe and Central Asia and North America, whereas only 15 percent are in the Middle East and North Africa, South Asia, and Sub-Saharan Africa. Notably, 51 countries and territories, representing 5 percent of the world's population, are without an IXP. These are mainly small island states where the scale for an IXP may be lacking or countries with a monopoly telecommunication sector. The number of IXPs grew just over 20 percent between 2018 and 2022, with a notable slowdown since 2020 likely due to the impact of COVID-19.

Simply having an IXP is insufficient to accrue the benefits of lower costs and better internet performance. Although the number of IXPs has grown in low- and middle-income nations, many

FIGURE 3.4 **Number and distribution of IXPs, by country income group and region, 2022**

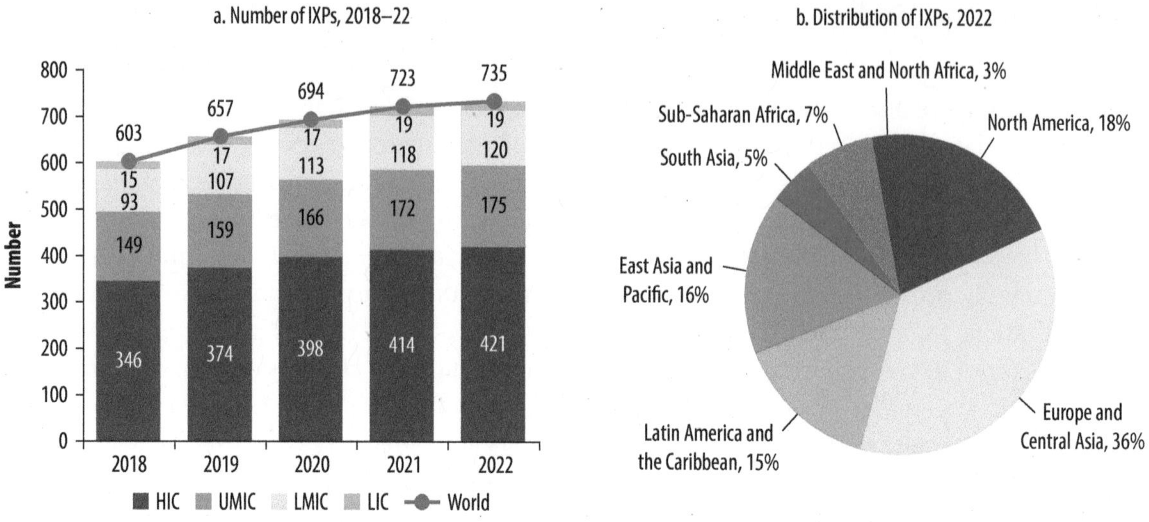

a. Number of IXPs, 2018–22

b. Distribution of IXPs, 2022

Source: Packet Clearing House (https://www.pch.net).
Note: HIC = high-income countries; IXP = internet exchange point; LIC = low-income countries; LMIC = lower-middle-income countries; UMIC = upper-middle-income countries.

of them have few members and generate little traffic. In 2022, average membership per IXP in low-income countries was just 20 percent of the world average (refer to figure 3.5, panel a). Markedly, average membership and traffic are higher in upper-middle-income countries than in high-income countries. Countries such as Brazil and the Russian Federation have among the largest IXPs in the world, befitting the fourth and sixth largest internet markets. Cost savings depend on the IXP's stage of maturity (that is, only allowing local ISPs to exchange traffic, allowing a diversity of participants, or locating an IXP in a co-location data center). As countries progress through the stages, prices drop, performance improves, and traffic increases. Lower-income and lower-middle-income countries are at different stages of maturity regarding IXPs. At one end of the scale are countries with no IXP, while at the other end are countries with a dense fabric of multiple IXPs located in connected data centers, typically operated by the private sector and with many different participants.

Regionally, Europe and Central Asia generate the most average traffic per IXP (refer to figure 3.5, panel b). This position is tied to the region's long history of membership-owned and -operated peering, with many of the first IXPs launched in the region (Lindqvist 2013). At the other extreme, Sub-Saharan Africa generates just 78 gigabytes per IXP (compared to a world average of 198 gigabytes). The figure is far lower when South Africa is excluded, with just 14 participants and 16 gigabytes of traffic per IXP.

Many IXPs in low- and middle-income countries have few members and limited traffic for various reasons. Some IXPs are located on government premises, typically in a small server room and, in some cases, using equipment provided through development assistance (World Bank 2021). They often generate limited amounts of traffic due to low participation of ISPs or lack of resources to upgrade equipment and train and retain staff. Regulatory restrictions may allow only ISPs to participate in the exchange, and onerous ISP licensing procedures may limit the number of ISPs. Some incumbent ISPs are reluctant to participate because of fears that their dominant market position will be weakened. IXPs operated by the government or located in state-owned facilities can inhibit international content and cloud providers from participating. Many IXPs in low- and middle-income countries are young, and only established in the last few years. In other markets, IXPs

FIGURE 3.5 **Average number of members and traffic per IXP, by country income group and region, 2022**

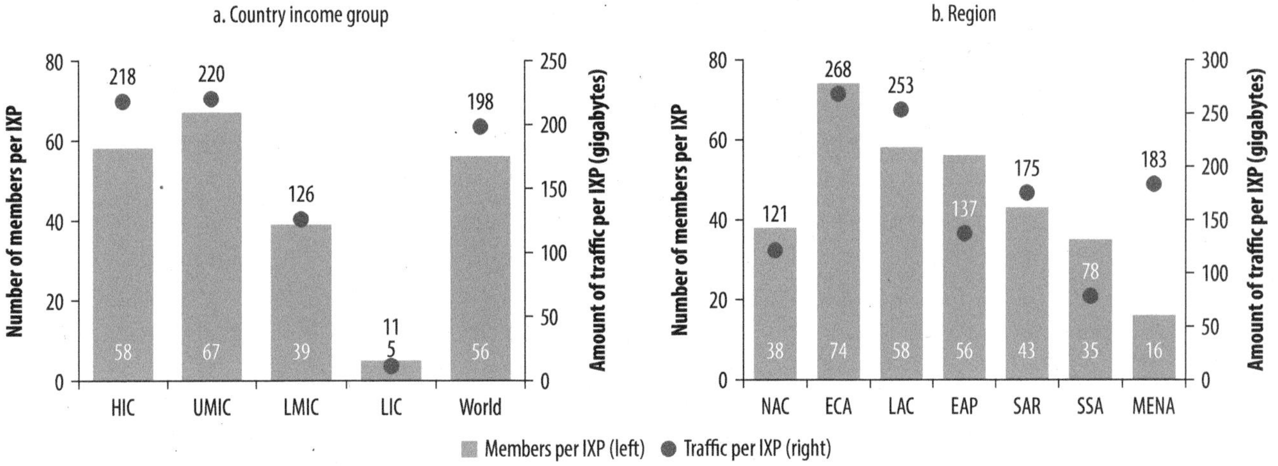

a. Country income group

b. Region

■ Members per IXP (left)   ● Traffic per IXP (right)

Source: Packet Clearing House (https://www.pch.net).
Note: Traffic refers to reported peak traffic. EAP = East Asia and Pacific; ECA = Europe and Central Asia; HIC = high-income countries; IXP = internet exchange point; LAC = Latin America and the Caribbean; LIC = low-income countries; LMIC = lower-middle-income countries; MENA = Middle East and North Africa; NAC = North America; SAR = South Asia; SSA = Sub-Saharan Africa; UMIC = upper-middle-income countries.

FIGURE 3.6 **Top companies and applications, by internet traffic generated, 2022**

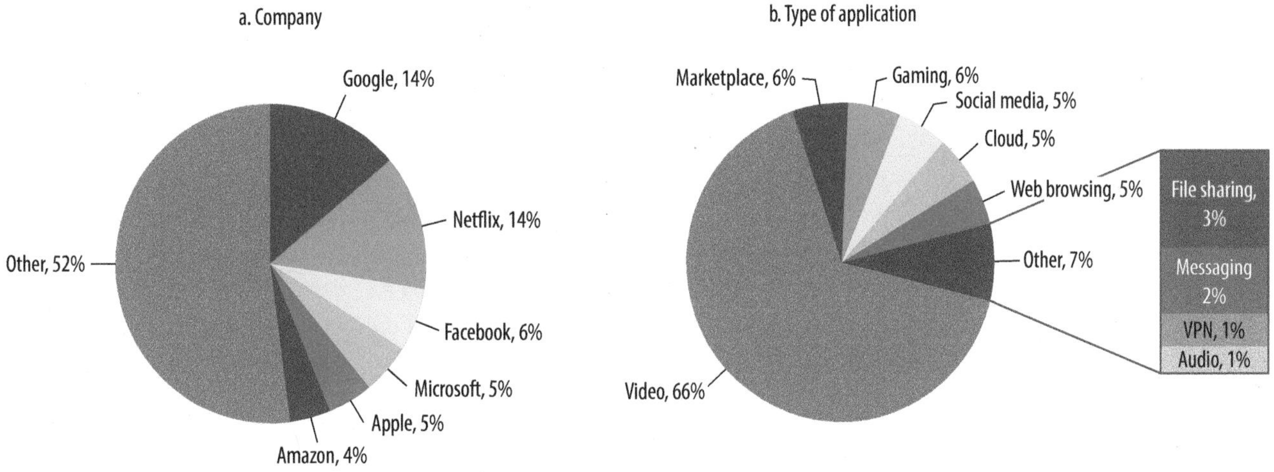

a. Company

b. Type of application

Source: Sandvine 2023.
Note: VPN = virtual private network.

grew over time, as larger ISPs realized the economic benefits of peering at the IXP to create better and faster connections at lower costs. This situation, in turn, attracts large content companies and cloud providers to the IXPs.

Most data traffic is generated by video, social media sites, and cloud computing providers. Almost half of internet traffic in 2022 was generated by just six companies (refer to figure 3.6). These companies have their own facilities to store content or provide cloud computing services. To exchange traffic with their users, they join IXPs to collect requests destined for them and backhaul the requested data back to the data center for free.

Several of the six companies are increasingly investing in global backbone infrastructure—four of the companies account for two-thirds of the world's fiber optic capacity—to haul traffic from where their data and services are stored to IXPs in connected data centers.[10] Their backbones can be envisioned as a highway for which the data centers provide an "on ramp" to the major content and cloud services.

This development marks a major transformational shift from the original reason that IXPs were created (that is, keeping locally destined traffic within the country). Today, hauling data traffic is about having an IXP that can attract major content and cloud providers that are able to handle the backhaul and, hence, lower the price of exchanging data with an overseas destination. At least one of the six major data traffic generating companies is a member of 316 IXPs in 66 countries, of which only 11 countries are low-income or lower-middle-income countries.[11]

Countries without IXPs residing in data centers and those that prohibit content and cloud providers from joining IXPs pay high costs to exchange traffic abroad. These costs are passed on to consumers (refer to figure 3.7). Data consumption per capita is also lower in countries without leading content providers at an IXP (Srinivasan, Comini, and Minges 2021). While some of the large data traffic companies offer a "cache" service in countries where they are not present in a data center, such a service can distort competition if these companies are not located in an IXP where every ISP can join.

Kenya is one of the only 11 low-income and lower-middle-income countries with major content providers present on its IXPs (refer to box 3.2). Five of the top six traffic generators exchange traffic at Kenyan IXPs. In addition to these companies, members also include government agencies, utilities, finance companies, and dozens of ISPs from Kenya, the region, and the world. Kenya has achieved this distinction by putting its IXPs in carrier-neutral multitenant data centers and ensuring that the IXPs are professionally operated. Kenya's abundant direct access to submarine cables is also an attraction, although it is not a prerequisite for leading internet traffic generators. For instance, Burkina Faso and Uganda, both landlocked, also have one or more leading traffic generators on their IXPs.

Connected data centers support the exchange of data among a diverse set of participants and thus form an essential building block of the digital economy. Estimates regarding the number of data centers in the world vary widely. One reason is the variety of data centers, ranging from small single-company-owned facilities to hyperscale centers operated by large multitenant operators. Due to such broad variety, this section focuses on "connected" data centers, which house the computing and networking equipment of tenants and include interconnection facilities.[12] Connected data

FIGURE 3.7 **Retail price and monthly consumption of internet data in low- and lower-middle-income countries, 2021–22**

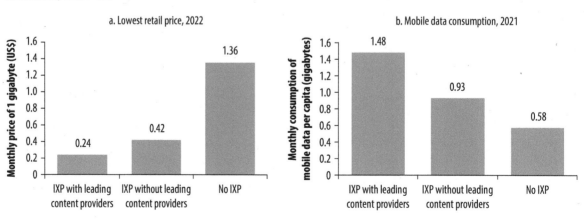

Source: PeeringDB (https://www.cable.co.uk/mobiles/worldwide-data-pricing).
Note: IXP = internet exchange point.

BOX 3.2 **Kenyan internet exchange point**

The Kenyan Internet Exchange Point (KIXP), managed by the Telecommunications Service Providers Association of Kenya (TESPOK), is one of the oldest among low- and lower middle-income countries. KIXP was originally launched in Nairobi in November 2000, but was shut down after two weeks because the incumbent operator, Telkom Kenya, filed a complaint.[a] Telkom Kenya argued that it had an exclusive monopoly on international traffic. However, given that KIXP was only exchanging domestic traffic, it was allowed to reopen again in February 2002 with five participants.

During the two weeks of the initial launch, latency was reduced from 1,200–2,000 milliseconds to 60–80 milliseconds, and monthly bandwidth costs for a 512 kilobytes per second circuit were reduced from US$9,546 to US$650.[b] Performance and cost savings have continued throughout KIXP's existence. In 2012, KIXP was saving internet service providers (ISPs) US$1.4 million in international bandwidth costs, with latency dropping further to 2–10 milliseconds. By 2020, the cost savings for international bandwidth was US$6 million a year (Kende 2020).

A major change in Kenya's digital connectivity occurred in 2009, when the country went from having no international fiber optic connectivity to having three high-speed undersea cables landing in Mombasa by the end of 2010 (Msimang 2011). In addition, phase one of the terrestrial national optical fiber backbone infrastructure was completed in 2008. Following the arrival of the submarine cables and in anticipation of further growth in local and regional internet traffic, a second IXP was launched in 2010 in Mombasa, site of the landing station for the cables.[c]

In 2014, KIXP added a second site at the East Africa Data Center (EADC), a tier III facility and part of the Africa Data Center group owned by Liquid Telecom, a pan-African wholesale fiber optic provider (Jones 2014). The data center provided the needed connectivity, security, and reliable power to support KIXP's growth. Renewable energy powers 73 percent of EADC's requirements, and backup is 100 percent solar, saving millions of dollars compared to the diesel-powered backup in place before and being more environmentally friendly.[d] The availability of renewable energy, which powers two-thirds of electricity in the country, makes Kenya an attractive location for investors keen on using reliable and clean energy (Kanali 2016).

Moving to privately operated, neutral co-location facilities made it easier to attract major international content players, including Meta and Alphabet, and cloud service providers, such as Amazon Web Services and Microsoft Azure. Beyond keeping domestic traffic local, KIXP also brings global companies into the country, reducing the cost of international bandwidth for ISPs and end users. By June 2023, TESPOK had more than 100 diverse members, including local ISPs, regional and international network service providers, government agencies, utilities, financial institutions, and others as well as major international content and cloud providers.

a. "Telecommunications Service Providers Comment on Internet Exchange Point Closure," *IFEX News*, December 21, 2000 (https://ifex.org/telecommunications -service-providers-comment-on-Internet-exchange-point closure.
b. TESPOK (Technology Service Providers of Kenya), "KIXP Background" (https://www.tespok.co.ke/?page_id=11651).
c. KIXP Mombasa was upgraded in 2016 following a grant from the African Union to become a regional exchange point as well as establishment of the first global system for mobile communication roaming exchange in Africa (https://au.int/sites/default/files/documents/32509-doc-axis-brochure_pida _january_2017.pdf).
d. "EADC Goes Solar for Power Back-up." *Africa Data Centres*, April 23, 2018 (https://www.africadatacentres.com/eadc-goes-solar-for-power-back-up/).

FIGURE 3.8 **Number and distribution of connected data centers, by country income group and region, 2018–22**

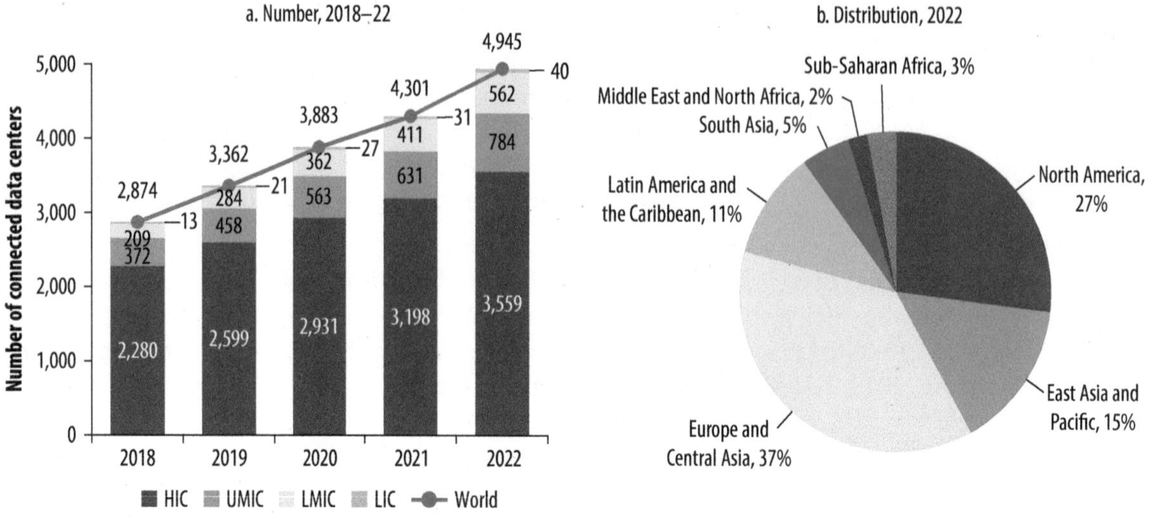

a. Number, 2018–22

b. Distribution, 2022

Source: PeeringDB data (https://www.peeringdb.com/).
Note: HIC = high-income countries; UMIC = upper-middle-income countries; LMIC = lower-middle-income countries; LIC = low-income countries.

centers serve a variety of tenants, including companies from a range of industries, governments, ISPs, and content and cloud providers as well as IXPs.

Connected data centers remain highly concentrated in high-income countries. Almost 5,000 data centers were connected to the internet in 2022. High-income economies accounted for the majority (72 percent), with nearly two-thirds (64 percent) located in North America and Europe and Central Asia (refer to figure 3.8). The number of connected data centers grew 72 percent between 2018 and 2022. Although low- and middle-income countries have a higher growth rate, they started from a small base (especially in low-income countries, with only 40 connected data centers in 2022).[13] Simply comparing data centers by the number of centers per capita is misleading. Data centers vary widely by size and the number of organizations connected to them. Just 132 connected data centers accounted for 75 percent of all hosted tenants in 2022.

Cloud computing has changed how data infrastructure and computing capacities are provisioned, shifting from fixed, physical infrastructure to a service-based, scalable, and on-demand model. This shift is important because it facilitates access to scalable computing resources, which, in turn, enables big data analytics and artificial intelligence, relying heavily on strong computational capabilities to store and process vast amounts of data for training and refinement. It is technically challenging and cost prohibitive for a single organization to establish and maintain secure and scalable data infrastructure for such purposes.

Developing countries need to accelerate investment in data infrastructure

Governments in low- and middle-income countries should liberalize the IXP environment and prevent ISPs from discouraging the use of IXPs (Qassrawi 2022). Large, foreign IXPs are one potential source of assistance. Such IXPs have been expanding in low- and middle-income economies.[14] For instance, Dutch-based AMS-IX has developed an IX-as-a-Service product that provides easy setup for an IXP and has been deployed in the Arab Republic of Egypt and India.[15] Germany's DE-CIX is also fostering IXPs in low- and middle-income countries and has created a "virtual" IXP for the Association of South East Asian Nations.[16]

To encourage private investment in data centers, governments need to create a favorable investment climate and introduce targeted financial and other instruments, such as state aid, venture capital, public-private co-financing mechanisms, and tax incentives. These instruments can vary depending on a data center's location, size, energy efficiency, and environmental footprint. For example, South Africa's Draft Policy on Data and Cloud proposes supporting local and foreign investment in data and cloud infrastructure and services by establishing a digital or ICT special economic zone.[17]

Aggregating demand at the regional level and bringing together stakeholders to achieve economies of scale is another potential solution for poorer countries to attract private sector investment. Regional harmonization of regulations for data security, data protection, and data sovereignty could help to encourage major cloud providers to establish a presence in low- and middle-income countries. This is one reason that South Africa has emerged as the de facto cloud hub for Sub-Saharan Africa. For example, in March 2019 Microsoft launched the first hyperscale data center in Africa, with locations in Cape Town and Johannesburg, South Africa.[18] In April 2020, AWS South Africa launched its own data center in Cape Town (Gilbert 2020). In October 2022, Alphabet also announced a plan to launch its first Google Cloud region in South Africa.[19] These data centers are relevant to the southern Africa region overall, not just South Africa.

Governments can serve as important catalysts in promoting cloud services through the adoption of cloud technologies for their own use. Government's use of the cloud validates the technology and sends a strong signal of trust and confidence. It also creates demand for cloud services, as governments, particularly in countries with a large public sector, are among the biggest consumers of cloud services. Government cloud or "Cloud First" policies prioritize the use of cloud computing technologies for delivering IT services and conducting digital operations, promoting a shift away from traditional on-premises infrastructure. Most high-income countries have adopted Cloud First policies and a growing number of middle-income countries have followed suit.

Greening digital infrastructure creates opportunities for low- and middle-income countries

Explosive growth in data and accelerating digitalization are contributing to rising electricity use and greenhouse gas emissions. The ICT sector currently accounts for a relatively small share of greenhouse gas emissions and electricity consumption. The emissions footprint of the ICT sector was estimated at between 467 million and 688 million tons of carbon dioxide equivalent (tCO_2e) in 2020 or 1.5–2.1 percent of the world total (figure 3.9, panel a). Electricity consumption of the sector was estimated at 825–926 terawatt-hours or 3.1–3.5 percent of the global total (refer to figure 3.9, panel b). Projections about future emissions stemming directly from the ICT sector vary, with some studies suggesting that emissions will remain largely stable, while others suggest that ICT could account for 14–24 percent of global emissions by 2030–40 (Godlovitch et al. 2021).

Governments in countries of leading data center hubs are already implementing measures to address concerns of rising electricity consumption (Fitri 2022). In Ireland, electricity consumption by data centers rose 32 percent between 2020 and 2021 alone. Data centers consumed 14 percent of the country's electricity in 2021, up from 5 percent in 2015 (refer to figure 3.10, panel a). Ireland's grid operator estimates that data centers could be using from a quarter to half the country's electricity by 2031 (EirGrid and SONI 2022). The rapid rise in electricity consumption by data centers is

FIGURE 3.9 **ICT sector greenhouse gas emissions and electricity consumption, 2020**

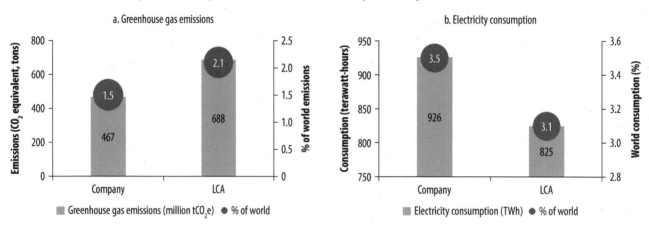

Source: Decoster, Minges, and Mudgal 2023.
Note: Company refers to reporting by major ICT firms to estimate operational as well as upstream and downstream emissions. ICT = information and communication technology; LCA = life cycle approach using ratios for estimates; TWh = terawatt-hour.

FIGURE 3.10 **Data center consumption of electricity in Ireland and the Netherlands**

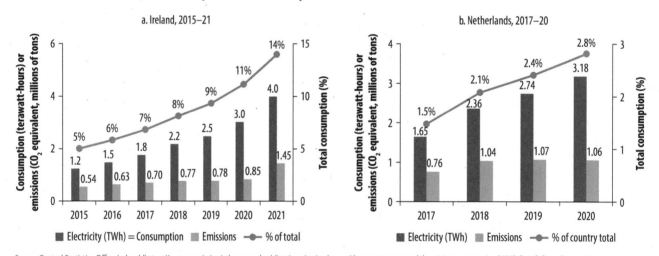

Source: Central Statistics Office Ireland (https://www.cso.ie/en/releasesandpublications/ep/p-dcmec/datacentresmeteredelectricityconsumption2022); Dutch Data Center Association (https://www.dutchdatacenters.nl/en).
Note: Emissions refer to scope 2 emissions from electricity. Scope 2 emissions are indirect greenhouse gas emissions associated with the purchase of electricity, steam, heat, or cooling. TWh = terawatt-hour.

particularly problematic because Ireland's electricity capacity is already constrained. To address this concern, in November 2021, Ireland's Commission for the Regulation of Utilities issued guidelines for electricity use by new data centers. New connections will be contingent on the data center providing its own onsite renewable generation or storage (CRU 2021). In the Netherlands, electricity consumption by data centers doubled from 2017 to 2020 (refer to Figure 2.10b). The government imposed a nine-month moratorium on the building of new hyperscale data centers in February 2022.[20] Due to the large number of data centers and concern about growing electricity consumption in Singapore, the government imposed a prohibition on new data centers in 2019.[21] The ban has ended, but new data centers must now follow strict regulations regarding power consumption and efficiency.

In a conscious effort to reduce its environmental impact, the ICT sector has become the world's biggest purchaser of renewable energy. The ICT sector accounted for an estimated 60 percent of

FIGURE 3.11 Volume of global renewable power purchase agreements, by sector and top 9 corporate purchasers of renewable energy, 2021

a. Volume of global renewable power purchase agreements

b. Top corporate purchasers of renewable energy

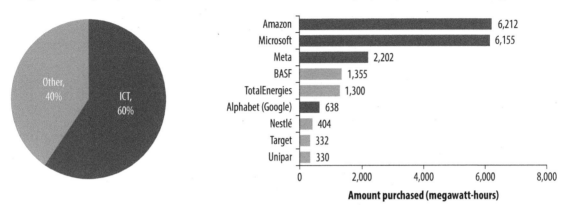

Sources: "Global Renewable Energy Power Purchase Agreements by Sector, 2010–2021," International Energy Agency, September 15, 2022 (https://www.iea.org/data-and-statistics/charts/global-renewable-energy-power-purchase-agreements-by-sector-2010-2021) and "Corporate Clean Energy Buying Tops 30GW Mark in Record Year." BloombergNEF, January 31, 2022 (https://about.bnef.com/blog/corporate-clean-energy-buying-tops-30gw-mark-in-record-year).

FIGURE 3.12 Price of electricity and grid emissions factor, various countries, 2021

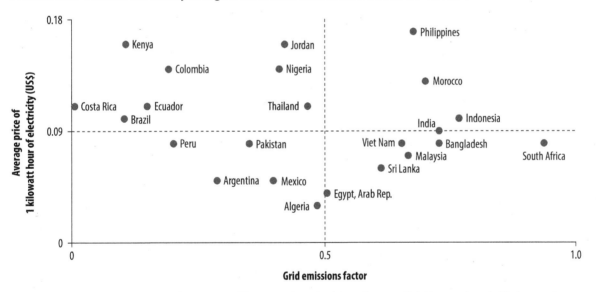

Sources: "ESG Addendum to the BT Group plc Manifesto Report 2022" (https://www.bt.com/bt-plc/assets/documents/digital-impact-and-sustainability/our-report/report-archive/2022/2022-esg-addendum.pdf) and "The Price of Electricity per KWh in 230 Countries" (https://www.cable.co.uk/energy/worldwide-pricing).

renewable power purchase agreements in 2021 (refer to figure 3.11, panel a). Further, digital companies are among the top 10 purchasers of renewable energy in the world (refer to figure 3.11, panel b). Increased focus on environmental, social, and governance issues has encouraged leading ICT companies to adopt emissions reductions targets. These targets extend to company subsidiaries in low- and middle-income countries, where multinational telecom and data center groups are using their scale to drive renewable energy use, where markets permit.

Countries with green grids and favorable investment policies in the energy markets are increasingly attracting investments from multinational ICT companies. Countries are in different quadrants, depending on how green their grid is (measured by the grid emissions factor[22]) and the price of electricity. Latin America tends to have greener grids mainly due to its rich hydropower resources (refer to figure 3.12). When combined with favorable investment policies, these countries can be attractive investment destinations for ICT companies. For instance, Costa Rica has attracted investment by digital companies, despite its relatively small market. One factor has been its commitment to sustainability and its clean grid (99 percent is powered by renewables). This factor is particularly relevant for companies with targets committing them to using 100 percent renewable energy in their operations. ICT companies with operations in Costa Rica include Amazon, Intel, Microsoft, and VMWare. VMWare notes, "Being installed in a country that already provides energy from renewable sources is key" (CINDE 2022).

Other countries can leverage the expertise and scale of ICT companies to expand the use of renewable energy by liberalizing their energy markets. ICT companies with operations in low- and middle-income countries are working to scale up renewable energy solutions. However, some countries have restrictive energy markets that limit the options for renewables. Given the energy-intensive nature of the digital sector, investors may be reluctant to invest if it is not possible to procure renewables; this reluctance will affect the development of digital economies in low-and middle-income countries. By liberalizing their energy markets, governments could tap into the scale that ICT companies can provide. Box 3.3 highlights the example of South Africa.

BOX 3.3 Liberalizing energy markets to attract ICT companies

In South Africa, information and communication technology companies began using electricity "wheeling" to power their data and cloud centers with renewable energy after the government liberalized the renewable energy market. South Africa is the data hub of the continent, with more than 50 data centers, and the number is increasing (Moyo 2022). These facilities use significant amounts of electricity, with consequent greenhouse gas emissions. Plagued by high electricity prices and load shedding (Dludla 2023), data center operators are building their own solar farms or procuring renewable energy from producers. Energy market reform has facilitated this effort, separating grid distribution from generation. One outcome of the reform is the emergence of wheeling, where a company builds a renewable energy plant and has electricity delivered to where it needs it (refer to figure B3.3.1). Data centers and cloud providers are making use of this feature.

FIGURE B3.3.1 Electricity wheeling

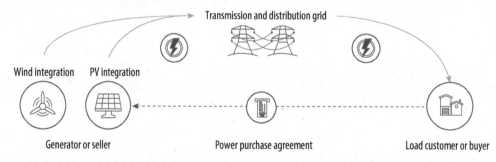

Source: "What You Need to Know about Wheeling of Electricity" (https://www.eskom.co.za/distribution/wheeling/).
Note: PV = photovoltaic.

(Continued)

BOX 3.3 **Liberalizing energy markets to attract ICT companies** *(Continued)*

Amazon, which has committed to power its operations with 100 percent renewable energy by 2030, contracted the largest solar wheeling arrangement ever in South Africa in 2020.[a] Its solar plant in the Northern Cape Province will power its cloud center and is expected to generate up to 28,000 megawatts of renewable energy per year, avoiding an estimated 25,000 tons of carbon dioxide-equivalent (CO_2e).

Other data center companies have followed since then. Vantage Data Centers is opening its first hyperscale data center (60,000 square meters) in South Africa at a reported cost of US$1 billion. Vantage has signed a renewable purchase power agreement providing 80 megawatts of solar energy, covering around a third of its needs.[b] South Africa's largest data center company, Teraco, aims to source half of its energy needs from renewables by 2027, using its own onsite solar facilities as well as renewable energy suppliers, wheeling arrangements, and renewable energy certificate purchases.[c] Africa Data Centers signed a 20-year power purchase agreement for 12 megawatts of solar energy, which will supply more than 30 percent of its power requirements (Hako 2023). The aggregate solar capacity of these deals is equivalent to around a third of South Africa's solar generation.

a. "SOLA Gets Approval for Largest Solar PV Wheeling Agreement in South Africa" (https://solagroup.co.za/sola-gets-approval-for-largest-solar-pv-wheeling-agreement-in-south-africa).
b. "Vantage Data Centers Enters Power Purchase Agreement with SolarAfrica to Secure 87MWp of Solar Energy for Johannesburg Data Center Campus" (https://vantage-dc.com/news/vantage-data-centers-enters-power-purchase-agreement-with-solarafrica-to-secure-87mwp-of-solar-energy-for-johannesburg-data-center-campus/).
c. "Sustainability at Teraco" (https://www.teraco.co.za/about-us/sustainability/environment/).

Notes

1. A zettabyte is 2^{70} bytes. It is equal to 1 trillion gigabytes.
2. "5G Global Launches & Statistics," *GSMA Future Networks* (blog) (https://www.gsma.com/futurenetworks/ip_services/understanding-5g/5g-innovation/).
3. "Consortium Led by Safaricom Wins Ethiopian Operating Licence," *Reuters*, May 7, 2021 (https://www.reuters.com/world/africa/ethiopias-ethio-telecom-launch-mobile-money-service-2021-05-07/).
4. "Safaricom Telecommunications Ethiopia Officially Launched," Safaricom press release, October 6, 2022 (https://www.safaricom.co.ke/media-center-landing/press-releases/safaricom-telecommunications-ethiopia-officially-launched).
5. The mile framework is useful for understanding the telecommunication value chain, which stretches from the point where the internet enters a country (the first mile), passes through the country (the middle mile), and eventually reaches the end user (the last mile), with certain hidden elements in between (the invisible mile) (World Bank 2016).
6. "Annual Capital Expenditures Survey (ACES)," *US Census Bureau, Our Surveys and Programs* (blog) (https://www.census.gov/programs-surveys/aces.html).
7. "Capex Analysis—Growth in Hyperscale and Enterprise Spending; Telco Remains in the Doldrums," Synergy Research Group press release, January 26, 2023 (https://www.srgresearch.com/articles/2022-capex-analysis-growth-in-hyperscale-and-enterprise-spending-telco-remains-in-the-doldrums).
8. US International Development Finance Corporation, "Public Information Summary" (https://www.dfc.gov/sites/default/files/media/documents/9000093563.pdf).
9. Public IXPs provide open traffic exchange among participants. Connected data centers without IXPs provide interconnection services, but these services are generally more restrictive and can result in higher costs.

10. For instance, Alphabet, Amazon, Meta, and Microsoft account for 66 percent of global fiber optic capacity, up from less than 10 percent a decade earlier (Mims 2022).

11. All 6 are on 36 IXPs.

12. PeeringDB, "PeeringDB Data Ownership Policy Document" (https://docs.peeringdb.com/gov /misc/2020-04-06_PeeringDB_Data_Ownership_Policy_Document_v1.0.pdf).

13. Notably China ranks low in connected data centers. Although the country has thousands of data centers, very few are connected to the global internet. With just 0.03 connected data center per 1 million population, China ranks 153 out of 156 countries. This situation is largely due to the country's firewall, which restricts the entry and exit of data.

14. "Internet Exchanges—How Does It Work and What's the Importance of It?" *Greenhouse Data Centers* (blog), September 30, 2021 (https://www.greenhousedatacenters.nl/en/news/30 -09-2021).

15. AMS-ix, "IX-as-a-Service" (https://www.ams-ix.net/ams/service/ix-as-a-service).

16. DE-CIX, "DE-CIX Asia Locations" (https://www.de-cix.net/en/asia#Locations).

17. South African Government, "Electronic Communications Act: National Data and Cloud Policy: Comments Invited" (www.gov.za).

18. "Microsoft Opens First Datacenters in Africa with General Availability of Microsoft Azure," *Microsoft Azure* (blog), March 6, 2019 (https://azure.microsoft.com/en-us/blog/microsoft-opens -first-datacenters-in-africa-with-general-availability-of-microsoft-azure/)."

19. "Amazon Web Services to Pump $1.8 Billion into South Africa," *Telecom Review Africa,* April 18, 2023 (https://www.telecomreviewafrica.com/en/articles/general-news/3345-amazon-web-services -to-pump-1-8-billion-into-south-africa).

20. "Dutch Call a Halt to New Massive Data Centres, While Rules Are Worked Out," *DutchNews*, February 17, 2022 (https://www.dutchnews.nl/news/2022/02/dutch-call-a-halt-to-new-massive -data-centres-while-rules-are-worked-out/).

21. "Launch Pilot Data Centre—Call for Application (DC-CFA) to Support Sustainable Growth of DCs," Singapore Economic Development Board and Info Media Development Authority press release, July 20, 2022 (https://www.imda.gov.sg/resources/press-releases-factsheets-and-speeches/press -releases/2022/launch-of-pilot-data-centre---call-for-application-to-support-sustainable-growth-of -dcs).

22. The grid emissions factor measures the carbon emissions on the electrical grid: tons of CO_2 equivalent divided by megawatt-hours of electricity.

References

Cappella, Nicole. 2022. "M&A: An Emerging Strategy in the African Data Centre Market." *TECHERATI*, January 14, 2022. https://www.techerati.com/news-hub/africa-data-centre-expansion/.

CINDE (Investment Promotion Agency). 2022. "Costa Rica's Commitment to Becoming a 'Greenshoring' Destination of Choice." *Investment Monitor*, July 12, 2022. https://www.investmentmonitor.ai /sponsored/costa-ricas-commitment-to-becoming-a-greenshoring-destination-of-choice/.

CRU (Commission for Regulation of Utilities). 2021. *CRU Consultation on Data Centre Measures.* Dublin: CRU. https://www.cru.ie/publications/27402/.

Decoster, Xavier, Michael Minges, and Shailendra Mudgal. 2023. "Consortium Led by Safaricom Wins Ethiopian Operating License." *Reuters*, May 7, 2021. https://www.reuters.com/world/africa /ethiopias-ethio-telecom-launch-mobile-money-service-2021-05-07/.

Dludla, Nqobile. 2023. "South Africa Fights to Keep Phone Networks Up as Lights Go Out." *Reuters*, April 5, 2023. https://www.reuters.com/business/media-telecom/south-africa-fights-keep -phone-networks-up-lights-go-out-2023-04-05.

EirGrid and SONI (System Operator Northern Ireland). 2022. *Ireland Capacity Outlook 2022–2031.* Dublin: EirGrid Group. https://www.eirgridgroup.com/site-files/library/EirGrid/EirGrid_SONI _Ireland_Capacity_Outlook_2022-2031.pdf.

Ericsson. 2023. *Mobility Report.* Stockholm: Ericsson, June 2023. https://www.ericsson.com/en /reports-and-papers/mobility-report/reports/june-2023.

Fitri, Afiq. 2022. "Inside the Data Centre Moratorium Movement." *TECHMONITOR*, October 13, 2022. https://techmonitor.ai/technology/cloud/inside-the-data-centre-moratorium-movement.

Gilbert, Paula. 2020. "AWS Cape Town Data Centers Officially Live." *Connecting Africa*, April 22, 2020. https://www.connectingafrica.com/author.asp?section_id=761&doc_id=759063.

Godlovitch, lsa, Aurelie Louguet, Dajan Baischew, Matthias Wissner, and Anaelle Pirlot. 2021. 2021. *Environmental Impact of Electronic Communications.* Bad Honnef, Germany: Final Study Report. WIK-Consult and Ramboll. https://www.berec.europa.eu/sites/default/files/files/document_register _store/2022/3/BoR%20%2822%29%2034_External%20Sustainability%20Study%20on%20 Environmental%20impact%20of%20EC.pdf.

GSMA. 2021. "Keeping Everyone and Everything Connected: How Temporary Access to Spectrum Can Ease Congestion during the COVID-19 Crisis." *Newsroom*, August 12, 2021. https://www.gsma.com /newsroom/blog/keeping-everyone-and-everything-connected-how-temporary-access-to-spectrum -can-ease-congestion-during-the-covid-19-crisis/.

GSMA. 2022. *The Mobile Economy 2022.* Zurich: GSMA. https://www.gsma.com/mobileeconomy /wp-content/uploads/2022/02/280222-The-Mobile-Economy-2022.pdf.

Hack, Ulrike. 2021. "What Is the Real Story behind the Explosive Growth of Data?" *Redgate* (blog), September 8, 2021. https://www.red-gate.com/blog/database-development/whats-the-real-story -behind-the-explosive-growth-of-data.

Hako, Nasi. 2023. "South Africa: Data Centres to Be Supplied with 12MW of Solar Energy." *ESI Africa*, March 14, 2023. https://www.esi-africa.com/business-and-markets/south-africa-data-centres-to-be -supplied-with-12mw-of-solar-energy/.

ITU (International Telecommunication Union). 2020a. *Connecting Humanity: Assessing Investment Needs of Connecting Humanity to the Internet by 2030.* Geneva: ITU. https://www.itu.int/dms_pub /itu-d/opb/gen/D-GEN-INVEST.CON-2020-PDF-E.pdf.

ITU (International Telecommunication Union). 2020b. *Economic Impact of OTTs on National Telecommunication/ICT Markets.* Geneva: ITU. https://www.itu.int/hub/2020/06/itu-launches-new -study-paper-on-economic-impact-of-otts/.

Jones, Penny. 2014. "East Africa Data Center Hosts Kenya Internet Exchange Point." *Data Centre Dynamics News*, January 20, 2014. https://www.datacenterdynamics.com/en/news/east-africa-data -center-hosts-kenya-Internet-exchange-point/.

Kanali, Nixon. 2016. "EADC Launches New Power Plant to Push It Up the 'Green' Ladder as a Green Data Center." *TechTrendsKE*, October 26, 2016. https://techtrendske.co.ke/eadc-launches-new -power-plant-in-nairobi/.

Kende, Michael. 2020. *Anchoring the African Internet Ecosystem: Lessons from Kenya and Nigeria's Internet Exchange Point Growth.* Reston, VA: Internet Society. https://www.internetsociety.org /resources/doc/2020/ixp-report-2020/.

Kolmar, Chris. 2023. "75 Incredible Email Statistics (2023): How Many Emails Are Sent per Day?" *Zippia (Research)*, March 30, 2023. https://www.zippia.com/advice/how-many-emails-are-sent -per-day/#:~:text=Approximently%20347.3%20billion%20emails%20are,billion%20were%20 sent%20each%20day.

Lindqvist, Kurt Erik. 2013. "Internet Exchange Points." *ITAC Newsletter*, May 28, 2013. https://www .internetac.org/archives/1520.

Mbugua, Caroline. 2022. "Rwanda Reverses Decision to Depend on a Single Wholesale Network." *GSMA* (blog), November 15, 2022. https://www.gsma.com/spectrum/rwanda-reverses-decision-to -depend-on-a-single-wholesale-network.

McKinsey Global Institute. 2020. *What's Next for Remote Work: An Analysis of 2,000 Tasks, 800 Jobs, and Nine Countries.* New York: McKinsey. https://www.mckinsey.com/featured-insights/future-of -work/whats-next-for-remote-work-an-analysis-of-2000-tasks-800-jobs-and-nine-countries.

Mims, Christopher. 2022. "Google, Amazon, Meta and Microsoft Weave a Fiber-Optic Web of Power." *Wall Street Journal*, January 22, 2022. https://www.wsj.com/articles/google-amazon-meta-and -microsoft-weave-a-fiber-optic-web-of-power-11642222824.

Mohsin, Maryam. 2023. "10 Google Search Statistics You Need to Know in 2023 (Infographic)." *Oberlo* (blog), January 13, 2023. https://www.oberlo.com/blog/google-search-statistics.

Moss, Sebastian. 2023. "Private Equity Leads 2022 Data Center M&A, in $48bn Year of Deals." *Data Center Dynamics*, January 31, 2023. https://www.datacenterdynamics.com/en/news/private-equity -leads-2022-data-center-ma-in-48bn-year-of-deals/.

Moyo, Admire. 2022. "'Meteoric Rise' of Local Data Centres Continues Unabated." *ITWeb*, June 15, 2022. https://www.itweb.co.za/content/WnxpEv4Yaza7V8XL.

Msimang, Mandla. 2011. *Broadband in Kenya: Build It and They Will Come.* Washington, DC: World Bank. http://www.infodev.org/articles/broadband-kenya-build-it-and-they-will-come.

O'Shea, Dan. 2021. "Facebook, Google Lead Latest Undersea Cable Boom." *FIERCE Telecom*, April 12, 2021. https://www.fiercetelecom.com/telecom/facebook-google-continue-to-lead-latest-undersea -cable-boom.

Parungo, Rob. 2022. "LatAm Top Groups: Despite Growing Subs, Mobile Revenues Decline." *S&P Global*, August 24, 2022. https://www.spglobal.com/marketintelligence/en/news-insights /research/2022-latam-top-groups-despite-growing-subs-mobile-revenues-decline.

Qassrawi, Zaher. 2022. "Internet Exchange Points—Beyond Configuration Issues." *RIPE Labs*, March 24, 2022. https://labs.ripe.net/author/zaher-qassrawi/internet-exchange-points-beyond-configuration -issues/.

Sandvine. 2023. *The Global Internet Phenomena Report.* Waterloo, Canada: Sandvine. https://www .sandvine.com/global-internet-phenomena-report-2023.

Srinivasan, Sharada, Niccolo Comini, and Michael Minges. 2021. "The Importance of National Data Infrastructure for Low and Middle-Income Countries." Paper prepared for TPRC49: The 49th Research Conference on Communication, Information, and Internet Policy, Washington, DC, September 24–25, 2021. https://ssrn.com/abstract=3898094.

World Bank. 2016. *World Development Report 2016: Digital Dividends.* Washington, DC: World Bank. https://elibrary.worldbank.org/doi/abs/10.1596/978-1-4648-0671-1.

World Bank. 2021. *World Development Report 2021: Data for Better Lives.* Washington, DC: World Bank. https://www.worldbank.org/en/publication/wdr2021.

PART 2
Emerging Trends

Digital Public Infrastructure: Transforming Service Delivery Across Sectors

4

Jonathan Marskell, Georgina Marin, and Minita Varghese

KEY MESSAGES

- Digital public infrastructure (DPI) is a new term referring to the basic capabilities that are building blocks for developing digital services at a societal scale. DPI is the intermediate layer between physical infrastructure (for example, broadband and data centers) and sectoral applications (for example, social protection and e-commerce). The most common types of DPI are platforms and systems for digital identification (ID), digital payments, and data sharing.

- DPI rose in prominence during the COVID-19 pandemic. The countries that had elements of DPI in place before the pandemic were generally more resilient. Research by the World Bank's Digitalizing Government-to-Person Payments initiative has found that these countries reached three times more beneficiaries with emergency cash transfers. Countries with good DPI in place could also keep government services, commerce, hospitals, schools, and other operations functioning through online channels.

- Globally, 850 million people lacked any form of official ID in 2021. Five billion people live in countries without a digital ID that can be used for secure online access to public and private sector services.

- Only 96 economies have fully operationalized both the legal frameworks and the technological infrastructure (for example, public key infrastructure) for e-signatures, which are a key source of trust in the digital economy. Two-thirds are high-income and upper-middle-income economies. Likewise, only 89 economies have a functional data exchange platform, with three-quarters being high-income and upper-middle-income economies.

- While the percentage of adults with a formal financial account in low- and middle-income countries jumped to 71 percent in 2021 (from 63 percent in 2017), only 57 percent of adults made or received some sort of digital payment and only 37 percent made one with a merchant. One significant opportunity is the rapid rise in fast or real-time payment systems, which have been launched or announced in about 100 jurisdictions.

Introduction

With a few taps on their mobile phone, remote area workers in India can apply for social benefits to be paid directly into their bank account and electronically sign an application for a loan. In Thailand, farmers can receive fertilizer subsidies into a bank account linked to their identification (ID).

In Singapore citizens and residents can conduct almost any transaction end-to-end online, no matter where they are, from registering a birth to filing taxes and opening a new business. These services are made possible through innovations catalyzed by digital public infrastructure.

This chapter introduces a new concept—digital public infrastructure (DPI)—and illustrates its growing significance to all aspects of the digital economy. The chapter also summarizes different models for developing certain DPI elements, notably ID and data exchange platforms. The chapter then identifies some key gaps in developing countries' DPI systems, and highlights general principles, risks, and challenges when developing DPI systems.

What is DPI, and why is it important?

DPI refers to the basic capabilities—such as for identification, payments, and data sharing—that are the building blocks for developing transformative digital services at a societal scale. At its simplest, DPI can be understood as an intermediate layer in the digital ecosystem (refer to figure 4.1). It sits atop a physical layer (including internet connectivity, devices, servers, data centers, the cloud, and routers) and enables applications across various sectors (for example, information systems and solutions to different verticals, e-commerce, social protection, remote education, and telehealth). The focus on reusable and horizontal foundations is a paradigm shift from conventional approaches to digitalization that have, in many cases, led to fragmentation and siloes. Some examples of DPI include India's Aadhaar identification system, Brazil's Pix fast payment system, and Australia's Consumer Data Right for consented sharing of personal data. Since reliable verification and the flow of money and information are at the core of most digital transactions, DPI prevents the need for the owner of an application to reinvent the wheel (Desai et al. 2023). Furthermore, when open and interoperable, DPI can promote innovation, competition, productivity gains, and other democratizing and multiplier effects at the application layer and across sectors (Global Partnership for Financial Inclusion 2023).

Awareness about the importance of DPI grew during the COVID-19 pandemic. As described later in this chapter, the countries that had elements of DPI in place before the pandemic were able to mount social protection responses more quickly, transparently, and effectively. For example, Thailand benefited from the ability of people to link their digital ID to a bank or e-wallet account.

FIGURE 4.1 The concept of digital public infrastructure

| a. Conventional approaches to digitalization | | | | | b. New approach to digitalization | | | |

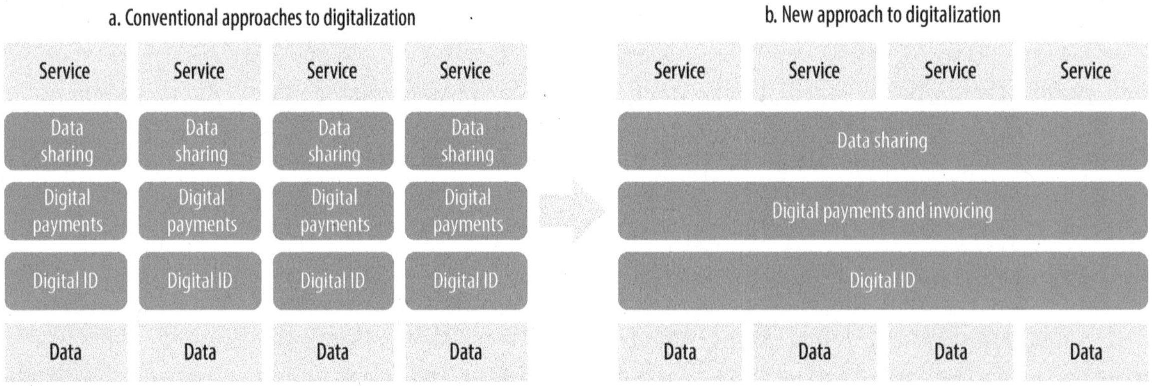

Source: World Bank.
Note: ID = identification.

When a new program for informal workers had to be rolled out quickly via online registration, this ability provided greater assurance that the right person was receiving emergency cash transfers. Countries with DPI were also better equipped to adapt as businesses, government agencies, schools, and hospitals shifted to digital and online channels.

However, while the term is new, the concept of DPI traces its roots to the earlier experience of advanced digital countries. Even before the pandemic, some of the fastest-growing digital economies and most dynamic digital governments—including Brazil, Estonia, Kenya, and the Republic of Korea—built much of their success in making lives easier and creating economic opportunities on cross-cutting platforms for identifying people and businesses (and related trust services such as e-signatures, consent, verifiable credentials, and data vaults), interoperable fast payments, and seamless and secure data sharing. Countries are also beginning to apply DPI to climate change mitigation and adaptation, such as to optimize energy generation using peer-to-peer energy trading. India's India Stack (refer to figure 4.2) and Singapore's Digital Utilities are examples of how countries have layered the elements of DPI with interoperability enabled by application programming interfaces (APIs), making the whole greater than the sum of the parts and creating opportunities for new products and services. The term DPI emerged in late 2021 (Rockefeller Foundation, Digital Public Goods Alliance, and Norway Ministry of Foreign Affairs 2021) and early 2022 (Metz et al. 2022).

FIGURE 4.2 **The India stack**

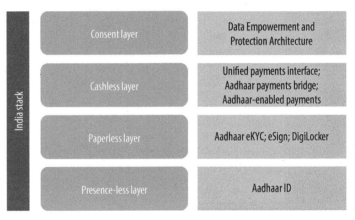

Source: Adapted from the India Stack website (https://indiastack.org).
Note: ID = identification.

In August 2023, the G-20 reached the first multilateral consensus on a description of DPI and suggestive guiding principles (refer to figure 4.3). This agreement was negotiated among the G-20 digital economy ministers, spearheaded by the Indian Presidency's Initiative and endorsed by the G-20 leaders. It lays a framework for a common understanding and future international cooperation. Notably, the G-20 outcome recognizes digital ID, digital payments, and data sharing as basic DPI, while also acknowledging that countries will have their own ways and architectures of implementing them. Furthermore, it recognizes that countries may have other forms of DPI to meet the same objectives of underpinning digital service delivery across sectors (refer to box 4.1). For example, India considers its Open Network for Digital Commerce, which is an open communication protocol that connects buyers and sellers across different platforms (from e-commerce to gig work), to be a DPI. Furthermore, the Global Partnership for Financial Inclusion has developed policy recommendations on how DPI can promote financial inclusion and productivity gains. Building on this global momentum, the World Bank has incorporated DPI in one of its five new global priority programs (on accelerating digitalization), and the United Nations has launched a high-impact initiative on DPI to spur progress across all 17 United Nations Sustainable Development Goals (SDGs).

The "public" in DPI refers to public benefit and common good, not government ownership. The intention is to convey that digital ID, digital payments, data sharing, and other foundational capabilities are just as important for the functioning and transformation of economies and societies in today's digital age as physical infrastructure like roads and railways were in previous centuries,

FIGURE 4.3 G-20 DPI outcomes in 2023

G20 description of DPI:
Under the Indian Presidency's initiative, we recognize that digital public infrastructure, hereinafter referred to as DPI, is described as a set of shared digital systems that should be secure and interoperable, and can be built on open standards and specifications to deliver and provide equitable access to public and / or private services at societal scale and are governed by applicable legal frameworks and enabling rules to drive development, inclusion, innovation, trust, and competition and respect human rights and fundamental freedoms. Considering the diverse approaches of G20 members to digital transformation, we recognize that DPI is an evolving concept that may not be limited to sets of digital systems with these characteristics and could be tailored to specific country contexts and can be referred to with different terminologies.

G-20 framework for systems of DPI: Suggested principles:
a. Inclusivity
b. Interoperability
c. Modularity and extensibility
d. Scalability
e. Security and privacy
f. Collaboration
g. Governance for public benefit, trust, and transparency
h. Grievance regress
i. Sustainability
j. Human rights
k. Intellectual property protection
l. Sustainable development

Indicative, voluntary, and nonbinding policy recommendations for advancing financial inclusion and productivity gains through the use of DPIs in the financial sector:
a. Enable and foster the use of DPIs to accelerate financial inclusion and productivity gains
b. Develop well-designed DPIs and the broader enabling environment through a widely accepted set of good practices
c. Encourage appropriate risk-based regulation, supervision, and oversight arrangements for financial sector use of DPIs
d. Promote sound internal governance arrangements
e. Enable DPIs to offer products and services in a way that no one is left behind and the interests of consumers are safeguarded

Sources: G20 India 2023; Global Partnership for Financial Inclusion 2023.
Note: DPI = digital public infrastructure.

BOX 4.1 Different approaches to DPI

The approach to governing and implementing digital public infrastructure (DPI), including individual layers, will differ markedly among countries, reflecting differences in the political economy, legal, and sociocultural circumstances of the country as well as the desired outcomes. Some factors that will be different include the level of private sector involvement, the extent of centralization or coordination of responsibilities in government, and how the different layers of DPI are architected and made interoperable (if at all).

In the case of digital identification, there are three well-established architectural approaches that, importantly, are not necessarily mutually exclusive:

• *Centralized.* A centralized approach has a single authority (typically a government agency) for issuing and authenticating identity credentials. Examples include India's Aadhaar and Singapore's Singpass. The advantage of this approach is its simplicity for users and service providers. The disadvantage is the absence of choice for users and service providers, potentially monopolistic effects on pricing, and the possibility of limited incentives for innovation.

• *Federated.* A federated approach has an ecosystem of authentication providers (from the public or private sectors or both) that users can choose from, operating according to common standards to achieve interoperability and portability. Although there are several providers of

(Continued)

BOX 4.1 **Different approaches to DPI** *(Continued)*

identity credentials and authentication services, the data they use are typically from a centralized source, such as a national identification (ID) system or civil registry. Examples include France's FranceConnect and Thailand's National Digital ID platform. The advantages of this approach are the provision of choice, incentivization of innovation, and lower pricing through competition. The disadvantages are potential complexity for users and the need for strong supervisory and regulatory capabilities, which are often lacking in low- and middle-income countries.

- *Decentralized.* This emerging approach involves authentication against a credential that is fully controlled by the user (for example, a digital wallet on a smartphone). In contrast to the other two architectures, the issuer of the identification (for example, a national ID or driving license authority) will not know about authentications that take place, since this verification is done against the credential, typically using asymmetric cryptography. To date, there are no known national-scale implementations; however, the approach is proposed as part of the new European digital wallet initiative and was launched in mid-2023 in Bhutan. The advantages are the increased privacy and potential for greater interoperability and portability. The disadvantage is the complexity for users and service providers, especially vis-à-vis the other architectures.

For data sharing, there is not yet a well-established taxonomy. However, different approaches reflect local political and legal contexts. For example, countries with centralized approaches to digital identification are more likely to have centralized approaches to data sharing. Three factors can vary between countries:

- *Level of centralization.* Some countries, like Belgium (Federal Service Bus), Estonia (X-Tee), Singapore (APEX), and Uganda (UGHub), have developed central mechanisms to facilitate data sharing. These central mechanisms take different technological approaches. For example, Singapore's APEX is simply an application programming interface marketplace for government to facilitate bilateral point-to-point data sharing, whereas Estonia's X-Tee involves middleware and a central service bus or hub that orchestrates data sharing. Other approaches, such as those taken in Australia and the United Kingdom, are more sectoral, federated, and standards based.

- *Level of user-centricity.* The first dimension is the extent to which consent is required for the sharing of personal data, which will be a function of the applicable personal data protection law. Singapore's Singpass and Estonia's Digital ID are examples of how consent is provided. The second dimension is the amount of control that data subjects have over the process of sharing their data. For example, India's DigiLocker and the United Arab Emirates' UAE Pass Digital Vault allow data subjects to store and share their digital documents (that is, data) inside their own devices. Emerging standards for verifying credentials, such as by the World Wide Web Consortium, are taking this a step further by following an approach similar to decentralized identity, described above. One of the first implementations of such an approach at a national scale is Cambodia's Verify.gov.kh system.

- *Approach to cross-border data flows.* There are three broad approaches to cross-boarder data flows: open transfer (typically regulated by industries and with no mandatory conditions or approvals for data transfers); conditional transfer (with white listing of recipient countries, incorporation of standard contractual clauses, adoption of domestic certification, and consent); and limited transfer (localization requirements and mandatory explicit regulatory approval). These approaches apply not only to personal data, but also to other forms of data that fuel digital and other trade—for example, data flowing from Internet of Things devices in a factory in country B and going to controllers or supervisors at a company's headquarters in country A.

with nondiscriminatory access in accordance with governance rules. Additionally, Poole, Toohey, and Harris (2014) argue, "'Public' infrastructure is an investment where the government has the primary role in, and responsibility for, deciding on whether and how the infrastructure is provided in the interests of the broader community and … extends beyond infrastructure that is owned or directly funded by the public sector." This definition can be expanded to cover this new concept of DPI. In fact, the private sector has a key role to play in the design and implementation of DPI—for example, as developers of use cases and services that drive adoption, as service providers and sources of innovation for development of DPI, as operators of DPI, and as participants in public-private partnerships and other collaborations to achieve scale.

As recognized by the G-20, DPI is just as much about governance and community as it is about technology. The paradigm shift toward a horizontal mind-set for digitalization can only be realized if there is a whole-of-country approach that facilitates coordination across government (including regulators) and collaboration with the private sector, civil society, and other stakeholders. The other necessary elements of governance include transparency and accountability, political will to clarify roles and responsibilities, and legal and institutional safeguards to protect against misuse. With many good-practice examples around the world and a growing number of open standards, open-source software, and other digital public goods, technology may be the easiest part of DPI to solve. For example, as of August 2023, 22 countries are using the X-Road open-source software as the platform for exchanging data (Nordic Institute for Interoperability Solutions 2023), and 11 countries are using the Modular Open Source Identity Platform.[1]

DPI plays a fundamental role in using digital technologies to enhance service delivery in various domains. Box 4.2 summarizes some emerging evidence on the impact of DPI.

BOX 4.2 **Growing evidence on the impact of DPI**

Digital public infrastructure (DPI) represents a transformative shift in a country's approach to digitalization. The broad theory portrayed in figure B4.2.1 can be applied to any element of DPI. Implementation of one or more elements of DPI is expected to act through various mechanisms to improve individual welfare, facilitate public services and efficiency, and enable commerce and innovation. As the adoption of DPI continues to scale up, it may become possible in the future to measure the distinct impact of applying a DPI approach in addition to studying the effects of its specific subcomponents.

FIGURE B4.2.1 **Theory of change**

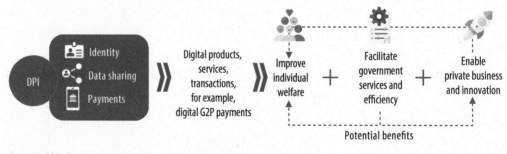

Source: World Bank.
Note: G2P = government-to-person.

(Continued)

BOX 4.2 **Growing evidence on the impact of DPI** *(Continued)*

The examples that follow provide early evidence to support this hypothesis. However, these interventions entail the same risks as any digitalization: exclusion of persons with low digital access, skills, or literacy; misuse or mismanagement of personal data; and system lock-in and waste. It is important for research to attempt to capture both negative and positive consequences of DPI design.

Benefits for people

Digital government-to-person (G2P) payments offer a gateway to financial inclusion and other benefits:

- According to the Global Findex 2021, digitalizing G2P payments has contributed to 865 million people worldwide opening their first financial institution account to receive money from the government (Demirgüç-Kunt et al. 2022).

- *Brazil.* Pix plus digital wallets with remote onboarding plus pro-digital policies contributed to 75 percent of Auxilio Emergencial cash transfer beneficiaries using the funds digitally (Lara de Arruda et al. 2022).

- *Mozambique.* Beneficiaries spent less than 30 minutes waiting for mobile money payments versus more than one hour waiting for cash payments (World Bank, forthcoming).

- *India.* The use of digital payments reduced delays in the payment of maternal health conditional cash transfers by 43 percent.[a]

DPI can empower women by ensuring that they receive and *control* G2P transfers:

- *Pakistan.* Digital identification–linked cash transfers increased women's reported control over cash by 9 percentage points (Clark et al. 2022).

- *Niger.* Households where women received digital social assistance payments had 16 percent higher diet diversity than those who received benefits in cash (Aker et al. 2016).

- *India.* Digital payments increased female employment outside the household (Field et al. 2021).

DPI for online services can make lives easier:

- *Singapore.* eKYC, facilitated by the Singpass consented data-sharing service, reduced the time to complete digital transactions by 80 percent (OECD 2022).

- *Estonia.* The government, citizens, and residents save 820 years of working time every year thanks to the X-Tee data-sharing platform (Vainsalu 2017).

Benefits for businesses

Digitalization of G2P payments can expand access and improve services:

- *Zambia.* Choice-based payments under the Girls Education and Women's Empowerment and Livelihoods project allowed for greater competition among payment service providers, improved customer service (travel time dropped from six to two hours), and lowered transaction fees (cash-out fees dropped from US$3.35 to US$2.34) (Baur-Yazbeck, Hobson, and Chirmba 2021).[b]

DPI can lower the cost of doing business:

- *India.* The typical firm's onboarding cost is about Re 1,500 (US$23), which, through increased queriability, digitization, and interoperability of the Aadhaar system, is estimated to reduce onboarding costs to as little as Re 10 (US$0.15) (World Bank 2018).

(Continued)

BOX 4.2 Growing evidence on the impact of DPI *(Continued)*

- *Singapore.* Financial service providers saved up to US$50 to acquire each customer online using Singpass (Cooper, Marskell, and Chan 2022).

Benefits for government

DPI can achieve savings by lowering transaction and disbursement costs, improving targeting, and reducing leakages and identity-related fraud:

- *Zambia.* The cost to deliver payments fell from 4 percent to 2.8 percent of the payment value (Baur-Yazbeck, Hobson, and Chirmba 2021).

DPI can also strengthen trust by verifying data and identities and improving transparency:

- *India.* The introduction of biometric-based digital payments in employment and pension social programs reduced leakages by 41 percent (Muralidharan, Niehaus, and Sukhtankar 2016).

- *Türkiye.* Through the use of a common identifier and interoperable digital databases, the Integrated Social Assistance Service Information System, which is linked to 28 public databases, reduced the number of documents needed for applicants of social assistance programs from 17 to just 1, the time to apply from days to minutes, and the time to process applications and deliver the benefits from months to days (World Bank 2023).

During the COVID-19 pandemic, DPI enabled safe and effective scale-up of social protection:

- Analysis using data from 85 countries showed that, during the COVID-19 pandemic, countries that had elements of DPI in place (such as digital databases or ID records and data-sharing platforms) reached more than three times more beneficiaries than countries that had to collect new information (World Bank 2022b).

a. "Bihar India: Digitizing Cash Transfers Improves Women's Health," *World Bank Feature Story,* December 8, 2015 (https://www.worldbank.bihar-india-digitizing-cash-transfers-improves-womens-healthorg/en/news/feature/2015/12/08/).

b. For information on the Girls Education and Women's Empowerment and Livelihoods project, refer to https://projects.worldbank.org/en/projects-operations/project-detail/P151451.

Key gaps remain in access to IDs, e-signatures, data exchange, and digital payments

Government-recognized digital identification and authentication (that is, digital ID) for people and businesses are a critical function for digital interactions with governments, businesses, and other service providers—and thus the digital economy more broadly—yet they are still not widely available.[2] Their absence presents a significant barrier, as having a secure way to prove identity online is an important gateway for full participation in the digital economy. One estimate has found that digital ID can unlock economic value equivalent to 3–13 percent of gross domestic product (White et al. 2019). More fundamentally, a digital ID to transact securely online, especially through a mobile phone, can help citizens, small merchants, farmers, and poor households in rural and remote areas to access more services, markets, formal employment (for example, some gig work), and other opportunities being created by the digital economy. This equalizing effect is why countries such as Brazil, Indonesia, and Rwanda, for example, have recently launched digital ID initiatives with support from the World Bank. Box 4.3 elaborates on the example of Fayda (Ethiopia), FranceConnect (France), and eFaas (Maldives).

BOX 4.3 **Examples of digital IDs: Ethiopia's Fayda, France's FranceConnect, and Maldives' eFaas**

Ethiopia's Fayda

Fayda (meaning "value" or "utility" in several local languages) is Ethiopia's voluntary foundational digital identification (ID) system. Launched as a pilot in 2022, Fayda is addressing the fragmentation and exclusion caused by the existing IDs issued by local governments (*kebeles*), which cannot be verified, are not very secure, and cannot provide assurance as to the uniqueness of an individual (for example, to support delivery of social transfers). Fayda intends to be the basis for a broader digital public infrastructure ecosystem, including for consented data sharing and digital payments.

Using the Modular Open Source Identity Platform as the foundation of the system, much of the development and integration with specialized components for biometric recognition and other functions have been done in-house. Apart from the ID card, registered users can also download a digital equivalent of their ID in applications maintained by partners, such as mobile network operators and banks. More than 3 million people have registered with Fayda to date.

FIGURE B4.3.1 **Sample Fayda card issued by the Government of Ethiopia**

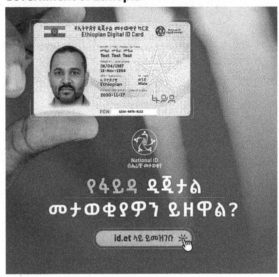

Source: National ID Program of Ethiopia, https://id.gov.et/services.

France's FranceConnect

Launched in 2016, FranceConnect is a federated digital ID ecosystem that allows French citizens and residents to access more than 1,500 public services online with their choice of digital ID provider from the public and private sectors. When users access a service through a website or application, they can select a digital ID provider with which they already have an account (for example, the post office or a mobile network operator) to authenticate themselves or create an account, with their identity verified based on data in relevant government registries and the "strength" of the digital ID (low, substantial, and high level) based on which data sources and documents they are using to log in. Some higher-risk public services, such as tax returns, may require a minimum strength of substantial or high.

FIGURE B4.3.2 **Screenshot of a menu of public services available through the FranceConnect system**

Source: FranceConnect, Interministerial Digital Department, Office of the Prime Minister, Government of France.

Interoperability is enabled by following the OpenID Connect open standard, and FranceConnect can be used to access public services anywhere in the European Union since it is part of the Electronic Identification and Trust Services (eIDAS) regulation trust framework. The FranceConnect

(Continued)

BOX 4.3 **Examples of digital IDs: Ethiopia's Fayda, France's FranceConnect, and Maldives' eFaas** *(Continued)*

connector, which orchestrates the transactions, is maintained by the Interministerial Digital Directorate. The government is also building a digital ID application (similar to eFaas and Singpass) called France Identité, which will be free to users and could comply with the eIDAS 2 regulation creating a decentralized digital ID ecosystem in the European Union.

Among all digital ID providers, FranceConnect facilitates 330 million transactions per year for 43 million users. In 2022, 30 million users authenticated themselves at least once.

Maldives' eFaas

eFaas is a digital ID service, built and maintained by the National Centre for Information Technology of Maldives. It is based on the physical national identity card, which is issued by the Department of National Registration. It has evolved from a simple single sign-on for online government services into a smartphone application.

Inspired by Singapore's Singpass in both functionality and design, eFaas allows citizens and residents to prove their identity in person by displaying a digital version of the

FIGURE B4.3.3 **Screenshot of a login page for eFaas**

Source: National Centre for Information Technology, Republic of Maldives, https:// efaas.egov.mv/.

national identity card and a verifiable quick response code or online through a single sign-on to access more than 450 online services, using a personal identification number and selfie verification. eFaas enables citizens and residents to transact with government and businesses without the need to travel between islands. It also functions as a digital wallet, allowing users to store their digital driving license, family card, and vaccination certifications, among others.

The eFaas login has more than 159,000 users (nearly half of the population ages 15–64), and the smartphone application version, which launched in June 2023, has 28,000 users. During the COVID-19 pandemic, the adoption of eFaas quadrupled (from 28,000 in 2019 to nearly 100,000 in 2021).

Note: Images do not depict actual IDs; they are examples generated by the agency issuing the ID.

An estimated 850 million people globally still do not have any official ID, an additional 220 million do not have a digital record of their identity, and an additional 400 million do not have a digitally verifiable identity document or identity records. These gaps are heavily concentrated in groups that may be vulnerable and marginalized, such as women, youth, low-income individuals, those in rural locations or with less education, and people out of the workforce (refer to figure 4.4). Closing this gap is key to achieving SDG target 16.9 to, "by 2030, provide a legal identity for all, including birth registration." More than 5 billion people (or 3.5 billion adults) do not have access to systems and credentials that would enable secure, remote digital authentication to facilitate access to online services and transactions. Even in the 75 economies where such digital identity solutions exist for transacting online—mostly in high-income countries—there are gaps in the ease of obtaining and using the required digital credentials, the ease of subsequent authentications when accessing a service or conducting a transaction, and the range of services and transactions that are accessible remotely, online.

Similarly, the use of e-signatures is limited in lower-middle-income and low-income countries for various reasons. E-signatures—when paired with proper regulation—have the same legal standing as traditional signatures, enabling contracts to be signed remotely and facilitating greater

FIGURE 4.4 **Gaps in access to official identification, by demographics and country income group, 2021**

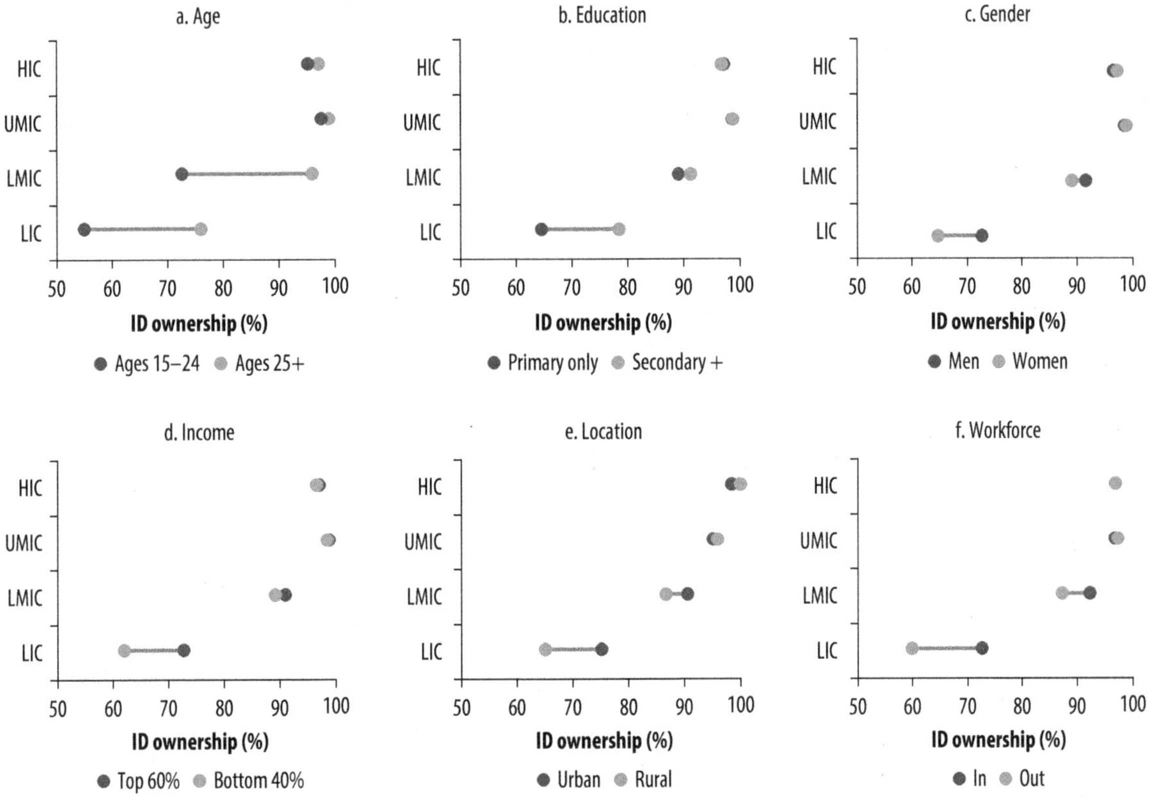

Sources: Clark, Metz, and Casher 2022; Demirgüç-Kunt et al. 2022.
Note: Information on rural versus urban location was only available for the subset of economies where face-to-face data collection was possible in 2021. Includes respondents ages 15 and older who are over the eligible age for obtaining an ID. HIC = high-income countries; ID = identification; LIC = low-income countries; LMIC = lower-middle-income countries; UMIC = upper-middle-income countries.

trust and assurance in remote transactions, which are essential for a vibrant digital economy. Only 96 economies have fully operationalized both the legal frameworks and the technological infrastructure (for example, public key infrastructure and certificate authorities) for e-signatures. Of these, 42 are high-income countries (of 62 high-income countries) and a further 27 are upper-middle-income countries. An additional 28 economies have both the necessary legal frameworks and the infrastructure but have not yet operationalized them. Some of the key challenges include the limited set of use cases for e-signatures, the cost and complexity of developing sustainable public key infrastructure, and low supervisory capacity to create a competitive marketplace of third-party e-signature providers. For instance, 35 economies have regulations, but are still developing the technological infrastructure.

Enabling seamless exchange and reuse of data, with appropriate safeguards against risks of misuse, is key to improving government services, as well as enabling businesses to reuse responsibly the data that government holds. The "Once Only" principle dictates that people and businesses should only have to provide information to the government on a single occasion and that data can be reused for other transactions. Interoperability frameworks and data exchange platforms (for example, government service buses and API gateways) facilitate data to move both horizontally (such as across ministries) and vertically (across different levels of government). Moreover, when governments can make the data it holds available to people, academia, civil society, and businesses—again, with appropriate safeguards to protect personal data—doing so can unlock innovation. For example, if people can share information about their official driving history, they may be able to access less expensive and more tailored insurance products. Similarly, if they can share their health information with health care providers, they may receive higher-quality and better-informed care.

Data exchange is an area for improvement: although 89 economies reportedly have a functional data exchange platform, 65 of them are high-income or upper-middle-income countries. Good examples of such data exchange platforms include Singapore's APEX (Cooper, Marskell, and Chan 2022) and Estonia's X-Tee, both of which are widely used and depend on consent of the data subject for triggering the exchange of personal data. Estonia has made the underlying technology for X-Tee available as a digital public good (open-source software), which has been used by or has inspired countries such as Cambodia, Finland, Mauritius, and Namibia. A further 24 economies are in the process of building data exchange platforms, leaving 85 economies without this important DPI element. Box 4.4 highlights a few data-sharing examples.

BOX 4.4   **Data-sharing examples: India's DigiLocker, Singapore's APEX, and Uganda's UGHub**

India's DigiLocker

Launched in 2015, DigiLocker is a secure personal document wallet and 1 gigabyte of cloud storage that the government of India offers to every person registered with Aadhaar. Digital documents shared via DigiLocker can be securely verified and have the same legal effect as physical equivalents. Users can either upload scans of documents or request documents to be uploaded on their behalf. Sharing is based on consent of the individual, and users can revoke their consent to third-party access. As of September 2023, there are 197 million users, 6.3 billion issued documents, 1,684 document issuers, and 187 requesters. The COVID-19 pandemic drove significant adoption, with 23 million users in 2019.

Singapore's APEX

APEX is a governmentwide application programming interface (API) management solution (Cooper, Marskell, and Chan 2022) that enables government agencies to publish and manage access to their APIs and to discover other APIs. Unlike the enterprise service bus approach, which creates a central infrastructure that data may pass through, APEX facilitates bilateral connections between systems and databases, which can provide more flexibility and scalability.

The number of APIs supported through APEX has surpassed 2,000, including more than 45 agencies, approximately half of all government agencies in Singapore. The level of traffic has surpassed 100 million transactions per month, with peaks, on average, exceeding 300 million transactions per month. APEX is a backbone of Singapore's national digital ID (Singpass) and is integrated with the Singpass consented data-sharing service, which empowers Singapore citizens, residents, and businesses to grant access to trusted data that the government holds about them. APEX eases access to services by saving time and lowering costs and improves the quality of data submitted to government agencies and businesses. Singpass is estimated to save as much as S$50 per eKYC transaction conducted for opening a financial account.

Uganda's UGHub

Following the enterprise service bus model of a central infrastructure and using the open-source WSO2 technology stack, UGHub is a systems and data integration platform. As of August 2023 and following two years of operations, 47 public entities and 66 private entities (for example, banks and universities) connected to exchange personal and nonpersonal data in a secure, seamless manner more than 100 million times. UGHub was developed by the National IT Authority, with financing from the World Bank's Regional Communications Infrastructure Program.

One of the most critical economic development objectives that digital technologies can enable is financial inclusion, which in many low- and middle-income countries has manifested in the form of mobile money accounts and payments. Its aim of "banking the unbanked" has overhauled financial services, especially for individuals in rural areas with no access to formal finance, improving financial inclusion in lower-income countries (Demirgüç-Kunt et al. 2022), and this trend increased during the global pandemic. According to World Bank Findex data collected from around 130 countries, more people had a mobile money account than an account at a financial institution in low-income countries in 2021 (26 percent versus 25 percent; refer to figure 4.5, panel a). Ownership of a mobile money account also grew faster than ownership of an account in a formal financial institution in lower-middle-income and low-income countries from 2017 to 2021.

While the percentage of adults with a formal financial account in low- and middle-income countries jumped to 71 percent in 2021 (from 63 percent in 2017), only 57 percent of adults in low- and middle-income countries made or received some sort of digital payment, and only 37 percent did so with a merchant (Demirgüç-Kunt et al. 2022). In China and Mongolia, more than 80 percent of adults made digital merchant payments in 2021 (refer to figure 4.5, panel b). By contrast, in India, only 12 percent of adults made a digital merchant payment, and two-thirds of those who made a digital merchant payment did so for the first time after the onset of COVID-19. One significant opportunity is the rapid rise of fast or real-time payment systems, which have been launched or announced in about 100 jurisdictions. Together, the 24/7/365 availability of these systems and the instant availability of funds to recipients boost trust and convenience for users, while spurring competition and innovation from a diverse range of providers, including banks and nonbanks.

The COVID-19 crisis highlighted how DPI can play a critical role for governments to deliver social assistance quickly and safely. DPI not only allowed governments to reach an unprecedented number of new beneficiaries, but also allowed them to make payments remotely. Millions of

FIGURE 4.5 **Adoption of digital financial services**

a. Mobile money and financial account ownership, 2017 and 2021

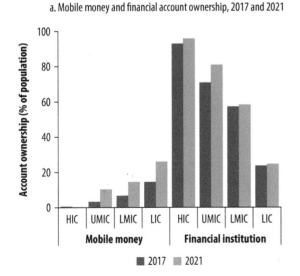

b. Digital merchant payments made, 2021

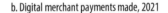
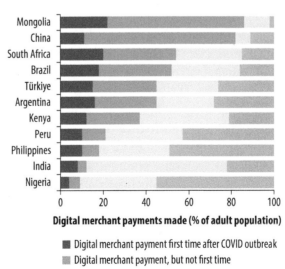

Source: Demirgüç-Kunt et al. 2022.
Note: HIC = high-income countries. UMIC = upper-middle-income countries; LMIC = lower-middle-income countries; LIC = low-income countries.

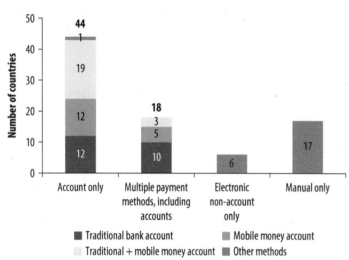

FIGURE 4.6 Number of payment methods used during the COVID-19 response, by number of countries, as of May 2021

Source: World Bank 2022b.

people were brought into the social protection and financial system for the first time. Scaling up social assistance presented two separate but related challenges: first, adapting targeting and registration to reach individuals not commonly included in social assistance databases, such as urban informal workers, and second, delivering G2P payments safely and securely in the context of the pandemic.

Countries also used digital systems to tackle the second challenge, with 80 percent of the countries analyzed starting to use digital payments for delivering at least one of their new or expanded social assistance programs as of May 2021 (refer to figure 4.6). Most countries that used digital payments to deliver COVID-response payments had already implemented digital payments to some extent prior to the pandemic; however, several countries used them for the first time, facilitating a long-term shift to modern social assistance payments.

When G2P payments are deposited digitally into accounts—mobile money or traditional accounts, such as banks or microfinance institutions—they not only reach more people quickly and safely and reduce leakages and corruption, but also create a pathway to financial inclusion and women's economic empowerment. The Global Findex 2021 finds that 865 million account owners (or around 18 percent), including 423 million women in low- and middle-income economies, opened their first financial institution account for the purpose of receiving money from the government. Among those who reported receiving government transfers, around 65 percent received it digitally, with no significant difference between men and women, and around 15 percent did so in cash.

Opening an account and receiving payments into it are just the first step toward financial inclusion. The Global Findex 2021 also shows that in low- and middle-income economies around 7 out of every 10 persons who received government transfers into an account also made a digital payment compared to only about half in 2017. Such payments included using the internet to pay bills or make a purchase (49 percent) or using a mobile account to make an in-store purchase (54 percent). Beyond digital payments, 34 percent also saved in a formal financial institution or through a mobile money account. The increasing use of accounts by beneficiaries for more than taking out cash indicates strong progress toward bridging the gap between access and use of formal financial services.[3]

Countries that shifted to digital payments during the pandemic, even if partially, now can leverage that investment to facilitate a long-term shift to modern G2P payments. The digitalization of COVID-19 response programs led to an increase in account ownership, and provided a pathway to increasing financial inclusion only if this momentum was leveraged to develop and sustain the necessary enablers. At least 62 countries have leveraged account-based transfers for their COVID-19 response social assistance programs to some extent. Many of them are using accounts as their method of paying social assistance for the first time. Yet in many cases, these account-based payments have been adopted only for temporary COVID-19 programs. Unless governments make conscious efforts to adopt these account-based payments across other social assistance programs and government payment streams, there is a risk of reversing the important strides made in building the ecosystem needed to deliver digital payments.

How to build good DPI

A growing body of experiences, evidence, and principles is cultivating a shared understanding of what is generally needed to make DPI work at scale and what are the risks and challenges (refer to exhibit 4.1). However, what works in a particular country will depend on the local context.

EXHIBIT 4.1 **How to build good digital public infrastructure**

Success factors	Challenges and risks
• *Focus on use cases.* Building digital public infrastructure (DPI) for its own sake is unlikely to achieve high adoption. The design of DPI should be driven by solving real-world problems that people, firms, and government agencies face.	• *Exclusion from services.* Poorly designed DPI can create unnecessary barriers for people and firms to access services. Systems and processes need to be reimagined, since digitalizing poor practices will lead to poor digital practices.
• *Prioritize inclusion and universal accessibility.* DPI should be designed to work for all parts of society, which means accommodating various factors (for example, access to digital infrastructure and devices, awareness, skills, and trust in technology) and ensuring accessibility for individuals with different needs, including those with disabilities.	• *Data protection and security breaches.* Leaks and misuse of data, not just of DPI but also of the applications using DPI, can erode public trust and have potentially disastrous consequences. Continuous investment in security postures and in legal and institutional frameworks for protecting personal data can reduce these risks.
• *Build public trust and accountability.* Adoption is enabled at a faster rate when all stakeholders have confidence that DPI works as intended and is in their best interests and that grievance redress mechanisms are in place.	• *Vendor and technology lock-in.* Inadequately selected or procured technology can lead to a dependence that makes it harder to adapt DPI and can increase the total cost of ownership in the medium and long terms. The risk can be reduced substantially by building capacity to manage procurement and contracts effectively, by using modular designs, and by adopting open standards.
• *A whole-of-country approach and public-private partnership.* The shift in mind-set requires coordination and collaboration across a wide range of stakeholders; a whole-of-country approach benefits from having a singular vision.	• *Inertia and legacy legal frameworks.* Resistance to the changes that can be brought about by DPI can come from a variety of sources. A comprehensive review and reform of laws and regulations may be needed to address this key bottleneck.
• *Promote interoperability.* The true power of DPI comes when different layers or elements can work together to enable exponential innovation. The adoption of common standards and open application programming interfaces can help to address this need.	
• *Strengthen capacity and culture in government.* Civil servants need incentives to take risks and to think and act boldly. Budget and procurement policies may also need to be made fit-for-purpose.	
• *Cross-border use of DPI.* As DPI gains global traction, there is an opportunity for enhanced regional and international cooperation to establish standards for cross-border use. This cooperation includes mutual recognition of digital IDs, interoperable fast payment systems, and secure data sharing. Such cooperation can lower the costs and risks associated with international transactions, such as remittances, access to services across borders, and cross-border data flows.	

Source: World Bank.

Notes

1. "Digital IDs Are an Effective Tool against Poverty," Bill and Melinda Gates Foundation (https://www.gatesfoundation.org/ideas/articles/mosip-digital-id-systems).
2. Such services can be provided through multiple digital identity ecosystems, operated by governments or the private sector, or provided through centralized, federated, or decentralized architectures. In some cases, they are provided by the same entity responsible for traditional forms of official identification (for example, a digital version of a national ID or population register); in others, they are built on top of such systems and leverage them for digital ID onboarding (for example, Europe's eIDAS federation or new e-wallet or Australia's Trusted Digital Identity Framework). For a typology of architectures for government-recognized digital identity, refer to World Bank (2022a).
3. This analysis is based on Desai, Klapper, and Natarjan (2022).

References

Aker, Jenny C., Rachid Boumnijel, Amanda McClellan, and Niall Tierney. 2016. "Payment Mechanisms and Antipoverty Programs: Evidence from a Mobile Money Cash Transfer Experiment in Niger." *Economic Development and Cultural Change* 65 (1): 1–37.

Baur-Yazbeck, Silvia, Emma Wadie Hobson, and Mutale Chirmba. 2021. "The Future of Government-to-Person (G2P) Payments: 3 Years of Learning about G2P Choice in Zambia." CGAP Background Document, *FinDev Gateway*, April 2021. https://www.findevgateway.org/paper/2021/04/future-government-person-g2p-payments-three-years-learning-about-g2p-choice-zambia.

Clark, Julia Michal, Muhammad Haseeb, Umm E. Amen Jalal, Bilal Murtaza Siddiqi, and Kate Vyborny. 2022. "Using Biometrics to Deliver Cash Payments to Women: Early Results from an Impact Evaluation in Pakistan." ID4D Evidence Note, World Bank Group, Washington, DC. http://documents.worldbank.org/curated/en/099155004142238180/P1763410d1e1af00108e170e5754d04fed9.

Clark, Julia Michal, Anna Metz, and Claire Casher. 2022. *ID4D Global Dataset—Volume 1 2021: Global ID Coverage Estimates*. Washington, DC: World Bank Group. http://documents.worldbank.org/curated/en/099705012232226786/P176341032c1ef0b20adf10abad304425ef.

Cooper, Adam Kenneth, Jonathan Daniel Marskell, and Cheow Hoe Chan. 2022. *National Digital Identity and Government Data Sharing in Singapore: A Case Study of Singpass and APEX*. Washington, DC: World Bank Group. http://documents.worldbank.org/curated/en/099300010212228518/P171592079b3e50d70a1630d5663205bf94.

Demirgüç-Kunt, Asli, Leora Klapper, Dorothe Singer, and Saniya Ansar. 2022. *The Global Findex Database 2021: Financial Inclusion, Digital Payments, and Resilience in the Age of COVID-19*. Washington, DC: World Bank.

Desai, Vyjayanti, Leora Klapper, and Harish Natarjan. 2022. "Does Digitizing Government Payments Increase Financial Access and Usage?" *Brookings* (blog), November 15, 2022. https://www.brookings.edu/blog/future-development/2022/11/15/does-digitizing-government-payments-increase-financial-access-and-usage/.

Desai, Vyjayanti, Jonathan Marskell, Georgina Marin, and Minita Varghese. 2023. "How Digital Public Infrastructure Supports Empowerment, Inclusion, and Resilience." *Digital Development* (blog), March 15, 2023. https://blogs.worldbank.org/digital-development/how-digital-public-infrastructure-supports-empowerment-inclusion-and-resilience.

Field, Erica, Rohini Pande, Natalia Rigol, Simone Schaner, and Charity Troyer Moore. 2021. "On Her Own Account: How Strengthening Women's Financial Control Impacts Labor Supply and Gender Norms." *American Economic Review* 111 (7): 234–75.

G20 India. 2023. "Digital Economy Ministers' Meeting—Outcome Statement and Chair's Summary." G20 India, Bengaluru, August 19, 2023. https://www.g20.org/content/dam/gtwenty/gtwenty_new/document/G20_Digital_Economy_Outcome_Document%20_and_Chair%27s_Summary_19082023.pdf.

Global Partnership for Financial Inclusion. 2023. *G20 Policy Recommendations for Advancing Financial Inclusion and Productivity Gains through Digital Public Infrastructure.* Washington, DC: Global Partnership for Financial Inclusion. https://www.g20.org/content/dam/gtwenty/gtwenty_new /document/G20_POLICY_RECOMMENDATIONS.pdf.

Lara de Arruda, Pedro, Marina Lazarotto de Andrade, Tiago Falcao, Diana Teixeira Barbosa, and Matteo Morgandi. 2022. "The Payment System Used by Auxilio Emergencial: Introduction of the Digital Social Account, and the Banking of More than 100 Million People in 9 Months." Technical Note 2, World Bank, Brasilia. http://hdl.handle.net/10986/36837.

Metz, Anna, Georgina Marin, Jonathan Marksell, Julia Clark, and Karol Karpinski. 2022. "A Digital Stack for Transforming Service Delivery: ID, Payments, and Data Sharing." ID4D/G2Px Practitioner's Note, World Bank Group, Washington, DC. https://documents1.worldbank.org /curated/en/099755004072288910/pdf/P1715920edb5990d60b83e037f756213782.pdf.

Muralidharan, Karthik, Paul Niehaus, and Sandip Sukhtankar. 2016. "Building State Capacity: Evidence from Biometric Smartcards in India." *American Economic Review* 106 (10): 2895–929.

Nordic Institute for Interoperability Solutions. 2023. *X-Road World Map.* Tallin: Nordic Institute for Interoperability Solutions. https://x-road.global/xroad-world-map.

OECD (Organisation for Economic Co-operation and Development). 2022. "Singapore's National Digital Identity—Singpass." *Observatory of Public Sector Innovation* (blog), November 16, 2022.

Poole, Emily, Carl Toohey, and Peter Harris. 2014. "Public Infrastructure: A Framework for Decision-Making." *Reserve Bank of Australia (RBA) Annual Conference,* 97–135. Sydney: Reserve Bank of Australia. https://www.rba.gov.au/publications/confs/2014/pdf/poole-toohey-harris.pdf.

Rockefeller Foundation, Digital Public Goods Alliance, and Norway Ministry of Foreign Affairs. 2021. *Co-Develop: Digital Public Infrastructure for an Equitable Recovery.* New York: Rockefeller Foundation. https://www.rockefellerfoundation.org/wp-content/uploads/2021/08/Co-Develop -Digital-Public-Infrastructure-for-an-Equitable-Recovery-Full-Report.pdf.

Vainsalu, Heiko. 2017. "How Do Estonians Save Annually 820 Years of Work without Much Effort?" *e-Estonia* (blog), December 12, 2017. https://e-estonia.com/how-save-annually-820-years-of-work/.

White, Olivia, Anu Madgavkar, James Manyika Mumbai, Deepa Mahajan, Jacques Bughin, Michael McCarthy, and Owen Sperling. 2019. *Digital Identification: A Key to Inclusive Growth.* New York: McKinsey Global Institute. https://www.mckinsey.com/capabilities/mckinsey-digital/our-insights /digital-identification-a-key-to-inclusive-growth.

World Bank. 2018. *Private Sector Economic Impacts from Identification Systems.* Washington, DC: World Bank.

World Bank 2022a. *ID4D Federated Ecosystems for Digital ID.* Washington, DC: World Bank Group. http://documents.worldbank.org/curated/en/099745012232218303/P17159208cf1d501a0af6f 001e4852997fc.

World Bank. 2022b. *The Role of Digital in the COVID-19 Social Assistance Response.* Washington, DC: World Bank. http://hdl.handle.net/10986/38104.

World Bank. 2023. *Deep Dive into the Ecosystem for the Delivery of Social Assistance Payments: Türkiye Case Study.* Washington, DC: World Bank.

World Bank. Forthcoming. *Mozambique SP COVID-19 Response Survey.* Washington, DC: World Bank.

Artificial Intelligence: Revolutionary Potential and Huge Uncertainties | 5

Yan Liu, Hans Christian Boy, Saloni Khurana, and Anshuman Sinha

KEY MESSAGES

- The development of large language models (LLMs) represents a remarkable stride in the field of artificial intelligence (AI). LLMs' ability to interpret natural language prompts correctly and generate completely original text, audio, image, and video content that is indistinguishable from human-made content has propelled them to the forefront of AI research and commercialization.

- AI holds potential to accelerate productivity growth, expand opportunities, improve consumer welfare, and bring vast benefits to the global economy and society. However, the use of AI systems and tools could also cement big tech's market dominance, displace workers, widen inequality, strengthen the state's surveillance abilities, erode privacy, turbocharge misinformation, manipulate democratic processes, and increase security vulnerabilities.

- AI can help low- and middle-income countries to tackle a range of development challenges. However, AI may also devalue the comparative advantages of low- and middle-income countries, lead to a deterioration of their terms of trade, divert investment, and eventually widen the technology, productivity, and income gaps between rich and poor countries.

- Countries are adopting divergent approaches and priorities in AI governance. Regulatory strategies must navigate the complexities and potential biases inherent in AI, addressing the juxtaposition of economic growth, efficiency, transparency, privacy, national security, and societal impacts. Regulatory fragmentation may hinder AI innovation and development, create enforcement gaps and trade barriers, lead to regulatory arbitrage, and diminish the effectiveness of such regulations.

- Low- and middle-income countries are formulating AI strategies to accelerate safe and inclusive AI adoption, with a focus on building infrastructure, developing digital skills, and adopting AI solutions. Such efforts echo with the views of industry leaders, who emphasize the urgency for low- and middle-income countries to invest in digital infrastructure and prepare the workforce for the disruptions that AI may bring.

Transformer models and large language models mark a new stage in artificial intelligence development

OpenAI's release of ChatGPT in late 2022 immediately caused a sensation, and generative artificial intelligence (AI) became a hot topic for technologists, investors, policy makers, and society. While the concept of AI dates to the 1950s, it was only in recent years that the capabilities of AI have improved significantly thanks to the availability of massive data, better algorithms, and more powerful computer hardware. AI is already pervasive in many aspects of our everyday lives, from image and speech recognition to personalized ads, robots, and self-driving vehicles. Generative AI, a category of system that can create wholly novel content, is much newer. It has spurred a new wave of AI investment, stirred fear about job displacement, and raised important questions for society, the economy, and governance. This chapter delves into the most recent breakthroughs in AI, summarizes the empirical evidence and projections of its potential benefits and risks, and highlights the regulatory trends and debates.

AI has evolved from rules-based systems in the 1970s and 1980s to machine learning and more recently to deep learning. As a subfield of machine learning, deep learning refers to algorithms inspired by the structure and function of the human brain called artificial neural networks. The adjective "deep" in deep learning refers to the use of multiple layers in the network. Unlike conventional machine learning models that reach a performance plateau after ingesting a certain amount of data, deep learning models continue to improve. This feature has established deep learning as a vital tool in sectors flooded with unstructured data.

The progress of large language models (LLMs)—foundational models that use deep learning in processing and generating natural language—represents a remarkable stride in the AI field. LLMs are a type of neural network model, and they usually consist of hundreds of billions of parameters. LLMs are based on the transformer architecture. The transformer model, a groundbreaking method in the field of natural language processing, was proposed by Alphabet in 2017 and gained widespread popularity. Transformers revolutionized neural networks by introducing self-attention, allowing them to capture intricate relationships in sequences in a parallelized manner. This departure from sequential processing, coupled with positional encoding and transfer learning, underpins their success across diverse tasks, making transformers a cornerstone of modern machine learning (Vaswani et al. 2017). LLMs have attained a level of sophistication previously unimaginable. Their ability to interpret natural language prompts correctly and to generate completely original text, audio, image, and video content that is indistinguishable from human-made content has propelled them to the forefront of AI research and commercialization (Brown et al. 2020).

When compared to other AI disciplines, the growth and adoption of LLMs are striking. The number of published significant LLMs has multiplied recently, and LLMs are now among the most sophisticated and costliest AI developments, with the number of model parameters growing exponentially (refer to figure 5.1, panel a). While academia dominated the development of AI models until the early 2010s, industry-led developments have since taken the lead (refer to figure 5.1, panel b).

New generative AI start-ups have been entering the market at a swift pace, with content generation and generative AI infrastructure gaining the most traction from investors. In the first half of 2023, the space received US$14.1 billion in equity funding (including US$10 billion to OpenAI), more than five-fold compared to full-year 2022. Even excluding the OpenAI deal, investment in this area increased 30 percent from full-year 2022 (CB Insights 2023a). Eighteen generative AI companies have hit unicorn status. Text and visual media generation is the most crowded space. Solutions in

FIGURE 5.1 **Number of model parameters for significant published AIs, by domain and type of institution, 1940–2020**

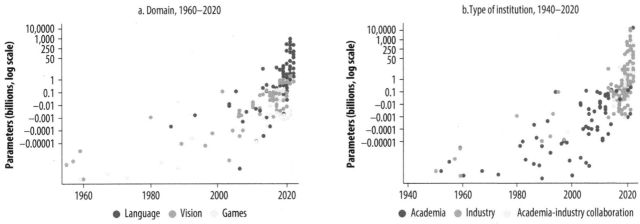

Source: HAI 2023.
Note: AI = artificial intelligence.

these areas primarily target social media and marketing content, enterprise AI avatars, and text summarization. Investors are also betting big on generative AI infrastructure, including foundational models and application programming interfaces, machine learning operations platforms, and vector databases.[1] These solutions enable the development, scale, and use of generative AI. Likely due to the capital-intensive nature of developing LLMs, generative AI infrastructure has received more than 70 percent of funding since the third quarter of 2022 across just 10 percent of all generative AI deals (CB Insights 2023b).

Various start-ups are also using generative AI for industry-specific applications. In health care, start-up firms like Cradle and Insilico Medicine help biologists to design proteins and drugs using generative AI (Zhavoronkov et al. 2019). Legal start-up Harvey creates custom LLMs for law firms to facilitate processes like contract analysis, due diligence, litigation, and regulatory compliance (Merken 2023). Other legal AI start-ups build tools that search for case-related information and assist in writing drafts. In finance, start-ups use generative AI to assist in investment research and create financial models. In education, start-ups use AI to generate quizzes and questions, create personal study tools, and train employees. In industry and manufacturing, vendors use generative AI to design construction sites, building architecture, floor plans, parts, and components (CB Insights 2023b).

Potential benefits and risks of AI

As a potential general-purpose and transformative technology, AI promises to accelerate productivity growth and bring vast benefits to the global economy and society. However, it also presents new risks and pitfalls. Just like other technologies, AI will affect different people, firms, and geographies differently, potentially exacerbating inequality and polarization within and across countries. AI and underlying data can also aggravate rising concerns over privacy, algorithm bias, political control, and surveillance. AI could erode an already embattled information ecosystem by flooding it with inaccuracies and misinformation and deepening social divides and political polarization. AI also poses new cybersecurity risks and vulnerabilities. Low- and middle-income countries may have more reasons to be concerned than high-income economies, as AI threatens to devalue their comparative advantages and undermine their terms of trade, potentially arresting or even reversing their convergence in standards of living with rich countries.

While large-scale deployment of AI is still in the early stages, empirical evidence on the impacts of AI is emerging. Theoretical modeling and projections on the potential benefits and risks of AI have also proliferated. This section summarizes the potential benefits and risks of AI.

Potential benefits

Driving innovation and productivity growth

AI has become a competitiveness differentiator for firms. AI enhances firm performance through two main channels: (1) product innovation and (2) process innovation and operating cost reduction (Babina et al. 2022). By embracing AI, firms can streamline and automate tasks, optimize resource deployment, produce better and novel products, and mitigate risks. Such improvements underpin potential growth in revenue and profits, better customer relationships, and market expansion (Babina et al. 2022). Several studies have shown that firms that have invested in and deployed AI have experienced higher growth in product innovation, labor force, sales, profits, net operating efficiency, and market valuations (Babina et al. 2022; Mikalef and Gupta 2021; Mishra and Pani 2021; Mishra et al. 2022).

Generative AI is also expected to enhance productivity across industries. For example, Industrial GPT (Generative Pre-trained Transformer) leverages industrial data sets for pretraining, industrial scenarios for fine-tuning, and domain knowledge for reinforcement learning. To enhance its use in the manufacturing industry, a new service mode called Model as a Service has been incorporated into cloud computing, enabling efficient and flexible delivery of customized industrial and general-purpose technology models for specific businesses (Wang, Liu, and Shen 2023). Generative AI is also being used in computer-aided design to create product plans in 2D and 3D, a concept known as generative design. The technology can help to optimize designs for specific uses and be employed to create custom parts and products across various industries, including aerospace, automotive, and medical equipment (Mondal, Das, and Vrana 2023). In many white-collar occupations, generative AI can empower workers to perform a wide range of tasks more efficiently and free them up to do more meaningful things.

Creating new and better jobs

The introduction of innovative technologies frequently expands job opportunities and gives rise to novel and better-paid occupations. Autor et al. (2022) highlight the quantitative significance of this phenomenon, revealing that more than 60 percent of employment in the United States in 2018 was attributed to job titles that did not exist in 1940. These new jobs may hold higher value than traditional ones due to the initial scarcity and premium associated with novel expertise and specialization. Acemoglu et al. (2022) report an observable surge in AI-related vacancies in the United States since 2010, driven by establishments whose workers engage in tasks compatible with AI's current capabilities. An analysis of LinkedIn data from Latin American countries by Collett, Gomes, and Neff (2022) suggests that half of the 20 fastest-growing skills (including AI) are linked directly to technological advancements. In India, the demand for AI-related skills has been growing exponentially since 2016, and these roles offer substantially higher wages than other white-collar service jobs (Copestake et al. 2023).

Many new clerical service jobs have been created as part of the AI ecosystem, and many of these jobs are in low- and middle-income countries. In supervised learning, which is the prevalent form of AI, algorithms require millions of prelabeled images to recognize images accurately. This process necessitates substantial human effort. For example, according to a report from Axios, 1 hour of video data pertaining to autonomous driving could require up to 800 hours of human labor for data labeling (Waddell 2019). Data labelers manually annotate and categorize data to train AI models. They are found across the globe, influenced by factors like labor costs, language proficiency, and access to digital infrastructure. These individuals perform tasks that can be done remotely and do not require specialized training, expanding their presence across a wide range of locations. The size of the data-labeling market is estimated at between US$1 billion and US$3 billion and is likely to experience double-digit growth for the remainder of the decade.

AI is also leading to gains in economic efficiency by optimizing the hiring process and improving the quality of job-candidate matching. For instance, companies employ AI platforms to match candidates' skills and experience automatically with suitable job openings, resulting in substantial time and cost reductions in recruitment. This matching not only accelerates onboarding but also decreases training costs and productivity ramp-up time. Moreover, these AI-driven job platforms facilitate a more inclusive hiring process by discovering diverse talent pools and mitigating bias in job descriptions and communications (Mearian 2023).

Increasing consumer welfare

AI can improve consumer welfare by offering cheaper, better, and personalized products and shopping experiences (Mondal, Das, and Vrana 2023). For example, Google's AI-driven Shopping Graph tool enables highly personalized shopping experiences by analyzing billions of product listings and aligning them with consumer preferences (Rockinson 2023). Consumers benefit from this tailored approach, which saves them time and effort in finding the products they need. At the same time, retailers can sell their products more efficiently by reaching the right customers, reducing surplus inventory, and enhancing sales turnover.

Improving government efficiency and effectiveness

AI integration within public institutions offers considerable benefits, enhancing public service delivery and aiding in effective governance. This integration can occur in three main ways: influencing policy making, streamlining government operations, and improving core functions within government organizations (Van Noordt and Misuraca 2022). AI's capacity for data analysis and interpretation enables a more data-driven approach to policy making. This approach facilitates the swift identification of social issues and allows for informed analysis of potential policy solutions, fostering a more responsive and effective decision-making process. Through process automation and augmentation of staff via AI recommendations, governments can improve their productivity.

Risks and uncertainties

Job automation or augmentation?

AI could augment workers in some tasks and replace workers entirely in some other tasks. It is challenging to determine precisely what proportion of labor across different economies can be augmented or replaced by current or future AI systems. Several recent studies have assessed the automation and augmentation potential of various occupations based on job definitions and typical tasks (Eloundou et al. 2023; Gmyrek, Berg, and Bescond 2023; WEF 2023).

Clerical support roles, such as typists and data entry clerks, showed the highest automation potential, with more than 50 percent of the tasks being automatable. In contrast, elementary

FIGURE 5.2 **Automation and augmentation potential, by gender and country income group**

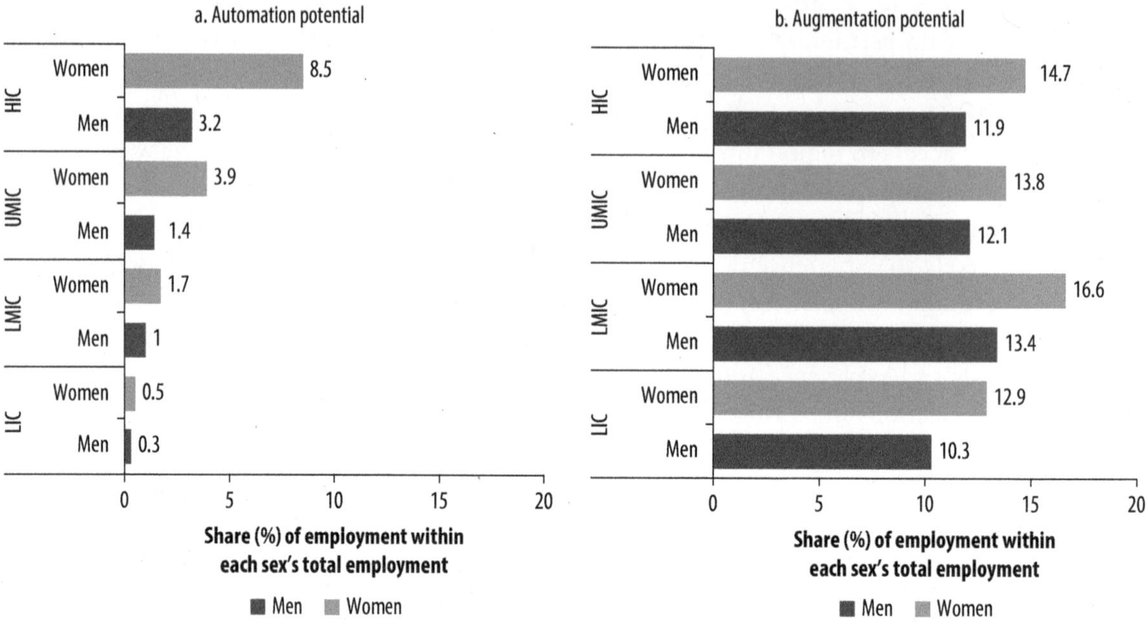

Source: Gmyrek, Berg, and Bescond 2023.
Note: HIC = high-income countries; UMIC = upper-middle-income countries; LMIC = lower-middle-income countries; LIC = low-income countries.

occupations, agricultural workers, and crafts-related workers demonstrated minimal automation potential, with less than 10 percent of tasks being susceptible to automation. Many professional service occupations that require abstract reasoning skills have the highest augmentation potential.

When these results are aggregated into country-level estimates, high-income countries have the largest share of jobs with automation potential. Low- and middle-income countries have a similar share of jobs with high augmentation potential as high-income countries (refer to figure 5.2). However, such projects are inherently limited. They cannot predict the capabilities of future AI technologies. There is, therefore, a conceivable risk that the automation potential may be systematically underestimated.

Widen or reduce income inequality?

AI could increase inequality as the benefits of technological advances often flow primarily to highly skilled labor and capital owners (Moll, Rachel, and Restrepo 2022). Yang (2022) found that AI innovations in electronics companies in Taiwan, China, favor high-skilled labor, reducing the share of the workforce with educational qualifications of college level and below. Tyson and Zysman (2022) found a polarization of income and jobs due to sluggish growth of wages for low- and middle-skilled workers and wage premiums for highly educated workers. These trends, they argued, lead to a dissociation of wage growth from productivity growth, a drop in the share of labor in value added, and an escalation of wage inequality. The researchers predicted that AI not only will sustain these adverse labor trends, but could even exacerbate them, driving further employment polarization, wage stagnation for low-skilled workers, increasing income inequality, and a dwindling supply of quality jobs.

Moreover, the advantages of scale and being early adopters of AI can exacerbate the income gap within and between countries (Ernst, Merola, and Samaan 2019). Drawing from industry and patent data across 283 regions in 32 European countries, Pinheiro et al. (2022) suggested that AI technologies may heighten regional disparities. They found that regions with lower income and less complex technology adopt simpler technologies, whereas regions with higher income and more complex technology lean more toward intricate technologies and industries. This pattern, observed over a 15-year period, implies that AI-driven diversification could intensify, rather than alleviate, regional economic inequalities, deepening the divide between regions in terms of income and technological complexity. This situation jeopardizes the progress made in poverty reduction and access to technology in low- and middle-income nations. Without a fairer international system, low-income countries may not fully benefit from lower capital costs due to barriers set by leading innovative firms, hindering technology diffusion.

However, experimental evidence shows that generative AI can boost labor productivity and expand job opportunities, especially for lower-skilled and less-experienced workers, which could ultimately lower inequality among workers and expand the middle class (Agrawal, Gans, and Goldfarb 2023; Webb 2020). Three recent empirical studies tested the effect of adopting generative AI tools by very different types of users. Brynjolfsson, Li, and Raymond (2023) found that call center agents who used ChatGPT tools could handle 14 percent more customer inquiries per hour. Noy and Zhang (2023) documented that business professionals who used ChatGPT could write much faster and that the quality of writing improved significantly. Peng et al. (2023) showed that programmers who use GitHub Copilot could code 56 percent faster. All three studies consistently found that lower-skilled and less-experienced workers benefited the most. This result is driven mainly by the ability of generative AI to embody the best practices of high-skilled workers, which traditional, human-based organizational processes in businesses have had difficulty disseminating because these best practices involve tacit knowledge.

Big tech's market dominance

AI's digital nature has created an environment where first-mover advantages can be significant, potentially amplifying the disparity between early adopters operating at the forefront of technology and other companies (Agrawal, Gans, and Goldfarb 2019; Brynjolfsson, Jin, and McElheran 2021; Ernst, Merola, and Samaan 2019). This dynamic has led to a shift in market structures, where a handful of firms reap most of the benefits from AI and big data.

The current dominance of Chinese and US companies in AI creates dependencies at both the company and country levels. Even though a wave of new generative AI start-ups has secured handsome funding, big tech is well positioned to win the AI arms race due to its ubiquitous ecosystems, vast data sets, and deep pockets. Customers of AI products face the risk of being effectively locked into their supplier relationships, because AI products are intertwined with a range of software solutions and switching suppliers creates information technology migration risks and requires costly retraining of employees. Low- and middle-income countries increasingly face the choice of whether to join a China-centric or a United States–centric internet space. The *Financial Times* recently reported that the submarine cable market is in danger of splitting into "Eastern" and "Western" blocs (Gross et al. 2023). Such stark choices, if they come to pass, could limit further commercial opportunities for countries.

Privacy concerns

Individuals regard privacy as valuable for economic, psychological, social, and political reasons (Acemoglu 2021). The advent of big data and AI has complicated privacy concerns due to inexpensive data storage, nonrivalry, and data externalities (Agrawal, Gans, and Goldfarb 2019). Data externalities happen when one individual's data reveal information about other individuals.

This shared information diminishes the value of other people's data, not only for the individual but also for prospective data buyers (Acemoglu 2021).

The issue of information misuse becomes prominent as firms capitalize on their customers' personal data and privacy. Through AI-driven systems, firms use personal information to enhance discrimination between customer groups. This detailed prediction, based on previous consumer and search patterns, facilitates individualized pricing or personalized price-service quality combinations, leading to first-degree price discrimination. Such practices permit firms to appropriate a larger part of the consumer surplus at the expense of consumers (Acemoglu 2021; Ernst, Merola, and Samaan 2019).

Firms are also developing and buying increasingly intrusive AI tools to monitor and analyze their workers, often without the worker even knowing. Based on a survey of 1,000 business leaders in March 2023, 96 percent of US firms with a primarily remote or hybrid workforce use employee monitoring software, up from 10 percent before the COVID-19 outbreak. Three in four companies have fired workers over data collected by the monitoring software (Tan 2023). The tools used range from keystroke and computer activity monitoring to video monitoring and even eye-tracking software (which tracks a user's eyes to show whether he or she is looking at the screen and at which part of the screen) (Lazar and Yorke 2023).

Algorithmic bias

Algorithmic management and algorithmic bias pose another critical risk. Bias in algorithms can emanate from unrepresentative or incomplete training data or from flawed information that reflects historical inequalities. If left unchecked, biased algorithms can lead to decisions that can have a collective, disparate impact on certain groups of people even without the programmer's intention to discriminate. For instance, LinkedIn's recruitment algorithms, developed to bridge job seekers with employers, were found in 2018 to be generating gender-biased results, favoring men over women owing to the increased job-seeking activity of men (Wall and Schellmann 2021). In the health care sector, Obermeyer et al. (2019) disclosed that an algorithm intended to discern high-risk patients allotted lower risk scores to poor patients than to wealthier patients suffering from similar ailments, suggesting economic and racial bias.

Cybersecurity challenges

AI creates new cybersecurity risks and vulnerabilities. Data leaks from AI use can expose confidential and sensitive information. Increasingly complex AI algorithms also make it difficult for developers to identify security flaws. In addition, AI enables sophisticated cyber threats ranging from phishing and social engineering exploits to the creation and deployment of stealthy malware and deepfakes (Gupta et al. 2023). For instance, ChatGPT can be used to craft seemingly legitimate phishing emails or messages designed to deceive people into revealing confidential data or engaging with malicious links. It can generate complex malware code capable of eluding standard security protocols. Voice and facial recognition are being used increasingly as a security measure to control access. AI is an opportunity for bad actors to create deepfakes that get around that security. Several cases have already been reported.

Misinformation

AI and especially generative AI can turbocharge misinformation, undermine decision-making processes, and distort economic activities (Hajli et al. 2022; Strasser 2023; Suciu 2023). AI has made it much easier to produce disinformation and misinformation, from fake images and fake news to deepfakes, which are highly manipulated imagery, video, and audio. In March 2022, a video that was circulated on social media and a Ukrainian news website purported to show Ukraine's president directing his army to surrender the fight against the Russian Federation. It was eventually revealed that the video was a deepfake (HAI 2023). AI-generated images and videos can be created much more quickly than fact checkers can review and debunk them. AI can also corrode trust by making the public believe that anything could be artificially generated.

Copyright issues

AI platforms rely heavily on extensive data, often sourced from the internet without explicit permissions, to train their models (Edelman et al. 2023). Such practices can lead to copyright infringements, posing potential liabilities for both AI platforms and their users. For instance, lawsuits have been lodged against AI platforms like Stable Diffusion for using copyrighted artists' images as training data. This "unauthorized" use is seen as creating derivative works, infringing on the original copyright. Conversely, companies using AI to generate content face a unique conundrum—the lack of copyright protection for AI-generated outputs. According to the US Copyright Office, AI-generated content lacks "human authorship" and hence does not qualify for copyright protection. This stance is currently under review, considering the degree of human intervention in AI output, but the legal landscape remains uncertain. The lack of copyright leaves such AI-generated content open to misappropriation and presents challenges in the transfer of rights between creative vendors and clients.

Implications of AI for low- and middle-income countries: a blessing or a curse?

AI can be either a blessing or a curse for low- and middle-income countries. This section examines each in turn, highlighting how AI can help countries to address key development challenges and how it can widen existing gaps between rich and poor countries.

Blessing: How AI can help address development challenges

Agriculture

Almost two-thirds of the working population of Africa is employed in agriculture, but agriculture contributes only about 15 percent of African gross domestic product (GDP). Farm productivity is a key driver in freeing labor for other, more productive uses in many low- and middle-income economies (World Bank 2023). Large untapped productivity potential lies in furthering mechanization and the use of modern crops. Drone- and satellite-based collection and classification of images enable farmers to oversee large swaths of land for signs of infestations, to assess crop growth, and to choose profit-optimal input levels of water, fertilizer, and pesticides. AI can also help to develop better seeds based on local conditions, advise farmers on the best seeds to plant based on the soil and weather in their area, and develop drugs and vaccines for livestock (Gates 2023).

Health care

Several diagnostic tasks in the medical professions have been shown to be highly automatable using AI systems. Machine learning and AI are particularly apt at recognizing pathological patterns in images (radiology) or from sets of symptoms in conjunction with blood or other specimen tests. This ability can be transformative in low- and middle-income countries. The average number of medical doctors per 10,000 people remains below 3 in low-income countries and just 8 in lower-middle-income countries, compared to 37 in high-income countries, based on World Health Organization data. Building a high-skilled medical workforce takes time and considerable resources, so readily deployable AI solutions have the potential to increase the provision of modern health care at a fraction of the cost. For example, Ada Health, an AI start-up with a presence in Africa, offers a mobile app that uses AI algorithms to provide personalized assessments of symptoms and health advice. By leveraging AI-driven triage systems, such start-ups are extending health care access to remote areas, reducing the burden on health care systems, and improving health outcomes.

Education

Many low- and middle-income countries face an acute shortage of teachers. The world needs 69 million teachers to achieve universal primary and secondary education by 2030, of which 58 million are needed in low- and middle-income countries (UIS 2016). There is also a pressing need for teachers who are well trained and well supported. AI can assist and empower teachers in various ways, such as automating administrative tasks, providing feedback, generating content, enhancing content delivery, and facilitating collaboration. In addition to the shortage of teachers, scarcity of learning materials, and overcrowded classrooms, child labor or household responsibilities also depress school enrollment and attendance. Long and hazardous journeys to and from school further increase the cost to attend school regularly. AI-supported learning platforms hold the power to relax these constraints: children may, using written or spoken prompts, interact with such systems at their own pace and at the time of day of their choosing. AI can also help students to access tutoring, mentoring, and coaching services, using platforms such as intelligent tutoring systems, conversational agents, and recommender systems. When overseen by humans, and likely supplemented with in-presence days at schools, AI-based solutions may offer a realistic way to achieve better educational outcomes for low- and middle-income economies.

Financial inclusion

Providing access to banking and associated financial services to all is crucial for economic development. For the longest time, setting up a bank account has involved tedious administrative steps, including identity checks and the registration of tax identification numbers. Lack of credit information also complicates risk assessment and limits the access of many people and small and medium enterprises to finance. AI is helping to get around the challenges of identification using tiered know-your-customer approaches to verification that allow an easier way of identifying people using face recognition. AI also uses data aggregated from digital activities, including an individual's social network, call history, and even the top-ups on their mobile phone to evaluate their credit score and offer loans.

Climate resilience and insurability

AI can be used to establish early warning systems and perform advanced predictive analysis of local climate events, enabling stakeholders to take a more data-centric approach to climate adaptation. Such enhanced predictive capabilities will enable insurers to assess and price risk better. This ability is key to providing insurance to businesses and individuals. For example, the One Million Farmers Platform has already seen success in promoting the uptake of crop insurance (World Bank 2022). In Kenya, farmers receive insurance scratch cards when they buy seeds or fertilizer and can activate coverage using their mobile phones. Farms are automatically geo-tagged based on the location of the phone. By analyzing satellite and weather station data, the system identifies farmers who are eligible for insurance payouts. Notifications are sent via text message, and cash transfers are made through the M-PESA mobile money transfer service.

Fair and efficient taxation

Collecting taxes effectively is key to modern statehood. Recent estimates suggest that many low- and middle-income countries have shadow economies amounting to more than 30 percent, and up to 60 percent, of their GDP (Medina and Schneider 2018). Current research on tax administration shows that verifying taxpayer reports against related sources, such as employer records or reports by trading partners, is more effective at increasing tax compliance than the classical, and labor-intensive, tool of tax audits (for example, Kleven et al. 2011; Kopczuk and Slemrod 2006; Pomeranz 2015). Using AI systems, such verification efforts could plausibly be made for the universe of tax filings and commercial records, hugely increasing tax compliance and limiting the size of the shadow economy as a result (Saragih et al. 2022).

Targeted social transfers

AI's benefits extend to better targeting of social welfare programs as well. Aiken et al. (2021) used machine learning to assess targeting accuracy in Togo's emergency cash transfer program during the COVID-19 crisis. The machine learning approach minimized exclusion errors by 4–21 percent, demonstrating how AI and novel data sources can augment traditional methods for targeting humanitarian aid, especially in crises, when conventional data are missing or outdated.

Curse: Will AI widen the income gap between rich and poor countries and reverse development gains?

AI could potentially widen the gap between rich and poor countries through two main channels. First, the productivity gains from AI are most likely to be concentrated in rich countries, where new technologies are first created, diffused, and adopted. Digital technologies including AI tend to give rise to natural monopolies, creating a small set of superstar firms that are headquartered in a few powerful countries but serve the entire world economy. There is a risk that the countries that lead in the advancement of AI may reap all of the benefits, becoming "superstar countries" and reaping all of the rents associated with the development of AI. The rest of the world, particularly most low- and middle-income countries, may be left behind.

Rich countries also have stronger incentives and better complementary skills and institutions to adopt AI than poor countries. A shrinking working-age population and high labor costs in rich countries compel firms to use AI and robots more intensively, while firms in poor countries often lack the incentive to adopt new technologies as the cost of labor might be even lower than the cost of machines. Lack of digital infrastructure, digital skills, adequate institutions, and sound regulations further impede AI adoption in low- and middle-income countries. The more powerful AI and robots become, the larger the divergence in productivity between rich and poor countries grows (Alonso et al. 2020).

Second, AI could deteriorate the terms of trade and devalue the comparative advantage of low- and middle-income countries, eventually reversing the convergence in standards of living between rich and poor countries. The comparative advantage of many poor low- and middle-income countries lies in their abundant cheap labor and natural resources. As the degree of automation increases with advances in AI, the economic rationale for trading with and investing in poorer countries becomes weaker, and cheap labor can be replaced by new technologies. As investment priorities in rich countries shift toward AI and automation, investments will be diverted from low- and middle-income countries. Declining returns to labor and natural resources could lead to further immiseration in the developing world (Korinek and Stiglitz 2021).

However, there is a lot of uncertainty about the direction, pace, scale, and effect of changes brought by AI. Some people believe that recent innovations including AI will only have a modest effect on economic growth and people's standards of living (Gordon 2016). Some optimists see AI as a truly transformative technology that will lead to significant productivity gains and dramatic changes across sectors (Gates 2023; Trajtenberg 2019). Some even warn that AI will advance into a superintelligence that poses an existential threat to humanity (Barten and Meindertsma n.d.). It is critical for the global community, including low- and middle-income countries, to work together to shape the direction of AI innovations, coordinate the pace and scale of their applications, forecast, monitor, and assess the impacts, and prepare for how to ameliorate the adverse effects.

AI governance principles and divergent regulatory trends

AI governance principles refer to a set of guidelines, ethics, and rules designed to guide the responsible and ethical development, deployment, and use of AI technologies. Various countries,[2] prominent private sector tech companies,[3] civil society organizations,[4] and multilateral organizations[5] share some common guiding principles on responsible AI and AI governance. Responsible AI refers to the ethical and accountable development, deployment, and use of AI technologies. It involves integrating principles and practices that prioritize human values, societal well-being, and the long-term impact of AI systems. The goal of responsible AI is to ensure that AI technologies are developed and used in a manner that aligns with ethical standards, respects human rights, and minimizes potential risks and harms.

While some common foundational principles guide AI regulation, distinct variations exist in the specific approaches and priorities adopted by different countries and private sector entities. A useful way to characterize these differences includes the concepts of "hard law," "soft law" (Abbott and Snidal 2000; Hagemann, Skees, and Thierer 2018), and "self-regulation," alongside the "risk-based approach," "technology-specific regulatory approach," and "responsible-use approach" (Gomes 2023).

Hard law, soft law, and self-regulation each vary in their degree of enforceability and governance mechanisms. The hard law approach entails enacting specific and binding legislation and rules that establish concrete obligations and consequences for AI development and use. In contrast, soft law refers to nonbinding guidelines, principles, or recommendations that offer guidance on ethical AI practices but lack legal enforceability. These instruments are often used to encourage voluntary compliance, industry self-regulation, and global cooperation without imposing strict legal requirements. Under self-regulation, industry stakeholders voluntarily set their own rules and standards for AI development and deployment.

The risk-based, technology-specific regulatory, and responsible-use approaches focus on distinct aspects of ethical and accountable AI development and use. The risk-based approach to AI regulation involves categorizing AI applications based on their potential risks and impacts on individuals and society. This approach focuses on identifying high-risk AI systems and subjecting them to more stringent regulations to mitigate potential harms. The technology-specific regulatory approach involves tailoring regulations to address the unique characteristics and challenges of specific AI technologies rather than applying general laws. The responsible-use approach largely involves interpreting existing laws while complementing them with voluntary agreements and public-private partnerships to ensure a responsible and value-aligned implementation of AI.

The European Union has opted for a structured and risk-based legislative framework, with the AI Act proposing exhaustive regulations governing AI applications across diverse sectors. This act classifies AI systems based on their associated risk levels and imposes corresponding obligations, focusing on mitigating potential harms. While lower-risk AI systems, like spam filters, are subject to minimal transparency requirements, high-risk systems, prevalent in sectors such as health care, must comply with stringent obligations before market placement. Additionally, the act prohibits AI systems that endanger safety and fundamental rights, like real-time biometrics and predictive policing. However, the extensive and costly compliance measures have raised concerns among businesses about the impact on firms' global competitiveness and productivity levels. The European Union's push for similar AI regulations in Asian countries has been met predominantly with a more cautious "wait and see" response.

The United States has adopted a more diverse and flexible approach to AI regulation, characterized by a combination of soft law, self-regulation, responsible use, and legislation at various levels within different domains. Federal initiatives include the AI Bill of Rights, AI risk management framework by the National Institute of Standards and Technology, and plans for a national AI research resource aimed at enhancing public access to AI infrastructure. Various federal agencies are formulating road maps and best practices for AI within their domains, addressing potential discrimination and other issues stemming from AI systems. At the state level, numerous laws related to AI use and protections are being either proposed or enacted. For instance, California's proposed act will allow citizens to opt out of AI systems, while New York City's local law mandates transparency in AI use during hiring processes and annual bias assessments. Several other states are either enacting or preparing AI-related legislation, and the US Congress is anticipated to pass the Algorithmic Accountability Act of 2022.

Japan is employing a soft law approach to AI, focusing not only on minimizing AI-related harm and stimulating economic growth but also on harnessing AI to achieve societal objectives such as human dignity, diversity, inclusion, and sustainability. Rather than imposing rigid obligations or prohibitions, Japan's AI strategies emphasize maximizing AI's societal benefits through a flexible, risk-based, and multistakeholder approach. The country has promulgated the Social Principles of Human-Centric AI, which seek to realize these values through AI use without imposing undue restrictions. Japan refrains from enacting extensive legal constraints on AI, with the Ministry of Economy, Trade, and Industry advocating for a nonrestrictive, agile governance structure that respects voluntary governance efforts by companies, offering nonbinding guidelines, and fostering multistakeholder dialogue.

China has developed a diverse regulatory framework, focusing on both hard and soft law, technology-specific AI regulations, encompassing draft rules for generative AI, guidelines for AI in various applications, and specific provisions regarding automated decision-making. The country has introduced rules to enhance consumer protection and maintain competition, with special provisions on biometric data privacy, albeit with exceptions for national security and law enforcement needs. The Cyberspace Administration of China and the Ministry of Science and Technology are crafting regulations and guidelines, emphasizing the responsibility of providers of generative AI products and services for the content generated.

Multistakeholder collaboration, regulatory balance, and trade-offs

Efforts characterized by multistakeholder collaboration, such as the Rome Call on AI Ethics and the United Nations Educational, Scientific, and Cultural Organization's Recommendation on the Ethics of AI, are pivotal in establishing comprehensive ethical frameworks for AI. The initiatives emphasize the synergy of foundational research, technological advancements, standardized norms, and balanced regulations in fostering responsible AI deployment. The conceptualization of a "CERN for AI" and potential international institutions for AI governance and safety underline the importance of international cooperation and unified policy trajectories to mitigate fragmentation and promote global collaboration.

The "bootleggers and Baptists" concept[6] illustrates the contrasting motivations underpinning support for regulations and emphasizes the need for balanced approaches amid rapid technological advancements. Regulatory strategies must navigate the complexities and potential biases inherent in AI, addressing the juxtaposition of economic growth, efficiency, transparency, privacy, national security, and societal impacts. The emergence of various biases in LLMs and the alignment of AI systems with specific ideologies emphasize the multifaceted nature of the challenges posed.

National security and ethical dilemmas

AI regulation within the spheres of national security and biotechnology entails intricate challenges and opportunities. The intensification of AI's role in defense and intelligence necessitates stringent cybersecurity measures and ethical considerations to counteract potential misuse, with overregulation posing risks to domestic AI advancements and international competitiveness.

Regulatory challenges and innovation dynamics

Increasing regulatory obligations may impede innovation, particularly for small-scale entities, with the potential for industry leaders to manipulate regulatory landscapes to curtail competition and innovation. The dichotomy between open-source and proprietary AI systems underscores the need for balanced approaches to foster innovation, collaboration, and ethical considerations.

Regulatory fragmentation and arbitrage

The disparities in regulatory frameworks across jurisdictions complicate compliance and hinder global innovation, with companies potentially exploiting regulatory discrepancies to gain a competitive advantage. A harmonized and cohesive international regulatory framework is imperative to circumvent enforcement disparities, trade obstacles, and innovation arbitrage.

Adequacy of existing regulations

The rapid evolution of AI technologies necessitates meticulous examination of the sufficiency of existing legal frameworks in addressing emerging challenges related to misinformation, freedom of speech, data privacy, bias, and discrimination. The precise determination of areas necessitating novel regulatory approaches is crucial to develop a comprehensive, agile, and effective legal ecosystem for AI.

Regulatory capture and inclusive governance

The phenomenon of regulatory capture highlights the susceptibility of regulatory entities to influence from the industries they are mandated to regulate, emphasizing the importance of inclusivity, diversity, public engagement, and multistakeholder collaboration in formulating balanced and effective AI regulations.

Strategies to accelerate safe and inclusive AI adoption

Some low- and middle-income countries, including the Arab Republic of Egypt, India, Kenya, Mauritius, Rwanda, and other Sub-Saharan African countries, have initiated efforts to develop national AI policies and strategies.[7] Egypt's national AI strategy, introduced in 2021, seeks to harness AI technology for sustainable development while fostering regional collaboration within Africa and the Arab world (National Council for Artificial Intelligence 2021). The strategy, overseen by the Ministry of Communications and Information Technology and the National Council for AI, focuses on four pillars: AI for government, AI for development, capacity building, and international engagement. Egypt's AI strategy emphasizes three key principles in its AI capacity-building efforts: augmenting human labor rather than replacing it, expanding the job market, and ensuring support for individuals unable to be upskilled or reskilled. Egypt's AI strategy seeks to establish a robust AI industry, enhance government efficiency through AI adoption, apply AI in key sectors aligned with the United Nations Sustainable Development Goals, and prepare the population for the AI era.

In 2021, Brazil introduced the Emerging Brazilian Artificial Intelligence Strategy (EBIA) as a significant addition to its technology-driven initiatives, alongside the Brazilian Strategy for Digital Transformation (E-Digital) and the General Data Protection Law.[8] EBIA plays a central role in directing the actions of the Brazilian government, prioritizing research, innovation, and the development of AI solutions, while emphasizing ethical and responsible use of AI. In line with principles of the Organisation for Economic Co-operation and Development, the EBIA focuses on inclusive growth, human-centered values, transparency, robustness, and accountability within its national AI plan. Its core objectives encompass fostering ethical AI principles, encouraging sustained investment in AI research and development, eliminating barriers to AI innovation, educating AI professionals, stimulating Brazilian AI development on the international stage, and promoting cooperation among public and private entities and research centers for AI advancement within Brazil's national AI plan.

India's national AI strategy, known as "AI for All," was initiated in response to the recognition of AI's transformative potential in the economy.[9] The strategy, established under the guidance of NITI Aayog, takes a three-prong approach. First, it includes exploratory proof-of-concept AI projects in key sectors like agriculture and health. Second, it aims to craft a national strategy to foster a thriving AI ecosystem in India. Third, it involves collaboration with various experts and stakeholders, including partnerships with leading AI technology firms. The government's role is clearly defined, emphasizing development of the research ecosystem, promoting AI adoption, and addressing AI skills in the population. Additionally, the strategy highlights the importance of addressing ethical, bias, and privacy concerns in AI technology through research and development efforts. Public investment will be channeled into sectors like agriculture, health, and education as part of this comprehensive AI strategy.

Rwanda's national AI policy seeks to leverage AI to power economic growth, improve quality of life, and position Rwanda as a global innovator for responsible and inclusive AI. The policy has six priority areas: AI skills development, reliable digital infrastructure and computer capacity, robust data strategy, AI adoption in the public sector, AI adoption in the private sector, and practical ethical guidelines. Rwanda is working on integrating internationally competitive science, technology, engineering, and mathematics skills into young learners' education to guarantee that future generations are proficient in AI, data, and digital technologies. Substantial investment in digital infrastructure and partnerships with international tech giants are also planned to ensure that the country has sophisticated technology and expertise. The government is also building a task force to establish ethical, responsible, and secure data governance frameworks and protocols.

Other Sub-Saharan African nations are also advancing their national AI plans. The African Union has endorsed a Data Policy Framework, emphasizing research and innovation in AI and related fields (Kpilaakaa 2023). Ethiopia, Ghana, Morocco, Rwanda, South Africa, Tunisia, and Uganda, are exploring AI's potential for economic growth. They are participating in projects like the Ethical Policy Frameworks for AI in the Global South and formulating national AI policies (IFG.CC 2023). Smart Africa, in collaboration with governments, is spearheading the development of national AI strategies in some African countries.

A new playbook for development in the AI era

The dawning AI era requires a new playbook for economic policy making to harness the potential and manage the effects of technological disruption. This section summarizes key policy responses in addition to the key areas already covered in countries' AI policies: investments in infrastructure and skills and data governance.

Innovation and adoption of AI to augment labor

Government policies can affect the incentives for innovation. Extremely low interest rates and restrictive migration policies in rich countries encourage excessive automation (Pritchett 2020; Stiglitz 2014). Tax policies that favor capital over labor distort the direction of progress toward saving labor (Acemoglu, Manera, and Restrepo 2020). Low- and middle-income countries can focus on steering the adoption of labor-using technologies that have been developed in rich countries and adapt them to their own circumstances and needs. These objectives could also inform decisions on what type of inward foreign direct investment to encourage (Korinek and Stiglitz 2021).

Taxation, redistribution, and social protection

Among the critical policies to combat rising inequality are those of taxation and redistribution. If AI augments skilled workers and automates unskilled workers like many previous technologies have done, it will contribute to even greater levels of wealth inequality within and across countries. Labor-saving technologies also reduce tax revenue from labor. This reduction has increased the importance of progressive taxation and necessitated a shift toward taxing other factors and rents. In particular, some of the monopoly rents of digital giants can be taxed without introducing major distortions into the economy (Korinek and Stiglitz 2021; Stiglitz 2018). It is similarly important to provide better systems of social protection for people displaced by AI.

New sectoral development strategies

AI and automation have posed challenges to the old and successful development strategies of the past half century, but they also open new opportunities. While low- and middle-income countries can still pursue a manufacturing-led growth strategy, more attention could be shifted toward carving out new areas of comparative advantage in services. A market for simple human services is growing and can be broken down into small components and fed into AI systems (for example, labeling images). However, what adds to the difficulty is that services that can be outsourced may also be automated more easily (Korinek and Stiglitz 2021). Other services such as tourism have proven to be a more automation-resistant source of revenue for some low- and middle-income countries. Low- and middle-income countries need to invest in digital infrastructure, raise aggregate productivity, and develop digital skills more urgently than ever before so that their labor force is augmented rather than substituted by AI and robots. Box 5.1 highlights the perspectives of industry leaders on AI and underscores the critical need for preparing the workforce for the AI age.

BOX 5.1 **Views of industry leaders on AI**

The World Bank surveyed dozens of industry leaders from a range of sectors on opportunities from and challenges to deploying artificial intelligence (AI) solutions. The following synthesizes their responses.

Economic opportunities

Industry leaders are brimming with optimism regarding AI's potential to drive meaningful innovations and unlock pivotal insights from the vast swathes of data, paving the way for societal and economic betterment. Industry leaders foresee substantial economic growth for economies that embrace AI and harness its full potential. They stress the significance of addressing the global and local discrepancies in AI approaches, particularly focusing on developing regions where the lack of infrastructure can accentuate AI's challenges and threats. Leaders are initiating and supporting ventures to tackle global issues such as digital literacy and health disparities through AI, highlighting the importance of transparency and public-private collaborations to employ AI efficaciously to address myriad societal challenges.

Responsible and ethical deployment

Among industry leaders, there is a unanimous and rigorous emphasis on the ethical and responsible deployment of AI technologies. Industry leaders stress aligning AI advancements with core organizational and societal values and focusing on transparency, inclusiveness, reliability, and accountability to cultivate and maintain trust and fairness. The insistence is on structured, robust governance measures and responsible use policies to uphold high standards of safety, quality, and information integrity in AI applications.

Advocacy for robust regulatory frameworks

Industry leaders advocate for a collaborative and multifaceted approach involving various stakeholders, nongovernmental organizations, and government entities to navigate the complexities of AI effectively. They call for cohesive international alignment and democratic law-making processes to establish balanced and reflective common policies and norms, emphasizing the formation of public-private partnerships for informed and rounded policy making on emerging technologies and ensuring the ethical and regulated development and deployment of AI solutions.

Challenges and concerns

While the optimism surrounding AI is palpable, industry leaders also recognize the substantial challenges and concerns that AI brings, including issues of information integrity, latent bias, and potential ramifications on the employment and education sectors. Industry leaders acknowledge the intrinsic legal and ethical dilemmas, emphasizing the need for a global, multistakeholder approach to tackle challenges like misinformation, discrimination, and misuse effectively and to frame efficacious governance structures around AI.

Skills development and education

Industry leaders recognize the acute shortage of requisite skills in software programming and information technology, which they perceive to be a hindrance to the advancement of AI. Leaders emphasize the critical need for substantial skill development initiatives and preparation of workforces for the transitions that AI would induce. Progress is noted in low- and middle-income countries, where steps are being taken to formulate national AI strategies, concentrating on responsible and ethical AI use and innovation leadership.

Source: World Bank summary of industry leader survey. The project team thanks the following organizations for participating in the Digital Industry Leader Survey and providing valuable inputs: Alphabet, Atos Africa, Bureau Veritas, Business Finland, Meta, Microsoft, Mouvement des Entreprises de France International (MEDEF International), MTN Group Limited, Orange, Secure Identity Alliance, Sofrecom, and Visa.

Notes

1. Vector databases provide enterprises with an easy way to store, search, and index unstructured data at a speed, scale, and efficiency that current relational databases cannot offer.

2. For China's AI governance principles, refer to "Governance Principles for the New Generation of Artificial Intelligence—Developing Responsible Artificial Intelligence," *China Daily,* June 17, 2019 (http://www.chinadaily.com.cn/a/201906/17/WS5d07486ba3103dbf14328ab7.html). For Japan's human-centric AI principles, refer to "Social Principles of Human-Centric AI" (https://www.cas.go.jp /jp/seisaku/jinkouchinou/pdf/humancentricai.pdf). For the United Kingdom's AI regulatory principles, refer to UK Secretary of State for Science, Innovation, and Technology (2023). For the United States AI blueprint, refer to US White House, Office of Science and Technology (n.d.). For the European Union harmonized AI rules, refer to European Commission (2021).

3. For Google's AI principles, refer to https://ai.google/responsibility/principles/. For Meta's AI pillars, refer to https://ai.meta.com/responsible-ai/#pillars. For Microsoft's AI principles and approach, refer to https://www.microsoft.com/en-us/ai/principles-and-approach. For Open AI's product safety standards, refer to https://openai.com/safety-standards.

4. For information about the Global Partnership on Artificial Intelligence's Working Group on Responsible AI, refer to https://gpai.ai/projects/responsible-ai/. For Amnesty International's Toronto Declaration, refer to "The Toronto Declaration: Protecting the Rights to Equality and Non-Discrimination in Machine Learning Systems" (https://www.amnesty.org/en/documents/pol30/8447/2018/en/).

5. For the G20 New Delhi Leaders' Declaration, refer to https://www.caidp.org/resources/g20 -india-2023/#:~:text=The%20G20%20guidelines%20call%20for,and%20internationally%20 recognized%20labor%20rights. For the AI perspective of UNESCO, refer to https://www.unesco .org/en/artificial-intelligence. For an overview of the OECD AI principles, refer to https://oecd.ai/en /ai-principles.

6. The "Bootleggers and Baptists" concept, introduced by regulatory economist Bruce Yandle, illustrates the phenomenon where regulations receive support from two seemingly opposite groups. On the one hand, there are those who advocate for the intended purpose of the regulation, often with the best of intentions. On the other hand, there are entities that stand to benefit by circumventing or undermining the very purpose they publicly endorse.

7. Egypt published its national AI strategy in 2021, Kenya created its Distributed Ledgers Technology and AI Task Force in 2018, Mauritius published a national AI strategy in 2018, Rwanda's cabinet approved its national AI policy in April 2023, and South Africa published an AI blueprint in 2021. Refer to Teleanu and Kurbalija (2022).

8. Refer to "Brazilian Strategy," *OECD.ai Policy Observatory* (https://oecd.ai/en/dashboards/policy -initiatives/http:%2F%2Faipo.oecd.org%2F2021-data-policyInitiatives-27104).

9. For information on India's strategy, refer to "Welcome to AI For All Program," Ministry of Education Digital Portal (https://ai-for-all.in/#/home) and OECD.AI Policy Observatory (https://oecd.ai/fr/dashboards/policy-initiatives/2019-data-policyInitiatives-24951.

References

Abbott, Kenneth W., and Duncan Snidal. 2000. "Hard and Soft Law in International Governance." *International Organization* 54 (3): 421–56.

Acemoglu, Daron. 2021. *Harms of AI.* Technical Report. Cambridge, MA: National Bureau of Economic Research.

Acemoglu, Daron, David Autor, Jonathon Hazell, and Pascual Restrepo. 2022. "Artificial Intelligence and Jobs: Evidence from Online Vacancies." *Journal of Labor Economics* 40 (S1): S293–340.

Acemoglu, Daron, Andrea Manera, and Pascual Restrepo. 2020. "Does the US Tax Code Favor Automation?" *Brookings Papers on Economic Activity* 2020 (1): 231–300.

Agrawal, Ajay, Joshua Gans, and Avi Goldfarb. 2019. "Economic Policy for Artificial Intelligence." *Innovation Policy and the Economy* 19 (1): 139–59.

Agrawal, Ajay, Joshua S. Gans, and Avi Goldfarb. 2023. "Do We Want Less Automation?" *Science* 381 (6654): 155–58.

Aiken, Emily, Suzanne Bellue, Dean Karlan, Christopher R. Udry, and Joshua Blumenstock. 2021. *Machine Learning and Mobile Phone Data Can Improve the Targeting of Humanitarian Assistance.* Technical Report. Cambridge, MA: National Bureau of Economic Research.

Alonso, Cristian, Andrew Berg, Siddharth Kothari, Chris Papageorgiou, and Sidra Rehman. 2020. "Will the AI Revolution Cause a Great Divergence?" *Journal of Monetary Economics* 127 (April): 18–37.

Autor, David, Caroline Chin, Anna M. Salomons, and Bryan Seegmiller. 2022. *New Frontiers: The Origins and Content of New Work, 1940–2018.* Technical Report. Cambridge, MA: National Bureau of Economic Research.

Babina, Tania, Anastassia Fedyk, Alex He, and James Hodson. 2022. "Artificial Intelligence, Firm Growth, and Product Innovation." *Journal of Financial Economics.* Available at SSRN 3651052.

Barten, Otto, and Joep Meindertsma. n.d. "An AI Pause Is Humanity's Best Bet for Preventing Extinction." *Time.* https://time.com/6295879/ai-pause-is-humanitys-best-bet-for-preventing-extinction/.

Brown, Tom B., Benjamin Mann, Nick Ryder, Melanie Subbiah, Jared Kaplan, Prafulla Dhariwal, Arvind Neelakantan, Pranav Shyam, Girish Sastry, Amanda Askell, et al. 2020. "Language Models Are Few-Shot Learners." arXiv preprint arXiv:2005.14165.

Brynjolfsson, Erik, Wang Jin, and Kristina McElheran. 2021. "The Power of Prediction: Predictive Analytics, Workplace Complements, and Business Performance." *Business Economics* 56 (October): 217–39.

Brynjolfsson, Erik, Danielle Li, and Lindsey R. Raymond. 2023. *Generative AI at Work.* Technical Report. Cambridge, MA: National Bureau of Economic Research.

CB Insights. 2023a. "The Generative AI Market Map: 35 Vendors Automating Content, Code, Design, and More." *CB Insights Research Brief,* July 12, 2023. https://app.cbinsights.com/research/generative-ai-startups-market-map/.

CB Insights. 2023b. "The State of Generative AI in 7 Charts." *CB Insights Research Brief,* August 3, 2023. https://app.cbinsights.com/research/generative-ai-funding-top-startups-investors/.

Collett, Clementine, Livia Gouvea Gomes, and Gina Neff. 2022. *The Effects of AI on the Working Lives of Women.* Paris: UNESCO Publishing.

Copestake, Alexander, Max Marczinek, Ashley Pople, and Katherine Stapleton. 2023. "AI and Services-Led Growth: Evidence from Indian Job Adverts." Working Paper, International Monetary Fund and World Bank, Washington, DC; University of Oxford, Oxford. https://copestake.info/workingpaper/akai/AKAI.pdf.

Edelman, Sara L., Paavana Kumar, Samantha G. Rothaus, Howard Weingrad, and Andrew Richman. 2023. "The Risks and Rewards of Generative AI." *Davis+Gilbert Alert, Emerging Issues,* March 31, 2023. https://www.dglaw.com/the-risks-and-rewards-of-generative-ai/.

Eloundou, Tyna, Sam Manning, Pamela Mishkin, and Daniel Rock. 2023. "GPTs Are GPTs: An Early Look at the Labor Market Impact Potential of Large Language Models." arXiv preprint arXiv:2303.10130.

Ernst, Ekkehardt, Rossana Merola, and Daniel Samaan. 2019. "Economics of Artificial Intelligence: Implications for the Future of Work." *IZA Journal of Labor Policy* 9 (1): n.p.

European Commission. 2021. "Proposal for a Regulation of the European Parliament and of the Council Laying Down Harmonised Rules on Artificial Intelligence (Artificial Intelligence Act) and Amending Certain Union Legislative Acts." European Commission, Brussels. https://eur-lex.europa.eu/legal-content/EN/TXT/?uri=CELEX:52021PC0206.

Gates, Bill. 2023. "The Age of AI Has Begun." *GatesNotes* (blog), March 21, 2023.

Gmyrek, Pawel, Janine Berg, and David Bescond. 2023. "Generative AI and Jobs: A Global Analysis of Potential Effects on Job Quantity and Quality." ILO Working Paper 96, International Labour Organization, Geneva.

Gomes, Andre Moura. 2023. "Artificial Intelligence." Cullen International, June 26, 2023. https://www.cullen-international.com/news/2023/06/Global-trends-in-Artificial-Intelligence-regulation.html.

Gordon, Robert J. 2016. *The Rise and Fall of American Growth.* Princeton, NJ: Princeton University Press.

Gross, Anna, Alexandra Heal, Chris Campbell, Dan Clark, Ian Bott, and Irene de la Torre Arenas. 2023. "Subsea Cables: How the US is Pushing China Out of the Internet's Plumbing." *Financial Times,* June 12, 2023. https://ig.ft.com/subsea-cables/.

Gupta, Maanak, Charan Kumar Akiri, Kshitiz Aryal, Eli Parker, and Lopamudra Praharaj. 2023. "From ChatGPT to ThreatGPT: Impact of Generative AI in Cybersecurity and Privacy." arXiv preprint arXiv:2307.00691.

Hagemann, Ryan, Jennifer Huddleston Skees, and Adam Thierer. 2018. "Soft Law for Hard Problems: The Governance of Emerging Technologies in an Uncertain Future." *Colorado Technology Law Journal* 17 (1): 37–129.

HAI (Institute for Human-centered Artificial Intelligence). 2023. *Artificial Intelligence Index Annual Report 2023.* Stanford, CA: Stanford University, HAI.

Hajli, Nick, Usman Saeed, Mina Tajvidi, and Farid Shirazi. 2022. "Social Bots and the Spread of Disinformation in Social Media: The Challenges of Artificial Intelligence." *British Journal of Management* 33 (3): 1238–53.

IFG.CC (Potsdam eGovernment Competence Center). 2023. "AI for Africa, by Africa: A Call to Action for Inclusive and Ethical Artificial Intelligence Policies." IFG.CC, Zurich. http://www.ifg.cc/aktuelles /nachrichten/regionen/153-afrika-africa/62325-ai-for-africa-by-africa-a-call-to-action-for-inclusive -and-ethical-artificial-intelligence-policies.html.

Kleven, Henrik Jacobsen, Martin B. Knudsen, Claus Thustrup Kreiner, Søren Pedersen, and Emmanuel Saez. 2011. "Unwilling or Unable to Cheat? Evidence from a Tax Audit Experiment in Denmark." *Econometrica* 79 (3): 651–92.

Kopczuk, Wojciech, and Joel Slemrod. 2006. "Putting Firms into Optimal Tax Theory." *American Economic Review* 96 (2): 130–34. https://doi.org/10.1257/000282806777212585.

Korinek, Anton, and Joseph E. Stiglitz. 2021. "Artificial Intelligence, Globalization, and Strategies for Economic Development." NBER Working Paper w28453, National Bureau of Economic Research, Cambridge, MA.

Kpilaakaa, Johnstone. 2023. "African Countries Rank Lowest on the AI Readiness Index Globally." Benjamindada.com, August 16, 2023.

Lazar, Wendi S., and Cody Yorke. 2023. "Watched While Working: Use of Monitoring and AI in the Workplace." *Reuters,* April 25, 2023. https://www.reuters.com/legal/legalindustry/watched-while -working-use-monitoring-ai-workplace-increases-2023-04-25/.

Mearian, Lucas. 2023. "How AI Can Help Find New Employees." *Computerworld,* March 6, 2023.

Medina, Leandro, and Friedrich Schneider. 2018. "Shadow Economies around the World: What Did We Learn Over the Last 20 Years?" IMF Working Paper 2018/017, International Monetary Fund, Washington, DC.

Merken, Lisa. 2023. "Legal AI Race Draws More Investors as Law Firms Line Up." *Reuters,* April 26, 2023. https://www.reuters.com/legal/legal-ai-race-draws-more-investors-law-firms-line-up-2023-04-26/.

Mikalef, Patrick, and Manjul Gupta. 2021. "Artificial Intelligence Capability: Conceptualization, Measurement Calibration, and Empirical Study on Its Impact on Organizational Creativity and Firm Performance." *Information & Management* 58 (3): 103434.

Mishra, Arindra Nath, and Ashis Kumar Pani. 2021. "Business Value Appropriation Roadmap for Artificial Intelligence." *VINE Journal of Information and Knowledge Management Systems* 51 (3): 353–68.

Mishra, Sagarika, Michael T. Ewing, and Holly B. Cooper. 2022. "Artificial Intelligence Focus and Firm Performance." *Journal of the Academy of Marketing Science* 50 (2022): 1176–97 (2022). https://doi.org/10.1007/s11747-022-00876-5.

Moll, Benjamin, Lukasz Rachel, and Pascual Restrepo. 2022. "Uneven Growth: Automation's Impact on Income and Wealth Inequality." *Econometrica* 90 (6): 2645–83.

Mondal, Subhra, Subhankar Das, and Vasiliki G. Vrana. 2023. "How to Bell the Cat? A Theoretical Review of Generative Artificial Intelligence towards Digital Disruption in All Walks of Life." *Technologies* 11 (2): 44.

National Council for Artificial Intelligence. 2021. "Egypt National Artificial Intelligence Strategy." Ministry of Communications and Information Technology, Cairo. https://mcit.gov.eg/en/Publication /Publication_Summary/9283.

Noy, Shakked, and Whitney Zhang. 2023. "Experimental Evidence on the Productivity Effects of Generative Artificial Intelligence." *Science* 381 (6654): 187–92.

Obermeyer, Ziad, Brian Powers, Christine Vogeli, and Sendhil Mullainathan. 2019. "Dissecting Racial Bias in an Algorithm Used to Manage the Health of Populations." *Science* 366 (6464): 447–53.

Peng, Sida, Eirini Kalliamvakou, Peter Cihon, and Mert Demirer. 2023. "The Impact of AI on Developer Productivity: Evidence from GitHub Copilot." arXiv preprint arXiv:2302.06590.

Pinheiro, Flavio L., Pierre-Alexandre Balland, Ron Boschma, and Dominik Hartmann. 2022. "The Dark Side of the Geography of Innovation: Relatedness, Complexity, and Regional Inequality in Europe." *Regional Studies*, September 7, 2022. https://doi.org/10.1080/00343404.2022.2106362.

Pomeranz, Dina. 2015. "No Taxation without Information: Deterrence and Self-Enforcement in the Value Added Tax." *American Economic Review* 105 (8): 2539–69.

Pritchett, Lant. 2020. "The Future of Jobs Is Facing One, Maybe Two, of the Biggest Price Distortions Ever." *Middle East Development Journal* 12 (1): 131–56.

Rockinson, Randy. 2023. "4 Ways Google's Shopping Graph Helps You Find What You Want." *Google Shopping* (blog), February 7, 2023.

Saragih, Arfah, Qaumy Reyhani, Milla Reyhani, Milla Setyowati, and Adang Hendrawan. 2022. "The Potential of an Artificial Intelligence (AI) Application for the Tax Administration System's Modernization: The Case of Indonesia." *Artificial Intelligence and Law* 31 (3): 491–514.

Stiglitz, Joseph E. 2014. "Unemployment and Innovation." NBER Working Paper 20670, National Bureau of Economic Research, Cambridge, MA.

Stiglitz, Joseph E. 2018. "From Manufacturing-Led Export Growth to a Twenty-First-Century Inclusive Growth Strategy: Explaining the Demise of a Successful Growth Model and What to Do about It." WIDER Working Paper 2018/176, UNU-WIDER, Helsinki.

Strasser, Anna. 2023. "On Pitfalls (and Advantages) of Sophisticated Large Language Models." arXiv preprint arXiv:2303.17511.

Suciu, Peter. 2023. "The Next Threat from Generative AI: Disinformation Campaigns." *Forbes,* June 9, 2023. https://www.forbes.com/sites/petersuciu/2023/06/09/the-next-threat-from-generative-ai -disinformation-campaigns/.

Tan, Huileng. 2023. "96% of Remote Companies Say They're Using Some Kind of Software to Monitor Employees Who Work from Home, Survey Finds." *Insider,* March 30, 2023. https://www .businessinsider.com/majority-remote-hybrid-work-companies-wfh-monitor-employees-rto-2023 -3?r=US&IR=T.

Teleanu, Sorina, and Jovan Kurbalija. 2022. *Stronger Digital Voices from Africa: Building African Digital Foreign Policy and Diplomacy.* Malta: Diplo. https://www.diplomacy.edu/resource/report-stronger -digital-voices-from-africa/ai-africa-national-policies.

Trajtenberg, Manuel. 2019. "Artificial Intelligence as the Next GPT: A Political-Economy Perspective." In *The Economics of Artificial Intelligence: An Agenda*, edited by Ajay Agrawal, Joshua Gans, and Avi Goldfarb, 175–86. Chicago: University of Chicago Press.

Tyson, Laura D., and John Zysman. 2022. "Automation, AI & Work." *Daedalus* 151 (2): 256–71.

UIS (UNESCO Institute for Statistics). 2016. "The World Needs Almost 69 Million New Teachers to Reach the 2030 Education Goals." UIS Fact Sheet 39, UNESCO, Paris. https://unesdoc.unesco.org /ark:/48223/pf0000246124#:~:text=Across%20the%20region%2C%20more%20than,of%20 rising%20demand%20for%20education.

UK Secretary of State for Science, Innovation, and Technology. 2023. "Policy Paper: A Pro-Innovation Approach to AI Regulation." Command Paper 815, UK Secretary of State for Science, Innovation, and Technology, London. https://www.gov.uk/government/publications/ai-regulation-a-pro-innovation -approach/white-paper.

US White House Office of Science and Technology. n.d. "AI Regulation: A Pro-Innovation Approach." White Paper, Office of Science and Technology, Washington, DC. https://www.gov.uk/government /publications/ai-regulation-a-pro-innovation-approach/white-paper.

Van Noordt, Colin, and Gianluca Misuraca. 2022. "Artificial Intelligence for the Public Sector: Results of Landscaping the Use of AI in Government Across the European Union." *Government Information Quarterly* 39 (3): 101714. https://doi.org/10.1016/j.giq.2022.101714.

Vaswani, Ashish, Noam Shazeer, Niki Parmar, Jakob Uszkoreit, Llion Jones, Aidan N. Gomez, Lukasz Kaiser, and Illia Polosukhin. 2017. "Attention Is All You Need." In *Advances in Neural Information Processing Systems 30*, edited by Ulrike Von Luxburg, Isabelle Guyon, Samy Bengio, Hanna Wallach, Rob Fergus, S. V. N. Vishwanathan, and Roman Garnett. Red Hook, NY: Curran Associates.

Waddell, Kaveh. 2019. "Data Labeling for AI Is Set to Become a Billion-Dollar Market by 2023." *Axios,* March 25, 2019. https://www.axios.com/ai-data-labeling-billion-dollar-market-409704bc-e63c -4af0-b0d0-44424abcd561.html.

Wall, Sheridan, and Hike Schellmann. 2021. "LinkIn's Job-Matching AI Was Biased. The Company's Solution? More AI." *MIT Technology Review,* June 23, 2021.

Wang, Han, Min Liu, and Weiming Shen. 2023. "Industrial-Generative Pre-Trained Transformer for Intelligent Manufacturing Systems." *IET Collaborative Intelligent Manufacturing* 5 (2): e12078. https://doi.org/10.1049/cim2.12078.

Webb, Michael. 2020. "The Impact of Artificial Intelligence on the Labor Market." Available at SSRN 3482150.

WEF (World Economic Forum). 2023. *Future of Jobs Report.* Cologny: WEF. https://www3.weforum .org/docs/WEF_Future_of_Jobs_2023.pdf.

World Bank. 2022. "Disruptive Innovations Boost Uptake of Agriculture Insurance Solutions in Kenya." *World Bank News,* June 15, 2022. https://www.worldbank.org/en/news/feature/2022/06/15/disruptive -innovations-boost-uptake-of-agriculture-insurance-solutions-in-kenya.

World Bank. 2023. *Emerging Technologies Curation Series Issue 5: Generative Artificial Intelligence.* Washington, DC: World Bank, Technical and Innovation Lab Korea.

Yandle, Bruce. 1983 "Bootleggers and Baptists—the Education of a Regulatory Economist." *Regulation* 7 (3): 12.

Yang, Chih-Hai. 2022. "How Artificial Intelligence Technology Affects Productivity and Employment: Firm-Level Evidence from Taiwan." *Research Policy* 51 (6): 104536. https://doi.org/10.1016/j .respol.2022.104536.

Zhavoronkov, Alex, Yan A. Ivanenkov, Alex Aliper, Mark S. Veselov, Vladimir A. Aladinskiy, Anastasiya V. Aladinskaya, Victor A. Terentiev, Daniil A. Polykovskiy, Maksim D. Kuznetsov, Arip Asadulaev, et al. 2019. "Deep Learning Enables Rapid Identification of Potent DDR1 Kinase Inhibitors." *Nature Biotechnology* 37: 1038–40. https://doi.org/10.1038/s41587-019-0224-x.

Appendix A
Data Sets Used in the Report

ICT Sector Data Set

While there is a clear and widely adopted definition of the information and communication technology (ICT) sector, measurement challenges and data gaps have hindered meaningful analysis and interpretation at the global level. Basic indicators such as value added, employment, wages, prices, and fixed capital formation are often not available at disaggregated industry levels in many low- and middle-income countries. Even when such data are available, the use of diverse industry classifications and differences in update frequency across countries complicate international comparisons.

While the European Union's PREDICT database,[1] the United Nations Conference on Trade and Development, and the Organisation for Economic Co-operation and Development all compile and harmonize ICT value added and employment statistics across countries, their coverage is confined largely to high-income economies. The estimates for some of the biggest ICT-producing economies—notably, China, the Republic of Korea, and Taiwan, China—can differ significantly from more reliable official statistics.

The report team gleaned national statistics from dozens of major ICT-producing economies and curated them into the ICT Sector Data Set (ICTD), providing a much more accurate, comprehensive, and updated picture of the global ICT landscape. The data set focuses on two main variables: value added and employment. It covers about 140 economies around the world and includes annual data from 2000 to 2022. As disaggregated data are either unavailable or outdated in many low- and middle-income countries, this report uses ISIC Rev. 4 division 26—Manufacture of computer, electronic, and optical products for ICT manufacturing, section J—Information and communication (58–63) for ICT services. ICTD uses a definition that is slightly different from the official definition of the ICT sector, which excludes optical products, publishing, broadcasting, and audiovisual activities and includes wholesale, retail, and repair of ICT goods.

The ICTD also breaks down ICT services into three subsectors: publishing, broadcasting, and audiovisual activities; telecommunication; and information technology services. A more detailed breakdown of subsectors for ICT manufacturing (electronic components, computers and peripheral equipment, communications equipment, consumer electronics, and optical products) is available for 44 economies, including China; European Union countries; Japan; the Republic of Korea; Taiwan, China; the United Kingdom; the United States; and others. Employment data are gender-disaggregated whenever possible.

Firm Level Adoption of Technology Survey

The Firm Level Adoption of Technology (FAT) survey collects firm-level information on technology use, drivers and barriers of technology adoption, and balance sheets. It is a nationally representative survey, with the exception of India, which focuses on two states (Tamil Nadu and Uttar Pradesh), and Brazil, which includes the state of Ceará. It covers establishments in agriculture, manufacturing, and services (except Bangladesh, which only covers manufacturing, and India, which excludes agriculture). The data offer an innovative tool for measuring the adoption and use of technologies at the firm level through three angles:

1. Standard measures of technology related to general-purpose technologies
2. Technologies applied to general business support functions
3. Use of sector-specific technologies.

For each business function, the survey examines the adoption of each technology from rudimentary to the most sophisticated following the ladder of technology sophistication. For the analysis in this report, a sample of 18,622 firms in 14 countries is used, with data collected from 2019 to 2022, as outlined in table A.1.

The survey was initially implemented face-to-face until the start of the COVID-19 pandemic, when implementation was shifted to phone interviews. To ensure the accuracy of the responses and comparability of the data collected across countries, a standardized process for implementation was used in all countries. The same questionnaire was administered through face-to-face or telephone interviews with computer-assisted personal interviewing or computer-assisted telephone interviewing in all countries. The survey was implemented at the establishment level in each country, and response rates varied between 24 percent and 80 percent, with rates often on the higher end when the survey was conducted by the country's national statistical agency. The sampling weights were adjusted to minimize response bias. For details on the overall protocol for sampling weights of the FAT data and several robustness checks implemented by the team, refer to Cirera et al. (2021).

TABLE A.1 Description of data used from the Firm Level Adoption of Technology Survey

Country	Region	Year	Mode
Bangladesh	South Asia	2019	Face-to-face
Brazil	Latin America and the Caribbean	2019	Face-to-face
Burkina Faso	Sub-Saharan Africa	2021	Telephone
Cambodia	East Asia and Pacific	2021	Face-to-face
Chile	Latin America and the Caribbean	2022	Telephone
Ethiopia	Sub-Saharan Africa	2022	Face-to-face
Georgia	Europe and Central Asia	2021	Online
Ghana	Sub-Saharan Africa	2021	Telephone
India	South Asia	2020	Face-to-face
Kenya	Sub-Saharan Africa	2020	Telephone
Korea, Rep.	East Asia and Pacific	2021	Telephone
Poland	Europe and Central Asia	2021	Telephone
Senegal	Sub-Saharan Africa	2019	Face-to-face
Viet Nam	East Asia and Pacific	2019	Face-to-face

Source: World Bank.

Business Pulse Survey and World Bank Enterprise Survey

The Business Pulse Survey is a World Bank questionnaire conducted in the pandemic period beginning in 2020 that checked the pulse of businesses by measuring several critical dimensions of business health, including operations of the business, sales, liquidity and insolvency, labor adjustments, firms responses, expectations and uncertainty about the future, and preferred mechanisms of public support.[2] The surveys were conducted in three phases (refer to table A.2).

In most countries interviews were conducted over the phone, but in a few countries, such as Colombia and Türkiye, the questionnaire was administered online. Respondents included micro, small, medium, and large businesses, across all main sectors. Most businesses in the data were in wholesale and retail, manufacturing, and food preparation services. The full data set of 35 harmonized indicators can be retrieved from the Business Pulse Survey website, which presents further methodological reference material, including a technical note with detailed information on data availability, sample representativeness, and the harmonization process.

TABLE A.2 **List of countries in the Business Pulse Survey used in this report**

Region	Phase 1 April–August 2020	Phase 2 September 2020–June 2021	Phase 3 July 2021–December 2022
East Asia and Pacific	Cambodia	Cambodia	Malaysia
	Indonesia	Indonesia	Philippines
	Philippines	Malaysia	Viet Nam
	Viet Nam	Philippines	
		Viet Nam	
Europe and Central Asia	Bulgaria	Bulgaria	Bulgaria
	Croatia	Croatia	Croatia
	Kosovo	Kosovo	Greece
	Kyrgyz Republic	Kyrgyz Republic	Kyrgyz Republic
	Poland	Poland	Poland
	Romania	Romania	Romania
	Tajikistan	Tajikistan	Tajikistan
	Türkiye	Türkiye	Türkiye
	Uzbekistan	Uzbekistan	Uzbekistan
Latin America and the Caribbean	Argentina	Argentina	
	Brazil	Brazil	
	Chile	Chile	
	Colombia	Paraguay	
	Paraguay		

(Continued)

TABLE A.2 List of countries in the Business Pulse Survey used in this report *(Continued)*

Region	Phase 1 April–August 2020	Phase 2 September 2020–June 2021	Phase 3 July 2021–December 2022
Middle East and North Africa	Algeria	West Bank and Gaza	Egypt, Arab Rep.
	Egypt, Arab Rep.		
	Tunisia		
	West Bank and Gaza		
South Asia	Afghanistan	Afghanistan	Bangladesh
	Bangladesh	Bangladesh	India
	India	India	Nepal
	Nepal	Nepal	Pakistan
	Pakistan	Pakistan	
	Sri Lanka	Sri Lanka	
Sub-Saharan Africa	Côte d'Ivoire	Benin	Lesotho
	Gabon	Burkina Faso	South Africa
	Ghana	Ghana	Sudan
	Kenya	Kenya	
	Liberia	Madagascar	
	Madagascar	Malawi	
	Mali	Senegal	
	Nigeria	Sierra Leone	
	Senegal	South Africa	
	South Africa	Sudan	
	Sudan	Tanzania	
	Tanzania		
	Togo		

Source: World Bank.

Identification for Development Global Data Set

The Identification for Development (ID4D) global data set was produced within the ID4D program at the World Bank. It uses a combination of metrics that take advantage of available data and align with the changing nature of identification (ID) access throughout a person's lifetime.[3] Coverage rates are calculated across 194 countries with available data and then summed to arrive at the global total. For 129 countries, the ID4D-Findex survey was used, which directly measures adult ID ownership in 2017 and 2021. For the remaining countries, a combination of administrative data on registrations collected directly from ID agencies, voter registration rates, birth registration rates—depending on the availability of data—and country income levels was used. In revising the methodology for estimating 2021 global ID coverage, the primary aim was to integrate the ID4D-Findex survey data with improved administrative data and to maximize the proportion of the world's population covered in the estimates. The expanded set of metrics and data sources allows multiple models to be used for estimating coverage, triangulating the ID coverage gap, and accounting for uncertainty.

GovTech Maturity Index

The GovTech Maturity Index (GTMI) was developed as part of the GovTech Initiative at the World Bank to introduce a measure of government use of technology in four focus areas—supporting core government systems, enhancing service delivery, mainstreaming citizen engagement, and fostering GovTech enablers—and to assist practitioners in the design of new digital transformation projects. Constructed for 198 economies, the GTMI aims for a comprehensive measure of digital transformation in the public sector. It is not intended to create a ranking or assess a country's readiness or use; rather, it is intended to complement existing tools and diagnostics by providing a baseline and benchmark for maturity of adoption and use of technology by governments and identifying areas for improvement. The 2022 version of the GTMI is the simple average of the normalized scores of four components:

- The Core Government Systems Index (17 indicators) captures key aspects of a whole-of-government approach, including government cloud, interoperability framework, and other platforms.
- The Public Service Delivery Index (9 indicators) measures the maturity of online public service portals, with a focus on citizen-centric design and universal accessibility.
- The Digital Citizen Engagement Index (6 indicators) measures aspects of public participation platforms, citizen feedback mechanisms, open data, and open government portals.
- The GovTech Enablers Index (16 indicators) captures strategy, institutions, laws, and regulations, as well as digital skills and innovation policies and programs to foster GovTech.

The 2022 GTMI update, which includes data presented in this report, is based on the same four components, but the number of key indicators used to calculate the GTMI groups is slightly different due to the inclusion of several new indicators.[4]

Global Findex Survey and Database

Since 2011, the Global Findex Database has been collecting data on the ways in which adults around the world use financial services—from payments to savings and borrowing—and manage financial events, such as a major expense or a loss of income. Results from the first survey were published in 2011 and have been followed in subsequent surveys. The 2021 edition, based on nationally representative surveys of about 128,000 adults in 123 economies during the COVID-19 pandemic, contains updated indicators on access to and use of formal and informal financial services, such as the use of cards, mobile phones, and the internet to make and receive digital payments—including the adoption of digital merchant and utility payments during the pandemic—and offers insights into the behaviors that enable financial resilience. The data also identify gaps in access to and use of financial services by women and poor adults. All regional and global averages presented are adult population weighted, and regional averages include only low- and middle-income economies as classified by the World Bank. Income group classifications reflect the World Bank income group classifications in 2020. The survey results reflect a snapshot in time based on questions that respondents answer about their habits and experiences in the previous year. Data for all economies for all figures are available on the Global Findex website.[5]

Data tables for core indicators

All-country data tables are by pillar.

TABLE A.3 Digital adoption

| ISO abbreviation or World Bank designation | Economy | Adoption by people | | | | | Adoption by governments | |
		Individuals using the internet (% of population)	Fixed broadband subscriptions (per 100 inhabitants)	Unique mobile internet subscriptions (% of population)	Monthly mobile broadband traffic per capita (gigabytes)	Made or received a digital payment (% of population ages 15+), 2021	ID ownership (% of population ages 15+), 2021	UN e-government index
AFG	Afghanistan	18	0	13	0.4	8	87	0.27
ALB	Albania	83	20	48	5.5	35	97	0.74
DZA	Algeria	71	10	46	6.4	34	97	0.56
ASM	American Samoa			59				
AND	Andorra	94	51	84	2.2			0.72
AGO	Angola	33	0	24	0.4	25		0.38
ATG	Antigua and Barbuda	96	9	53	0.9			0.61
ARG	Argentina	88	25	72	3.0	65	99	0.82
ARM	Armenia	79	18	66	7.8	47	75	0.74
ABW	Aruba	97	18	26	0.0			
AUS	Australia	96	35	84	12.4	99		0.94
AUT	Austria	94	29	88	35.1	99		0.88
AZE	Azerbaijan	86	20	64	2.3	43		0.69
BHS	Bahamas, The	94	20	78	0.0			0.73
BHR	Bahrain	100	12	66	41.6	77		0.77
BGD	Bangladesh	39	7	32	3.2	45	87	0.56
BRB	Barbados	86	38	60	0.0			0.71
BLR	Belarus	90	33	67	12.1	79		0.76
BEL	Belgium	94	44	87	5.4	97	99	0.83
BLZ	Belize	62	9	48	0.8	28		0.50
BEN	Benin	34	0	14	1.3	44	47	0.43

(Continued)

TABLE A.3 Digital adoption (Continued)

ISO abbreviation or World Bank designation	Economy	Adoption by people					Adoption by governments	
		Individuals using the internet (% of population)	Fixed broadband subscriptions (per 100 inhabitants)	Unique mobile internet subscriptions (% of population)	Monthly mobile broadband traffic per capita (gigabytes)	Made or received a digital payment (% of population ages 15+), 2021	ID ownership (% of population ages 15+), 2021	UN e-government index
BMU	Bermuda	98	36	65				
BTN	Bhutan	86	1	58	0.0	17		0.55
BOL	Bolivia	66	9	46		55	98	0.62
BIH	Bosnia and Herzegovina	79	27	41	2.3	67	97	0.63
BWA	Botswana	74	4	43	2.0	52		0.55
BRA	Brazil	81	21	67	2.8	77	96	0.79
BRN	Brunei Darussalam	98	20	48	0.0			0.73
BGR	Bulgaria	79	35	66	10.3	75	99	0.78
BFA	Burkina Faso	22	0	17	0.1	33	83	0.35
BDI	Burundi	6	0	11	0.0	4		0.32
CPV	Cabo Verde	70	6	46	3.7			0.57
KHM	Cambodia	60	3	66	18.1	26	90	0.51
CMR	Cameroon	46	2	25	0.1	50	83	0.45
CAN	Canada	93	43	81	4.3	98	98	0.85
CYM	Cayman Islands	81	47	91				
CAF	Central African Republic	11	0	7	0.0	9		0.14
TCD	Chad	18	0	11	0.0	18		0.19
CHI	Channel Islands							
CHL	Chile	90	23	74	21.0	84	99	0.84

(Continued)

TABLE A.3 Digital adoption *(Continued)*

ISO abbreviation or World Bank designation	Economy	Adoption by people					Adoption by governments	
		Individuals using the internet (% of population)	Fixed broadband subscriptions (per 100 inhabitants)	Unique mobile internet subscriptions (% of population)	Monthly mobile broadband traffic per capita (gigabytes)	Made or received a digital payment (% of population ages 15+), 2021	ID ownership (% of population ages 15+), 2021	UN e-government index
CHN	China	76	41	79	14.4	86	100	0.81
COL	Colombia	73	17	59	4.6	52	97	0.73
COM	Comoros	27	0	14	1.1	20		0.28
COD	Congo, Dem Rep.	23	0	13	0.4	26		0.31
COG	Congo, Rep.	9	0	23	0.0	44	63	0.37
CRI	Costa Rica	83	21	63	5.3	59	95	0.77
CIV	Côte d'Ivoire	35	1	26	2.3	48	72	0.55
HRV	Croatia	82	27	71	22.8	87	100	0.81
CUB	Cuba	71	3	41	1.9			0.49
CUW	Curaçao	68	32	53	131.3			
CYP	Cyprus	90	38	58	5.6	87	87	0.87
CZE	Czech Republic	85	38	81	6.6	94	99	0.81
DNK	Denmark	98	45	91	22.6	100	99	0.97
DJI	Djibouti	69	1	12	2.7	0		0.28
DMA	Dominica	81	19	50	1.2			0.58
DOM	Dominican Republic	85	11	72	2.1	39	91	0.64
ECU	Ecuador	70	15	51	3.1	47	98	0.69
EGY	Egypt, Arab Rep.	72	10	49	1.6	20	97	0.59
SLV	El Salvador	63	11	45	1.2	28	97	0.55

(Continued)

TABLE A.3 Digital adoption *(Continued)*

ISO abbreviation or World Bank designation	Economy	Adoption by people					Adoption by governments	
		Individuals using the internet (% of population)	Fixed broadband subscriptions (per 100 inhabitants)	Unique mobile internet subscriptions (% of population)	Monthly mobile broadband traffic per capita (gigabytes)	Made or received a digital payment (% of population ages 15+), 2021	ID ownership (% of population ages 15+), 2021	UN e-government index
GNQ	Equatorial Guinea	54	0	9	0.3			0.27
ERI	Eritrea	22	0	0	0.0			0.17
EST	Estonia	91	40	75	42.4	99	98	0.94
SWZ	Eswatini	59	2	27	0.6	65		0.45
ETH	Ethiopia	17	0	12	0.3	20		0.29
FRO	Faroe Islands	98	35	85	8.3			0.62
FJI	Fiji	88	2	49				
FIN	Finland	93	34	87	59.1	98		0.95
FRA	France	85	49	87	13.6	98	94	0.88
PYF	French Polynesia	73	26	43	9.0			
GAB	Gabon	72	3	25	1.3	66	73	0.55
GMB	Gambia, The	33	0	16	0.0	22		0.31
GEO	Georgia	79	29	47	9.9	62	95	0.75
DEU	Germany	92	45	84	6.7	99	96	0.88
GHA	Ghana	68	1	28	3.5	66	87	0.58
GIB	Gibraltar	94	70	85	0.0			
GRC	Greece	83	43	89	0.0	91	98	0.85
GRL	Greenland	69	30	79	1.3			
GRD	Grenada	78	24	24	0.5			0.73
GUM	Guam	81	2	55				
GTM	Guatemala	51	4	41	0.0	26		0.51

(Continued)

TABLE A.3 Digital adoption *(Continued)*

ISO abbreviation or World Bank designation	Economy	Adoption by people				Adoption by governments	
		Individuals using the internet (% of population)	Fixed broadband subscriptions (per 100 inhabitants)	Unique mobile internet subscriptions (% of population)	Monthly mobile broadband traffic per capita (gigabytes)	Made or received a digital payment (% of population ages 15+), 2021	ID ownership (% of population ages 15+), 2021	UN e-government index
GIN	Guinea	35	0	22	0.7	28	59	0.36
GNB	Guinea-Bissau	35	0	13	1.0			0.26
GUY	Guyana	85	12	30	0.0			0.52
HTI	Haiti	39	0	22	0.0	28		0.25
HND	Honduras	48	5	42	5.5	32	93	0.39
HKG	Hong Kong SAR, China	96	40	82	18.4	93	98	
HUN	Hungary	90	35	77	9.4	86	99	0.78
ISL	Iceland	100	38	80	27.7	100	100	0.94
IND	India	46	2	49	9.6	35		0.59
IDN	Indonesia	66	5	47	8.8	37	97	0.72
IRN	Iran, Islamic Rep.	79	12	51	9.9	84	87	0.64
IRQ	Iraq	79	14	34	0.4	14	94	0.44
IRL	Ireland	95	32	77	7.3	98		0.86
IMN	Isle of Man			78				
ISR	Israel	90	29	73	0.0	91	98	0.89
ITA	Italy	85	34	92	15.1	96	98	0.84
JAM	Jamaica	82	15	54	2.1	50	83	0.59
JPN	Japan	83	36	86	15.8	96		0.90
JOR	Jordan	86	7	57	3.6	36	97	0.61
KAZ	Kazakhstan	92	15	49	24.8	78	99	0.86
KEN	Kenya	29	1	32	1.8	78	91	0.56

(Continued)

TABLE A.3 Digital adoption *(Continued)*

ISO abbreviation or World Bank designation	Economy	Adoption by people					Adoption by governments	
		Individuals using the internet (% of population)	Fixed broadband subscriptions (per 100 inhabitants)	Unique mobile internet subscriptions (% of population)	Monthly mobile broadband traffic per capita (gigabytes)	Made or received a digital payment (% of population ages 15+), 2021	ID ownership (% of population ages 15+), 2021	UN e-government index
KIR	Kiribati	54	0	17	1.8			0.43
PRK	Korea, Dem. People's Rep.	0		0				0.29
KOR	Korea, Rep.	97	45	94	17.0	98	97	0.95
XKX	Kosovo			22			95	
KWT	Kuwait	100	1	79	83.9	75		0.75
KGZ	Kyrgyz Republic	78	4	42	7.2	39	94	0.70
LAO	Lao PDR	62	2	46	2.0	21	55	0.38
LVA	Latvia	91	26	77	52.7	95	99	0.86
LBN	Lebanon	87	8	53	0.8	14	97	0.53
LSO	Lesotho	48	0	29	0.3	59		0.44
LBR	Liberia	34	0	18	0.4	46	30	0.29
LBY	Libya	18	5	45	0.0	32		0.34
LIE	Liechtenstein	96	49	90	2.7			0.87
LTU	Lithuania	88	29	79	32.1	91	92	0.87
LUX	Luxembourg	98	39	86	9.7	98		0.87
MAC	Macao SAR, China	88	30	82	7.7			
MDG	Madagascar	20	0	17	0.4	24		0.36
MWI	Malawi	24	0	22	0.5	40	85	0.34
MYS	Malaysia	97	12	67	28.6	79	96	0.77
MDV	Maldives	86	17	42	2.4	68		0.59

(Continued)

TABLE A.3 Digital adoption *(Continued)*

ISO abbreviation or World Bank designation	Economy	Adoption by people					Adoption by governments	
		Individuals using the internet (% of population)	Fixed broadband subscriptions (per 100 inhabitants)	Unique mobile internet subscriptions (% of population)	Monthly mobile broadband traffic per capita (gigabytes)	Made or received a digital payment (% of population ages 15+), 2021	ID ownership (% of population ages 15+), 2021	UN e-government index
MLI	Mali	34	1	17	0.0	38	69	0.34
MLT	Malta	92	43	84	12.9	91	99	0.89
MHL	Marshall Islands	39	2	37				0.37
MRT	Mauritania	59	0	25	2.7	20		0.32
MUS	Mauritius	68	26	50	6.7	80	99	0.72
MEX	Mexico	76	19	64	3.6	44		0.75
FSM	Micronesia, Fed Sts.	40	5	15	0.0			0.36
MDA	Moldova	61	24	59	8.4	60	99	0.73
MCO	Monaco	86	59	88	16.6			0.72
MNG	Mongolia	82	13	36	11.8	97	98	0.72
MNE	Montenegro	88	31	77	14.1	60		0.73
MAR	Morocco	88	6	50	9.6	30	94	0.59
MOZ	Mozambique	17	0	21	0.2	42	58	0.31
MMR	Myanmar	44	2	37	0.1	40	88	0.50
NAM	Namibia	53	4	29	0.7	66	91	0.53
NRU	Nauru	84	9	35	0.0			0.45
NPL	Nepal	52	4	45	0.1	29	88	0.51
NLD	Netherlands	93	44	88	7.7	99	95	0.94
NCL	New Caledonia	82	19	43				
NZL	New Zealand	96	36	83	4.9	98		0.94
NIC	Nicaragua	57	5	48	0.0	21	90	0.50

(Continued)

TABLE A.3 Digital adoption *(Continued)*

ISO abbreviation or World Bank designation	Economy	Adoption by people					Adoption by governments	
		Individuals using the internet (% of population)	Fixed broadband subscriptions (per 100 inhabitants)	Unique mobile internet subscriptions (% of population)	Monthly mobile broadband traffic per capita (gigabytes)	Made or received a digital payment (% of population ages 15+), 2021	ID ownership (% of population ages 15+), 2021	UN e-government index
NER	Niger	22	0	14	0.0	10		0.24
NGA	Nigeria	55	0	28	0.2	34		0.45
MKD	North Macedonia	83	24	66	5.4	74	98	0.70
MNP	Northern Mariana Islands			33				
NOR	Norway	99	46	82	11.7	99	99	0.89
OMN	Oman	96	12	60	7.6	0		0.78
PAK	Pakistan	21	1	23	3.6	18	88	0.42
PLW	Palau	27	7	64				0.50
PAN	Panama	68	15	74	0.0	36	98	0.70
PNG	Papua New Guinea	32	0	23	0.0			0.32
PRY	Paraguay	76	11	58	0.0	51	99	0.63
PER	Peru	75	9	53	2.3	49	98	0.75
PHL	Philippines	53	8	43	5.2	43		0.65
POL	Poland	87	23	75	16.0	93	98	0.84
PRT	Portugal	84	44	92	6.8	91	96	0.83
PRI	Puerto Rico	85	21	71		64		
QAT	Qatar	100	14	89	20.1	0		0.71
ROU	Romania	86	32	72	8.1	64	99	0.76

(Continued)

TABLE A.3 Digital adoption (Continued)

ISO abbreviation or World Bank designation	Economy	Adoption by people				Adoption by governments	
		Individuals using the internet (% of population)	Fixed broadband subscriptions (per 100 inhabitants)	Unique mobile internet subscriptions (% of population)	Monthly mobile broadband traffic per capita (gigabytes)	Made or received a digital payment (% of population ages 15+), 2021	ID ownership (% of population ages 15+), 2021	UN e-government index
RUS	Russian Federation	90	24	80	20.5	87	99	0.82
RWA	Rwanda	30	0	25	0.8	39		0.55
WSM	Samoa	78	1	42	0.2			0.42
SMR	San Marino	75	36		7.9			0.65
STP	São Tomé and Príncipe	51	2	27	0.7			0.41
SAU	Saudi Arabia	100	37	66	44.2	73	99	0.85
SEN	Senegal	58	1	22	2.9	53	82	0.45
SRB	Serbia	84	26	71	10.4	87	99	0.82
SYC	Seychelles	82	35	52	7.5			0.68
SLE	Sierra Leone	18	0	22	0.0	27	61	0.26
SGP	Singapore	96	37	89	13.7	95	97	0.91
SXM	Sint Maarten (Dutch part)			56				
SVK	Slovak Republic	89	33	78	7.8	95	100	0.80
SVN	Slovenia	89	32	79	11.9	97	95	0.88
SLB	Solomon Islands	36	0	31	0.2			0.35
SOM	Somalia	2	1	11	0.0	38		0.13
ZAF	South Africa	72	3	57	3.6	81	94	0.74
SSD	South Sudan	7	0	7	0.0	5	13	0.09
ESP	Spain	94	36	93	10.7	98	96	0.88

(Continued)

TABLE A.3 Digital adoption *(Continued)*

ISO abbreviation or World Bank designation	Economy	Adoption by people				Adoption by governments	
		Individuals using the internet (% of population)	Fixed broadband subscriptions (per 100 inhabitants)	Unique mobile internet subscriptions (% of population)	Monthly mobile broadband traffic per capita (gigabytes)	Made or received a digital payment (% of population ages 15+), 2021	ID ownership (% of population ages 15+), 2021	UN e-government index
LKA	Sri Lanka	44	10	55	6.2	55	93	0.63
KNA	St. Kitts and Nevis	79	42	46	0.0			0.68
LCA	St. Lucia	78	21	47	0.9			0.56
MAF	St. Martin (French part)			24				
VCT	St. Vincent and the Grenadines	85	28	41	1.3			0.58
SDN	Sudan	28	0	20	0.0	12		0.30
SUR	Suriname	66	20	56	72.7			0.58
SWE	Sweden	95	40	87	18.8	99	100	0.94
CHE	Switzerland	96	50	92	16.7	98	95	0.88
SYR	Syrian Arab Republic	36	7	33	0.0	0		0.39
TJK	Tajikistan	22	0	41	0.0	33	86	0.50
TZA	Tanzania	32	2	26	1.0	50	60	0.42
THA	Thailand	88	18	71	28.0	92	99	0.77
TLS	Timor-Leste	39	0	49	0.0			0.44
TGO	Togo	35	1	23	0.6	44	40	0.42
TON	Tonga	72	6	34	0.1			0.52
TTO	Trinidad and Tobago	79	24	45	5.8	64		0.63
TUN	Tunisia	79	14	60	5.5	28	99	0.65

(Continued)

TABLE A.3 Digital adoption *(Continued)*

ISO abbreviation or World Bank designation	Economy	Individuals using the internet (% of population)	Fixed broadband subscriptions (per 100 inhabitants)	Unique mobile internet subscriptions (% of population)	Monthly mobile broadband traffic per capita (gigabytes)	Made or received a digital payment (% of population ages 15+), 2021	ID ownership (% of population ages 15+), 2021	UN e-government index
		Adoption by people					**Adoption by governments**	
TUR	Türkiye	83	22	75	10.7	68	96	0.80
TKM	Turkmenistan	21	6	40		34		0.48
TCA	Turks and Caicos Islands			53				
TUV	Tuvalu	72	4	22	0.0			0.38
UGA	Uganda	10	0	25	0.7	63	73	0.44
UKR	Ukraine	79	18	64	0.0	81	99	0.80
ARE	United Arab Emirates	100	40	90	19.6	77	90	0.90
GBR	United Kingdom	97	41	89	0.0	99		0.91
USA	United States	92	38	86	13.4	93		0.92
URY	Uruguay	90	33	73	12.2	68	100	0.84
UZB	Uzbekistan	77	26	46	4.4	42	92	0.73
VUT	Vanuatu	66	1	34	3.7			0.50
VEN	Venezuela, RB	62	9	50	1.1	81	99	0.51
VNM	Viet Nam	79	22	56	9.2	46	97	0.68
VGB	Virgin Islands (British)	78	25	50	0.0			
VIR	Virgin Islands (US)	64	9	51				
PSE	West Bank and Gaza			45	1.6		96	
YEM	Yemen, Rep.	27	1	11	0.0	9		0.29

(Continued)

TABLE A.3 Digital adoption (*Continued*)

ISO abbreviation or World Bank designation	Economy	Adoption by people					Adoption by governments	
		Individuals using the internet (% of population)	Fixed broadband subscriptions (per 100 inhabitants)	Unique mobile internet subscriptions (% of population)	Monthly mobile broadband traffic per capita (gigabytes)	Made or received a digital payment (% of population ages 15+), 2021	ID ownership (% of population ages 15+), 2021	UN e-government index
ZMB	Zambia	21	0	19	0.0	46	94	0.50
ZWE	Zimbabwe	35	1	28	0.6	58	85	0.47
HIC	High-income countries	92[a]	38	85	14	93	97	0.89
UMIC	Upper-middle-income countries	79[a]	28	70	12	74	98	0.77
LMIC	Lower-middle-income countries	56[a]	4	42	6	38	88	0.56
LIC	Low-income countries	26[a]	0	16	0.3	25	69	0.31
EAP	East Asia and Pacific	74	31	71	13	76	98	0.78
ECA	Europe and Central Asia	87	32	78	12	86	97	0.83
LAC	Latin America and the Caribbean	76	17	61	4	59	97	0.72
MENA	Middle East and North Africa	77	14	51	9	41	94	0.61
NAC	North America	92	38	85	12	94	98	0.91
SAR	South Asia	42	3	44	8	33	88	0.56
SSA	Sub-Saharan Africa	34	1	23	0.8	38	74	0.40
World	World	66	18	56	9	58	94	0.66

Source: World Bank.
Note: All values are for 2022 unless otherwise indicated. Per capita data for groups are weighted averages using population. Other data for groups are simple averages. Blank cells indicate that no information is available. ID = identification; UN = United Nations.
a. Value is from the International Telecommunication Union. It is slightly different from the population-weighted average based on World Bank fiscal year 2023 income classification.

TABLE A.4 Digital sector

ISO abbreviation or World Bank designation	Economy	Value added (US$, millions)		Employment (thousands)		Export and venture investment				Innovation: ICT patent publications, 2021
		ICT manufacturing	ICT services	ICT manufacturing	ICT services	ICT goods exports (US$, millions), 2021	ICT services exports (US$, millions)	VC deals in digital sector	VC funding value (US$, millions)	
AFG	Afghanistan		566	0	5	2				
ALB	Albania		539	0	14	8	164			
DZA	Algeria					6	88	1	150	0
ASM	American Samoa					1				
AND	Andorra		102			21				
AGO	Angola			0	36	2	22			
ATG	Antigua and Barbuda					1	5	1	0	
ARG	Argentina	1,045	13,589	46	162	22	2,746	57	213	220
ARM	Armenia		529	0	22	19	711	1	3	
ABW	Aruba		94			1	13			
AUS	Australia	4,560	36,500	37	564	2,961	5,049	339	2,732	4,330
AUT	Austria	5,599	16,381	27	140	9,979	10,076	80	662	51
AZE	Azerbaijan					5	135			
BHS	Bahamas, The		425			2	0	4	422	
BHR	Bahrain					32		8	51	
BGD	Bangladesh		4,519	22	168	24	721	33	121	
BRB	Barbados			0	2	2				
BLR	Belarus			33	116	436	2,707	2	1	
BEL	Belgium	1,839	24,538	11	136	6,082	18,421	121	643	66

(Continued)

TABLE A.4 Digital sector *(Continued)*

| ISO abbreviation or World Bank designation | Economy | Value added (US$, millions) | | Employment (thousands) | | ICT goods exports (US$, millions), 2021 | Export and venture investment | | | Innovation: ICT patent publications, 2021 |
		ICT manufacturing	ICT services	ICT manufacturing	ICT services		ICT services exports (US$, millions)	VC deals in digital sector	VC funding value (US$, millions)	
BLZ	Belize		83			1	91	3	4	
BEN	Benin		327			0		1	0	
BMU	Bermuda		148			0	27	1	7	
BTN	Bhutan			0	3	0	1			
BOL	Bolivia			0	28	7	51	3	3	
BIH	Bosnia and Herzegovina	21	1,042	1	31	14	355			0
BWA	Botswana		496	0	6	1	24			
BRA	Brazil	5,289	45,544	174	1,701	730	4,642	367	3,079	2,386
BRN	Brunei Darussalam	3	228	0	5	2	6			
BGR	Bulgaria	387	5,570	15	124	851	3,018	17	28	14
BFA	Burkina Faso		550	0	15	1				
BDI	Burundi			0	5	0				
CPV	Cabo Verde					0	10			
KHM	Cambodia	1	729	5	23	333	119	1	0	
CMR	Cameroon	6	940			11		3	10	
CAN	Canada	5,618	80,692	56	911	7,407	16,161	499	6,664	2,669
CYM	Cayman Islands		141			7		6	41	
CAF	Central African Republic					0		1	3	
TCD	Chad		166	0	2	1				
CHI	Channel Islands									

(Continued)

TABLE A.4 Digital sector (*Continued*)

ISO abbreviation or World Bank designation	Economy	Value added (US$, millions)		Employment (thousands)		Export and venture investment				Innovation: ICT patent publications, 2021
		ICT manufac- turing	ICT services	ICT manufac- turing	ICT services	ICT goods exports (US$, millions), 2021	ICT services exports (US$, millions)	VC deals in digital sector	VC funding value (US$, millions)	
CHL	Chile	5,500	5,969	25	159	233	529	67	358	173
CHN	China	327,130	757,362	10,056	13,783	857,505	82,923	4,004	22,911	432,505
COL	Colombia	616	7,042	8	320	120	783	84	936	246
COM	Comoros			0	1	0				
COD	Congo, Dem Rep.			0	0	1				
COG	Congo, Rep.			0	0	1		2	38	
CRI	Costa Rica	519	3,339	7	43	3,710	1,878	8	4	5
CIV	Côte d'Ivoire			0	0	2		3	19	
HRV	Croatia	271	3,373	4	53	462	1,531	9	24	11
CUB	Cuba					3				2
CUW	Curaçao					2	33			
CYP	Cyprus	39	2,159	0	15	81	5,869	16	48	0
CZE	Czech Republic	3,670	17,712	48	175	35,226	6,883	32	680	32
DNK	Denmark	2,907	15,640	7	123	4,931	7,427	104	783	58
DJI	Djibouti					1				
DMA	Dominica					0	11			
DOM	Dominican Republic		758	4	45	278	65			3
ECU	Ecuador		1,960	2	65	12	83	6	100	3
EGY	Egypt, Arab Rep.			15	221	1,173	1,655	100	385	0
SLV	El Salvador		841	5	27	24	387	2	20	0

(Continued)

```
```

TABLE A.4 Digital sector *(Continued)*

ISO abbreviation or World Bank designation	Economy	Value added (US$, millions)		Employment (thousands)		Export and venture investment				Innovation: ICT patent publications, 2021
		ICT manufacturing	ICT services	ICT manufacturing	ICT services	ICT goods exports (US$, millions), 2021	ICT services exports (US$, millions)	VC deals in digital sector	VC funding value (US$, millions)	
GNQ	Equatorial Guinea					0				
ERI	Eritrea					0				
EST	Estonia	265	2,757	9	32	2,184	2,449	85	1,390	0
SWZ	Eswatini		144	0	1	2				
ETH	Ethiopia			6	92	3	151	2	0	
FRO	Faroe Islands		67	0	1	1				
FJI	Fiji		197	0	1	17	22			
FIN	Finland	5,659	15,595	23	125	2,073	12,334	88	878	113
FRA	France	15,131	146,655	86	1,034	21,271	24,372	662	8,554	1,878
PYF	French Polynesia					1				
GAB	Gabon					0		1	0	
GMB	Gambia, The		61		3	0				
GEO	Georgia		539	0	19	64	597	2	2	2
DEU	Germany	48,365	193,739	419	1,438	82,118	41,258	627	7,878	6,533
GHA	Ghana		2,696	0	33	3		11	59	
GIB	Gibraltar					1		4	113	
GRC	Greece	277	6,504	8	110	1,434	1,315	22	34	21
GRL	Greenland					2				
GRD	Grenada					0	6			

(Continued)

TABLE A.4 Digital sector *(Continued)*

ISO abbreviation or World Bank designation	Economy	Value added (US$, millions)		Employment (thousands)		Export and venture investment				Innovation: ICT patent publications, 2021
		ICT manufacturing	ICT services	ICT manufacturing	ICT services	ICT goods exports (US$, millions), 2021	ICT services exports (US$, millions)	VC deals in digital sector	VC funding value (US$, millions)	
GUM	Guam					1				
GTM	Guatemala	3,172		0	37	42	623			0
GIN	Guinea					1	7			
GNB	Guinea-Bissau			0	13	0				
GUY	Guyana		126	0	2	1				
HTI	Haiti		199			1				
HND	Honduras			0	20	8	100			0
HKG	Hong Kong SAR, China	171	12,357			410,478	3,677	89	1,156	0
HUN	Hungary	2,722	8,307	68	182	17,346	3,109	14	26	512
ISL	Iceland	61	1,237	0	9	19	467	26	131	0
IND	India	6,465	166,532	401	6,344	8,793	99,233	1,275	15,110	0
IDN	Indonesia	4,100	47,979	125	789	6,752	2,377	211	3,500	0
IRN	Iran, Islamic Rep.		6,214	38	224	3				
IRQ	Iraq			0	22	4		5	16	
IRL	Ireland		85,716	27	149	28,022	206,589	118	741	
IMN	Isle of Man									11
ISR	Israel	11,263	36,053	78	256	8,431		347	7,009	983
ITA	Italy	11,351	64,589	104	679	12,070	9,620	141	1,747	351
JAM	Jamaica					3	128			

(Continued)

TABLE A.4 Digital sector *(Continued)*

ISO abbreviation or World Bank designation	Economy	Value added (US$, millions)		Employment (thousands)		Export and venture investment				Innovation: ICT patent publications, 2021
		ICT manufacturing	ICT services	ICT manufacturing	ICT services	ICT goods exports (US$, millions), 2021	ICT services exports (US$, millions)	VC deals in digital sector	VC funding value (US$, millions)	
JPN	Japan	84,212	255,515	578	2,720	65,202	10,300	859	2,791	54,022
JOR	Jordan			3	29	19	25	21	13	6
KAZ	Kazakhstan	43	3,270			45	470			0
KEN	Kenya		2,685	0	69	20		62	745	0
KIR	Kiribati			0	0	0				
PRK	Korea, Dem. People's Rep.					8				
KOR	Korea, Rep.	114,324	78,418	842	823	219,811	9,163	971	6,848	53,495
XKX	Kosovo			0	12					
KWT	Kuwait					14	4,609	13	22	
KGZ	Kyrgyz Republic			0	32	60	32			
LAO	Lao PDR	15	330	2	8	180				
LVA	Latvia	174	2,065	2	38	1,728	1,301	7	7	2
LBN	Lebanon		1,335	1	25	23		1	0	
LSO	Lesotho			0	0	0	0			
LBR	Liberia			0	5	1				
LBY	Libya					0				
LIE	Liechtenstein	113	131	1	1			7	272	
LTU	Lithuania	309	2,504	7	51	1,396	1,842	31	245	7
LUX	Luxembourg		3,588	1	21	273	4,334	20	72	163
MAC	Macao SAR, China					307	14			

(Continued)

TABLE A.4 Digital sector (Continued)

ISO abbreviation or World Bank designation	Economy	Value added (US$, millions)		Employment (thousands)		Export and venture investment				Innovation: ICT patent publications, 2021
		ICT manufacturing	ICT services	ICT manufacturing	ICT services	ICT goods exports (US$, millions), 2021	ICT services exports (US$, millions)	VC deals in digital sector	VC funding value (US$, millions)	
MDG	Madagascar			0	19	1		1	1	
MWI	Malawi					1				0
MYS	Malaysia	18,647	23,397	590	353	96,315	3,622	48	360	300
MDV	Maldives			0	1	0	37			
MLI	Mali			3	8	4				
MLT	Malta	204	1,439	3	13	1,148	90	5	36	0
MHL	Marshall Islands			0	0	18		4	10	
MRT	Mauritania		232	1	3	0				
MUS	Mauritius		518	1	14	15	161	6	4	
MEX	Mexico	18,933	20,339	869	211	71,000		130	1,022	0
FSM	Micronesia, Fed Sts.			0	0	0				
MDA	Moldova		608			6	513	1	0	13
MCO	Monaco									2
MNG	Mongolia		290	0	15	1	50			0
MNE	Montenegro		204	0	0	6	189			2
MAR	Morocco	182	3,354	0		903	2,098	18	9	84
MOZ	Mozambique		494	0	15	1	16			
MMR	Myanmar	398	1,889	5	30	89				
NAM	Namibia		211	1	6	3	23	2	18	
NRU	Nauru			0	0	0				

(Continued)

TABLE A.4 Digital sector *(Continued)*

ISO abbreviation or World Bank designation	Economy	Value added (US$, millions)		Employment (thousands)		Export and venture investment				Innovation: ICT patent publications, 2021
		ICT manufacturing	ICT services	ICT manufacturing	ICT services	ICT goods exports (US$, millions), 2021	ICT services exports (US$, millions)	VC deals in digital sector	VC funding value (US$, millions)	
NPL	Nepal		686	0	0	2	123			
NLD	Netherlands	5,369	44,996	29	364	69,250	37,334	282	1,234	206
NCL	New Caledonia			0	1	2				
NZL	New Zealand	643	5,006	3	93	735	1,111	44	231	185
NIC	Nicaragua			0	2	2	293			0
NER	Niger		385	0	2	1				
NGA	Nigeria		44,310	28	372	41	263	141	514	
MKD	North Macedonia	37	495	2	21	57	492			
MNP	Northern Mariana Islands					0				
NOR	Norway	1,298	18,271	8	114	1,192	3,519	80	1,938	37
OMN	Oman					226				
PAK	Pakistan		5,948	46	294	24	2,649	66	263	
PLW	Palau			0	0	2				
PAN	Panama			1	14	105	495	5	42	0
PNG	Papua New Guinea		354			5	1			
PRY	Paraguay		1,068			10	20			
PER	Peru	142	4,699	10	130	15	121	16	25	52
PHL	Philippines	6,674	12,857	184	163	36,174	6,673	40	679	594
POL	Poland	2,575	28,922	65	497	21,552	13,419	72	720	150
PRT	Portugal	499	9,954	12	129	2,615	3,934	52	398	20
PRI	Puerto Rico							4	24	

(Continued)

TABLE A.4 Digital sector *(Continued)*

ISO abbreviation or World Bank designation	Economy	Value added (US$, millions)		Employment (thousands)		Export and venture investment				
		ICT manufacturing	ICT services	ICT manufacturing	ICT services	ICT goods exports (US$, millions), 2021	ICT services exports (US$, millions)	VC deals in digital sector	VC funding value (US$, millions)	Innovation: ICT patent publications, 2021
QAT	Qatar					85	1,140	3	2	
ROU	Romania	1,385	17,903	50	197	2,683		74	103	55
RUS	Russian Federation	8,156	37,126	459	1,474	1,253	5,831	47	374	2,759
RWA	Rwanda		221	1	12	3	26	1	0	
WSM	Samoa		52	0	1	0	20			
SMR	San Marino					2				0
STP	São Tomé and Príncipe					0				
SAU	Saudi Arabia	105	57,700	3	127	78	1,752	79	645	1
SEN	Senegal	2	940	2	20	22	132	9	7	
SRB	Serbia	175	3,232	6	92	424	2,820	4	44	73
SYC	Seychelles		48	0	1	3	10	13	174	
SLE	Sierra Leone			0	10	3				
SGP	Singapore	4,806	22,876	10	120	82,236	23,188	457	5,665	3,007
SXM	Sint Maarten (Dutch part)					0	8			
SVK	Slovak Republic	743	5,321	11	80	12,580	1,946	4	11	20
SVN	Slovenia	457	2,385	6	35	962	981	3	24	5
SLB	Solomon Islands			0	2	0	4			

(Continued)

TABLE A.4 Digital sector *(Continued)*

ISO abbreviation or World Bank designation	Economy	Value added (US$, millions)		Employment (thousands)		Export and venture investment				Innovation: ICT patent publications, 2021
		ICT manufacturing	ICT services	ICT manufacturing	ICT services	ICT goods exports (US$, millions), 2021	ICT services exports (US$, millions)	VC deals in digital sector	VC funding value (US$, millions)	
SOM	Somalia			2	14	0				
ZAF	South Africa	560	13,156	31	276	259	944	65	308	15
SSD	South Sudan					0				
ESP	Spain	2,047	51,071	28	574	6,242	16,015	322	1,896	96
LKA	Sri Lanka		797	5	58	27	1,097	1	1	
KNA	St. Kitts and Nevis					15	4	1	0	
LCA	St. Lucia		77			3	12			
MAF	St. Martin (French part)									
VCT	St. Vincent and the Grenadines		28			0	5	2	0	
SDN	Sudan			0	40	3	1			
SUR	Suriname		162	0	4	2	17			
SWE	Sweden	2,847	47,519	22	222	11,257	20,646	313	3,718	117
CHE	Switzerland	23,598	33,141	108	182	3,777	14,753	245	3,010	76
SYR	Syrian Arab Republic					0				
TJK	Tajikistan		105			3	4			
TZA	Tanzania		1,034	32	43	4		2	0	
THA	Thailand	3,112	14,286	543	238	74,410	393	39	378	
TLS	Timor-Leste		61	0	8	2	1			
TGO	Togo			2	0	1				

(Continued)

TABLE A.4 Digital sector (*Continued*)

ISO abbreviation or World Bank designation	Economy	Value added (US$, millions)		Employment (thousands)		Export and venture investment				
		ICT manufacturing	ICT services	ICT manufacturing	ICT services	ICT goods exports (US$, millions), 2021	ICT services exports (US$, millions)	VC deals in digital sector	VC funding value (US$, millions)	Innovation: ICT patent publications, 2021
TON	Tonga			0	0	0	15			
TTO	Trinidad and Tobago			0	107	5	48			
TUN	Tunisia	373	1,794	9	20	824		7	11	6
TUR	Türkiye	3,009	22,550	68	247	1,986	2,596	190	1,773	718
TKM	Turkmenistan					0				
TCA	Turks and Caicos Islands					0				
TUV	Tuvalu			0	0	0				
UGA	Uganda			0	34	2	40	10	15	
UKR	Ukraine					448	7,521	17	9	3
ARE	United Arab Emirates			18	184	2,783	8,352	121	1,444	
GBR	United Kingdom	15,873	163,908	112	1,414	17,313	42,564	1,432	18,952	1,383
USA	United States	337,696	1,847,499	1,053	5,160	158,927	66,227	7,250	124,635	168,003
URY	Uruguay			1	48	6	1,172	5	25	0
UZB	Uzbekistan					22	270	2	2	
VUT	Vanuatu			0	0	1				
VEN	Venezuela, RB					6		3	52	
VNM	Viet Nam	23,964	5,203	857	340	160,629		79	428	0

(Continued)

TABLE A.4 Digital sector *(Continued)*

ISO abbreviation or World Bank designation	Economy	Value added (US$, millions)		Employment (thousands)		Export and venture investment				Innovation: ICT patent publications, 2021
		ICT manufacturing	ICT services	ICT manufacturing	ICT services	ICT goods exports (US$, millions), 2021	ICT services exports (US$, millions)	VC deals in digital sector	VC funding value (US$, millions)	
VGB	Virgin Islands (British)		42			9		12	45	
VIR	Virgin Islands (US)									
PSE	West Bank and Gaza			0	13	1				
YEM	Yemen, Rep.					0				
ZMB	Zambia			4	15	1	26	2	12	0
ZWE	Zimbabwe			0	19	1		2	16	0
HIC	High-income countries	724,548	3,478,026	4,011	19,629	1,337,404	667,488	16,296	218,002	298,844
UMIC	Upper-middle-income countries	391,920	1,036,008	13,056	20,419	1,116,455	122,759	5,327	35,184	439,318
LMIC	Lower-middle-income countries	38,081	266,555	1,660	8,668	209,897	123,291	1,903	18,603	693
LIC	Low-income countries		2,441	14	294	38	235	15	18	0
EAP	East Asia and Pacific	592,761	1,275,885	13,837	20,080	2,014,176	148,728	7,185	47,688	548,438
ECA	Europe and Central Asia	167,270	1,112,560	1,887	10,523	381,853	542,732	5,376	59,169	15,560
LAC	Latin America and the Caribbean	32,044	109,698	1,152	3,125	76,386	14,369	786	6,414	3,090

(Continued)

TABLE A.4 Digital sector *(Continued)*

ISO abbreviation or World Bank designation	Economy	Value added (US$, millions)		Employment (thousands)		Export and venture investment				Innovation: ICT patent publications, 2021
		ICT manufac-turing	ICT services	ICT manufac-turing	ICT services	ICT goods exports (US$, millions), 2021	ICT services exports (US$, millions)	VC deals in digital sector	VC funding value (US$, millions)	
MENA	Middle East and North Africa	12,127	107,890	168	1,134	15,753	19,810	729	9,794	1,080
NAC	North America	343,314	1,928,339	1,109	6,071	166,334	82,415	7,750	131,306	170,672
SAR	South Asia	6,465	179,047	474	6,873	8,872	103,861	1,375	15,494	0
SSA	Sub-Saharan Africa	568	69,611	114	1,204	420	1,857	340	1,941	15
World	World	1,154,549	4,783,030	18,741	49,010	2,663,794	913,773	23,541	271,806	738,855

Source: World Bank.
Note: All values are for 2022 unless otherwise indicated. Per capita data for groups are weighted averages using population. Other data for groups are simple averages. Blank cells indicate that no information is available. ICT = information and communication technology; VC = venture capital.

TABLE A.5 Digital infrastructure

ISO abbreviation or World Bank designation	Economy	Broadband infrastructure					Data infrastructure	
		4G+ mobile coverage (% of population)	Price of mobile broadband (2 gigabytes per month) (% of monthly GNI per capita)	Price of fixed broadband (5 gigabytes per month) (% of monthly GNI per capita)	Median mobile download speed (megabits per second), 2023	Median fixed broadband download speed (megabits per second), 2023	IXP monthly peak traffic per capita (kilobytes per capita)	Connected data centers (per million people)
AFG	Afghanistan	26	10.7	15.0	4.0	2	0.0	
ALB	Albania	99	2.2	1.3	41.9	46	2.2	1.4
DZA	Algeria	86	0.7	3.9	16.1	11		
ASM	American Samoa							
AND	Andorra	97	0.0	0.6	0.0	88		
AGO	Angola	33	2.7	12.2	19.3	15	0.4	0.2
ATG	Antigua and Barbuda	99	3.0	4.8	0.0	30		10.7
ARG	Argentina	98	0.5	5.7	24.0	54	0.4	1.1
ARM	Armenia	100	0.9	4.2	24.1	39	7.2	2.2
ABW	Aruba	64	1.4	3.2	0.0			
AUS	Australia	100	0.2	1.2	86.2	53	49.4	5.7
AUT	Austria	98	0.2	0.7	69.6	66	117.2	5.9
AZE	Azerbaijan	94	1.3	1.8	37.4	28		0.6
BHS	Bahamas, The	95	1.1	1.6	0.0	44		2.4
BHR	Bahrain	100	0.8	3.0	96.5	48	232.3	4.1
BGD	Bangladesh	98	1.0	1.5	16.1	36	1.0	0.2
BRB	Barbados	99	3.2	3.6	0.0	81		
BLR	Belarus	98	0.6	0.7	11.9	53	0.0	0.2
BEL	Belgium	100	0.4	0.7	57.5	87	22.3	3.5
BLZ	Belize	70	3.9	7.0	0.0	40	0.1	

(Continued)

TABLE A.5 Digital infrastructure (Continued)

ISO abbreviation or World Bank designation	Economy	Broadband infrastructure					Data infrastructure	
		4G+ mobile coverage (% of population)	Price of mobile broadband (2 gigabytes per month) (% of monthly GNI per capita)	Price of fixed broadband (5 gigabytes per month) (% of monthly GNI per capita)	Median mobile download speed (megabits per second), 2023	Median fixed broadband download speed (megabits per second), 2023	IXP monthly peak traffic per capita (kilobytes per capita)	Connected data centers (per million people)
BEN	Benin	46	5.7	23.0	0.0	17	0.1	0.1
BMU	Bermuda	100				i		
BTN	Bhutan	97	0.9	2.9	0.0	17	4.5	3.8
BOL	Bolivia	74		8.3		25	2.3	0.2
BIH	Bosnia and Herzegovina	99	1.2	2.1	24.6	27	1.5	0.3
BWA	Botswana	91	1.1	10.1	0.0	7	0.4	
BRA	Brazil	92	0.6	3.1	36.9	102	85.4	1.4
BRN	Brunei Darussalam	99	0.3	1.2	85.1	49	0.0	6.7
BGR	Bulgaria	100	0.5	1.5	97.6	69	314.6	3.6
BFA	Burkina Faso	37	9.9	31.1	0.0	43	0.5	0.2
BDI	Burundi	32	12.8	964.3	0.0	5	0.0	0.2
CPV	Cabo Verde	80	3.1	2.9	0.0	15	0.0	
KHM	Cambodia	92	2.3	11.6	21.1	21	1.4	0.4
CMR	Cameroon	16	3.7	19.8	10.7	8	0.0	0.3
CAN	Canada	99	0.9	1.1	84.9	149	46.9	3.7
CYM	Cayman Islands	100		1.9				
CAF	Central African Republic	0.3	23.8	1772.2	0.0			
TCD	Chad	36	22.5	577.2	0.0		0.0	0.1
CHI	Channel Islands							

(Continued)

TABLE A.5 Digital infrastructure (Continued)

ISO abbreviation or World Bank designation	Economy	Broadband infrastructure					Data infrastructure	
		4G+ mobile coverage (% of population)	Price of mobile broadband (2 gigabytes per month) (% of monthly GNI per capita)	Price of fixed broadband (5 gigabytes per month) (% of monthly GNI per capita)	Median mobile download speed (megabits per second), 2023	Median fixed broadband download speed (megabits per second), 2023	IXP monthly peak traffic per capita (kilobytes per capita)	Connected data centers (per million people)
CHL	Chile	89	0.4	1.8	24.1	224	343.4	2.1
CHN	China	100	0.5	0.5	116.7	227	2.1	0.0
COL	Colombia	100	1.5	3.8	11.9	93	14.3	0.3
COM	Comoros	93	7.8	29.2	0.0			0.0
COD	Congo, Dem Rep.	45	10.3		14.9	10	0.8	0.0
COG	Congo, Rep.	85	10.4	31.0	0.0	41	0.0	0.3
CRI	Costa Rica	93	1.0	1.6	25.7	67	5.9	1.5
CIV	Côte d'Ivoire	91	2.4	13.0	15.9	40	0.0	0.1
HRV	Croatia	100	0.4	0.5	75.4	47	27.0	2.9
CUB	Cuba	50	0.0	6.8	5.0	2	0.0	
CUW	Curaçao	100		4.4			130.7	13.3
CYP	Cyprus	100	0.3	0.9	60.4	52	0.0	1.6
CZE	Czech Republic	100	0.5	1.0	45.6	56	227.7	2.9
DNK	Denmark	100	0.4	0.7	123.7	201	73.0	5.6
DJI	Djibouti	90	6.2	8.8	0.0	8	5.4	2.7
DMA	Dominica	100	2.9	5.6	0.0	80	0.9	
DOM	Dominican Republic	98	1.5	2.7	20.2	20	0.0	0.2
ECU	Ecuador	94	2.0	4.7	20.3	51	13.5	0.5
EGY	Egypt, Arab Rep.	98	1.0	2.8	22.9	45	0.3	0.1
SLV	El Salvador	76	2.9	6.7	23.6	35	0.0	0.2

(Continued)

TABLE A.5 Digital infrastructure (*Continued*)

ISO abbreviation or World Bank designation	Economy	Broadband infrastructure					Data infrastructure	
		4G+ mobile coverage (% of population)	Price of mobile broadband (2 gigabytes per month) (% of monthly GNI per capita)	Price of fixed broadband (5 gigabytes per month) (% of monthly GNI per capita)	Median mobile download speed (megabits per second), 2023	Median fixed broadband download speed (megabits per second), 2023	IXP monthly peak traffic per capita (kilobytes per capita)	Connected data centers (per million people)
GNQ	Equatorial Guinea	60	10.3	12.9	0.0			0.6
ERI	Eritrea	0	0.0	213.8	0.0			
EST	Estonia	99	0.2	0.8	66.8	65	6.0	5.9
SWZ	Eswatini	80	3.8	13.4	0.0	5		
ETH	Ethiopia	20	3.4	16.3	16.1	6		0.0
FRO	Faroe Islands	100		1.2				
FJI	Fiji	80		1.8		15	0.0	
FIN	Finland	100	0.3	0.9	91.3	95	10.3	5.9
FRA	France	99	0.2	1.2	69.1	164	26.4	2.9
PYF	French Polynesia	90						
GAB	Gabon	98	1.6	7.2	0.0	41	0.3	1.3
GMB	Gambia, The	8	11.6	98.1	0.0	7	0.2	0.4
GEO	Georgia	100	0.7	2.4	30.5	25	0.0	1.1
DEU	Germany	100	0.3	1.0	57.2	83	149.3	3.5
GHA	Ghana	68	2.1	12.8	9.6	28	0.9	0.2
GIB	Gibraltar	100						
GRC	Greece	99	0.6	1.9	63.6	45	52.0	0.9
GRL	Greenland	100	0.0		0.0			
GRD	Grenada	99	4.7	4.9	0.0	74	12.4	
GUM	Guam	83					0.0	29.1
GTM	Guatemala	88	3.1	6.3	24.4	29	0.5	0.3

(Continued)

TABLE A.5 Digital infrastructure (Continued)

ISO abbreviation or World Bank designation	Economy	Broadband infrastructure					Data infrastructure	
		4G+ mobile coverage (% of population)	Price of mobile broadband (2 gigabytes per month) (% of monthly GNI per capita)	Price of fixed broadband (5 gigabytes per month) (% of monthly GNI per capita)	Median mobile download speed (megabits per second), 2023	Median fixed broadband download speed (megabits per second), 2023	IXP monthly peak traffic per capita (kilobytes per capita)	Connected data centers (per million people)
GIN	Guinea	29	5.9	11.3	0.0	11	0.0	0.1
GNB	Guinea-Bissau	31	8.0	67.0	0.0			
GUY	Guyana	50	2.4	3.7	0.0	49		
HTI	Haiti	35	14.8	42.3	7.2	20	1.0	
HND	Honduras	79	7.8	12.8	25.3	33	0.0	0.1
HKG	Hong Kong SAR, China	99		0.5		199		7.1
HUN	Hungary	99	0.6	0.7	44.2	139	34.9	0.7
ISL	Iceland	100	0.4	1.4	0.0		57.6	23.6
IND	India	99	1.1	2.8	31.0	51	4.2	0.1
IDN	Indonesia	97	1.1	6.1	20.2	26	5.1	0.5
IRN	Iran, Islamic Rep.	81	0.0	0.9	35.0	11	33.4	0.0
IRQ	Iraq	97	1.7	5.0	31.4	28	0.0	0.1
IRL	Ireland	90	0.4	1.5	31.0	83	152.5	4.9
IMN	Isle of Man							11.8
ISR	Israel	97	0.3	0.9	28.4	121	24.1	2.0
ITA	Italy	100	0.4	1.0	44.2	64	32.2	1.6
JAM	Jamaica	99	5.4	8.9	32.1	50	0.0	
JPN	Japan	93	1.2	1.1	44.2	147	53.2	0.7
JOR	Jordan	99	3.6	6.7	20.6	82	0.0	0.4
KAZ	Kazakhstan	85	0.8	0.6	23.5	40	2.5	0.3

(Continued)

TABLE A.5 Digital infrastructure (*Continued*)

ISO abbreviation or World Bank designation	Economy	Broadband infrastructure					Data infrastructure	
		4G+ mobile coverage (% of population)	Price of mobile broadband (2 gigabytes per month) (% of monthly GNI per capita)	Price of fixed broadband (5 gigabytes per month) (% of monthly GNI per capita)	Median mobile download speed (megabits per second), 2023	Median fixed broadband download speed (megabits per second), 2023	IXP monthly peak traffic per capita (kilobytes per capita)	Connected data centers (per million people)
KEN	Kenya	97	2.8	16.6	22.3	10	2.1	0.2
KIR	Kiribati	60	5.8	82.7	0.0			
PRK	Korea, Dem. People's Rep.							
KOR	Korea, Rep.	100	0.5	1.0	138.5	143	10.7	0.6
XKX	Kosovo					57		
KWT	Kuwait	100	0.5	1.2	119.8	131	6.6	0.7
KGZ	Kyrgyz Republic	85	1.2	6.2	20.3	48	2.8	0.1
LAO	Lao PDR	52	2.1	7.2	30.6	29	0.0	0.4
LVA	Latvia	95	0.4	1.4	58.9	76	12.8	3.2
LBN	Lebanon	99	10.0	1.0	29.6	7	0.0	0.7
LSO	Lesotho	85	4.9	6.1	0.0	19	0.0	
LBR	Liberia	35	15.5	324.3	0.0	9	0.0	
LBY	Libya	90	0.7	0.9	14.3	8		
LIE	Liechtenstein	100	0.1	0.4	0.0	153	45.3	101.7
LTU	Lithuania	100	0.2	0.8	68.3	93	46.2	2.8
LUX	Luxembourg	100	0.1	0.7	84.6	97	371.9	24.6
MAC	Macao SAR, China	100		0.8		159		1.4
MDG	Madagascar	27	9.3	92.6	0.0	25		0.0
MWI	Malawi	70	9.4	63.7	0.0	9	0.0	0.0
MYS	Malaysia	97	0.3	2.5	44.2	93	7.3	0.9

(Continued)

TABLE A.5 Digital infrastructure *(Continued)*

ISO abbreviation or World Bank designation	Economy	Broadband infrastructure				Data infrastructure		
		4G+ mobile coverage (% of population)	Price of mobile broadband (2 gigabytes per month) (% of monthly GNI per capita)	Price of fixed broadband (5 gigabytes per month) (% of monthly GNI per capita)	Median mobile download speed (megabits per second), 2023	Median fixed broadband download speed (megabits per second), 2023	IXP monthly peak traffic per capita (kilobytes per capita)	Connected data centers (per million people)
MDV	Maldives	100	2.5	2.5	74.3	10	5.4	1.9
MLI	Mali	53	9.7	24.1	0.0	20	0.0	0.1
MLT	Malta	100	0.5	0.9	53.4	101		1.9
MHL	Marshall Islands			11.9		0		
MRT	Mauritania	0		19.2		20		
MUS	Mauritius	99	0.8	1.4	23.2	28	0.3	3.2
MEX	Mexico	95	1.2	2.1	26.1	50	0.1	0.4
FSM	Micronesia, Fed Sts.	0	9.3	6.2	0.0	0		8.8
MDA	Moldova	99	0.6	2.0	32.6	98		1.2
MCO	Monaco	100	0.0	0.4	0.0	226		
MNG	Mongolia	99	1.4	1.7	18.4	54	0.0	
MNE	Montenegro	98	0.9	1.7	43.6	58	0.0	
MAR	Morocco	99	1.0	3.8	32.7	20	0.0	0.1
MOZ	Mozambique	52	9.4	33.7	17.2	7	0.0	0.2
MMR	Myanmar	94	3.1	15.3	26.7	20	0.2	0.1
NAM	Namibia	79	2.6	8.7	25.9	8	0.2	0.4
NRU	Nauru	30	0.0	3.5	0.0			
NPL	Nepal	45	2.4	10.3	14.4	52	0.5	0.1
NLD	Netherlands	99	0.5	1.1	114.3	123	966.2	8.6
NCL	New Caledonia	80						7.2
NZL	New Zealand	98	0.3	0.8	52.2	133	38.9	17.8

(Continued)

TABLE A.5 Digital infrastructure *(Continued)*

ISO abbreviation or World Bank designation	Economy	Broadband infrastructure					Data infrastructure		
		4G+ mobile coverage (% of population)	Price of mobile broadband (2 gigabytes per month) (% of monthly GNI per capita)	Price of fixed broadband (5 gigabytes per month) (% of monthly GNI per capita)	Median mobile download speed (megabits per second), 2023	Median fixed broadband download speed (megabits per second), 2023	IXP monthly peak traffic per capita (kilobytes per capita)	Connected data centers (per million people)
NIC	Nicaragua	69	4.9	12.5	17.1	44		0.1
NER	Niger	15		111.5		5		
NGA	Nigeria	81	1.8	19.3	22.4	14	2.0	0.1
MKD	North Macedonia	100	0.9	3.2	71.6	32	0.1	2.4
MNP	Northern Mariana Islands	10						40.4
NOR	Norway	100	0.4	1.1	131.2	107	29.7	8.6
OMN	Oman	98	0.7	3.7	51.7	59	0.0	1.1
PAK	Pakistan	76	0.5	12.7	15.2	10	0.0	0.1
PLW	Palau			5.0				
PAN	Panama	84	1.9	3.8	17.2	114	5.6	1.4
PNG	Papua New Guinea	50	6.0	12.0	24.1	15	0.0	0.2
PRY	Paraguay	98	2.1	4.0	18.2	70	2.6	0.9
PER	Peru	81	1.4	3.0	17.6	73	54.1	0.4
PHL	Philippines	80		11.3		90	0.7	0.1
POL	Poland	100	0.5	1.1	43.8	101	165.8	1.9
PRT	Portugal	100	0.7	1.5	69.1	132	10.1	0.8
PRI	Puerto Rico	90		1.5			0.6	3.1
QAT	Qatar	100	0.3	2.0	160.3	90	0.0	2.2
ROU	Romania	99	0.6	0.6	47.0	175	27.7	2.1
RUS	Russian Federation	93	0.7	0.7	22.9	78	59.9	0.6

(Continued)

TABLE A.5 Digital infrastructure *(Continued)*

ISO abbreviation or World Bank designation	Economy	Broadband infrastructure					Data infrastructure	
		4G+ mobile coverage (% of population)	Price of mobile broadband (2 gigabytes per month) (% of monthly GNI per capita)	Price of fixed broadband (5 gigabytes per month) (% of monthly GNI per capita)	Median mobile download speed (megabits per second), 2023	Median fixed broadband download speed (megabits per second), 2023	IXP monthly peak traffic per capita (kilobytes per capita)	Connected data centers (per million people)
RWA	Rwanda	99	3.0	41.6	0.0	31	0.2	0.2
WSM	Samoa	99	5.3	15.1	0.0			
SMR	San Marino	99	0.0	0.5	0.0	77		
STP	São Tomé and Príncipe	0		15.6				
SAU	Saudi Arabia	100	0.9	4.5	101.9	87	4.7	0.1
SEN	Senegal	83	2.8	17.8	20.0	22	0.0	
SRB	Serbia	99	0.8	2.3	48.2	64	14.8	1.3
SYC	Seychelles	99	2.5	1.1	0.0	27		
SLE	Sierra Leone	49	3.3	38.2	0.0	14		
SGP	Singapore	100	0.2	0.6	75.2	237	450.6	8.7
SXM	Sint Maarten (Dutch part)	74						
SVK	Slovak Republic	99	0.5	0.9	46.6	58	70.2	0.9
SVN	Slovenia	100	0.4	1.8	61.8	82	47.9	4.3
SLB	Solomon Islands	25	9.8	47.6	0.0			1.4
SOM	Somalia	30	5.3	80.0	9.8	9	0.0	0.1
ZAF	South Africa	98	1.8	3.9	35.1	44	56.7	0.4
SSD	South Sudan	15	0.0	25.8	0.0			0.1
ESP	Spain	100	0.2	1.3	38.4	180	49.0	1.1
LKA	Sri Lanka	97	0.3	0.8	14.7	21	0.0	0.0

(Continued)

TABLE A.5 Digital infrastructure *(Continued)*

ISO abbreviation or World Bank designation	Economy	Broadband infrastructure					Data infrastructure	
		4G+ mobile coverage (% of population)	Price of mobile broadband (2 gigabytes per month) (% of monthly GNI per capita)	Price of fixed broadband (5 gigabytes per month) (% of monthly GNI per capita)	Median mobile download speed (megabits per second), 2023	Median fixed broadband download speed (megabits per second), 2023	IXP monthly peak traffic per capita (kilobytes per capita)	Connected data centers (per million people)
KNA	St. Kitts and Nevis	100	2.5	3.2	0.0	43	0.0	
LCA	St. Lucia	96	4.7	4.7	0.0	81	0.0	
MAF	St. Martin (French part)							
VCT	St. Vincent and the Grenadines	90	5.6	6.7	0.0	77	0.0	
SDN	Sudan	35	4.5	7.6	17.6	5	0.0	0.1
SUR	Suriname	82	3.5	3.6	0.0	11	0.6	3.2
SWE	Sweden	100	0.3	1.1	89.0	111	173.9	5.1
CHE	Switzerland	100	0.3	0.8	82.1	157	17.7	8.7
SYR	Syrian Arab Republic	42	0.0	56.9	11.6	3		
TJK	Tajikistan	80	4.8	5.9	9.3	22		
TZA	Tanzania	58	4.6	20.7	20.3	15	0.6	0.1
THA	Thailand	98	1.4	3.5	40.1	203	2.3	0.4
TLS	Timor-Leste	45	4.3	30.3	0.0	5	0.0	
TGO	Togo	98	8.7	32.6	37.0	28	0.0	0.1
TON	Tonga	96	2.1	3.6	0.0			
TTO	Trinidad and Tobago	80	2.7	3.4	29.0	89	7.2	3.3
TUN	Tunisia	95	0.9	2.6	22.2	8	0.0	0.2
TUR	Türkiye	100	0.7	1.3	30.3	33	6.2	0.4

(Continued)

TABLE A.5 Digital infrastructure *(Continued)*

ISO abbreviation or World Bank designation	Economy	Broadband infrastructure					Data infrastructure	
		4G+ mobile coverage (% of population)	Price of mobile broadband (2 gigabytes per month) (% of monthly GNI per capita)	Price of fixed broadband (5 gigabytes per month) (% of monthly GNI per capita)	Median mobile download speed (megabits per second), 2023	Median fixed broadband download speed (megabits per second), 2023	IXP monthly peak traffic per capita (kilobytes per capita)	Connected data centers (per million people)
TKM	Turkmenistan	67		4.7		2		
TCA	Turks and Caicos Islands	95						
TUV	Tuvalu	0	2.7	13.7	0.0			
UGA	Uganda	31	5.4	50.5	23.1	11	0.1	0.1
UKR	Ukraine	92	1.3	1.9	20.6	63	102.3	1.3
ARE	United Arab Emirates	100	0.8	0.7	179.6	219	28.1	1.0
GBR	United Kingdom	100	0.4	1.2	48.3	73	75.0	3.5
USA	United States	100	0.7	0.9	82.3	198	44.1	3.7
URY	Uruguay	94	0.7	2.3	38.6	150	0.3	0.3
UZB	Uzbekistan	83	0.9	1.7	15.3	45	0.0	0.1
VUT	Vanuatu	70	3.4	30.0	0.0	8	0.3	3.1
VEN	Venezuela, RB	65	0.0	3.3	6.3	20		0.1
VNM	Viet Nam	100	0.4	2.6	42.7	92	0.3	0.1
VGB	Virgin Islands (British)	100	0.0		0.0		0.0	
VIR	Virgin Islands (US)	71						
PSE	West Bank and Gaza					55	0.4	0.6
YEM	Yemen, Rep.	0	6.1	4.0	8.5	5		0.0
ZMB	Zambia	91	2.4	14.7	14.5	9	0.0	0.2

(Continued)

TABLE A.5 Digital infrastructure *(Continued)*

ISO abbreviation or World Bank designation	Economy	4G+ mobile coverage (% of population)	Broadband infrastructure				Data infrastructure	
			Price of mobile broadband (2 gigabytes per month) (% of monthly GNI per capita)	Price of fixed broadband (5 gigabytes per month) (% of monthly GNI per capita)	Median mobile download speed (megabits per second), 2023	Median fixed broadband download speed (megabits per second), 2023	IXP monthly peak traffic per capita (kilobytes per capita)	Connected data centers (per million people)
ZWE	Zimbabwe	40	18.4	9.5	0.0	8	0.0	0.1
HIC	High-income countries	99	0.6	1.2	69.8	142	76.4	3.0
UMIC	Upper-middle-income countries	97	0.7	2.0	72.3	145	14.8	0.3
LMIC	Lower-middle-income countries	89	1.6	6.9	25.4	40	4.4	0.1
LIC	Low-income countries	34	7.4	94.1	11.0	10	0.2	0.1
EAP	East Asia and Pacific	97	0.7	2.5	89.5	171	6.9	0.3
ECA	Europe and Central Asia	97	0.6	1.2	44.1	85	80.8	2.1
LAC	Latin America and the Caribbean	89	1.4	4.4	25.7	74	45.5	0.9
MENA	Middle East and North Africa	85	1.3	5.5	35.5	36	10.5	0.2
NAC	North America	100	0.8	0.9	82.5	193	44.4	3.7
SAR	South Asia	93	1.2	4.3	26.7	43	3.2	0.1
SSA	Sub-Saharan Africa	55	5.2	56.2	15.6	15	4.2	0.1
World		89	1.6	10.7	48.1	91	19.6	0.7

Source: World Bank.
Note: All values are for 2022 unless otherwise indicated. Blank cells indicate that no information is available. GNI = gross national income; IXP = internet exchange point.

Notes

1. "Predict," *EU Science Hub* (https://joint-research-centre.ec.europa.eu/predict_en).

2. The Business Pulse Survey has an open online dashboard, which includes access to the data sets for download. The webpage includes further information about the methods employed, including a technical note. The website hosting these data sets and additional reference materials is located at https://www.worldbank.org/en/data/interactive/2021/01/19/covid-19-business-pulse-survey-dashboard.

3. The ID4D Global Data Set and further methodological details are available at https://id4d.worldbank.org/global-dataset.

4. Further details of the GovTech survey and index, including data sets, are available at https://www.worldbank.org/en/programs/govtech/gtmi-Intro.

5. The database, the full text of the report, and the underlying economy-level data for all figures—along with the questionnaire, the survey methodology, and other relevant materials—are available at https://www.worldbank.org/en/publication/globalfindex.

Reference

Cirera, Xavier, Diego A. Comin, Marcio Cruz, and Kyung Min Lee. 2021. "Anatomy of Technology in the Firm." NBER Working Paper 28080, National Bureau of Economic Research, Cambridge, MA. https://www.nber.org/system/files/working_papers/w28080/w28080.pdf.